C000140728

PSYCHOANALYSIS AND COVIDIAN LIFE

PSYCHOANALYSIS AND COVIDIAN LIFE
Common Distress, Individual Experience

Edited by

Howard B. Levine
and Ana de Staal

Contributors

Christopher Bollas, Patricia Cardoso de Mello,
Bernard Chervet, Joshua Durban, Antonino Ferro,
Serge Frisch, Steven Jaron, Daniel Kupermann, François Lévy,
Riccardo Lombardi, Alberto Rocha Barros, Elias Rocha Barros,
Michael Rustin, Jean-Jacques Tyszler

PHOENIX
PUBLISHING HOUSE
firing the mind

First published in 2021 by
Phoenix Publishing House Ltd
62 Bucknell Road
Bicester
Oxfordshire OX26 2DS

Copyright © 2021 to Howard B. Levine and Ana de Staal for the edited collection, and to the individual authors for their contributions.

The rights of the contributors to be identified as the authors of this work have been asserted in accordance with §§ 77 and 78 of the Copyright Design and Patents Act 1988.

All rights reserved. No part of this publication may be reproduced, stored in a retrieval system, or transmitted, in any form or by any means, electronic, mechanical, photocopying, recording, or otherwise, without the prior written permission of the publisher.

British Library Cataloguing in Publication Data

A C.I.P. for this book is available from the British Library

ISBN-13: 978-1-912691-77-7

Typeset by Medlar Publishing Solutions Pvt Ltd, India

www.firingthemind.com

"The oldest and strongest emotion of mankind is fear, and the oldest and strongest kind of fear is fear of the unknown."

—H. P. Lovecraft[1]

"If there is anything which is certain it is that certainty is wrong."

—W. R. Bion[2]

[1] Lovecraft, H. P. (1927, 1933–1935). *Supernatural Horror in Literature*. http://www. yankeeclassic.com/miskatonic/library/stacks/literature/lovecraft/essays/supernat/ supern01.htm (last accessed January 19, 2021).

[2] Bion, W. R. (1977). *Bion in New York and Sao Paulo*. F. Bion (Ed.). London: Roland Harris Trust/Clunie, 1980, p. 98.

Contents

Part III
The setting under pressure

Part IV
Reconfigurations and changes in practice

Part V
Clinical journals

Part VI
Conclusion

Acknowledgements

We would like to thank the publishers, Kate Pearce, from Phoenix Publishing House (Oxford), and Eduardo Blucher, from Editora Blucher (São Paulo), for the enthusiasm with which they welcomed the idea of this trilingual publication; our gratitude also goes, of course, to the fourteen authors of the chapters, eminent psychoanalyst colleagues—Italians, French, Brazilians, Americans, English, Israelis—who agreed to devote an important part of their thinking to respond to our request, thus allowing us to create this work with them.

We also would like to thank Daniel Conrod, who whispered in our ears the beautiful expression "Covidian life" and helped us to find the title of the book; Véronique Mamelli, from the photo agency of the Réunion des musées nationaux de France, who made it possible to use Edward Hopper's painting on the covers of the three international editions of the book; Gillian Jarvis for her always sympathetic availability and her help during the bibliographical research; all our translators, dedicated and efficient, among whom Jean-Baptiste Desveaux took care of a good part of the translations from English into French and Shahar Fineberg from French into English.

Finally, a special thanks goes to our colleague Daniel Kupermann, who valiantly coordinated the translation of the book into Brazilian, managing a team of eleven translator-analysts, whom we thank very warmly for their involvement, expertise, and generosity. More than thirty people were mobilised to bring this work to a successful conclusion, with the wish to make a humble contribution to the fascinating reflection on contemporary psychoanalysis, which we hope will always be up to date with the times.

Ana de Staal and Howard Levine

Translators

French and English target language team: Henrik Carbonnier, Jean-Baptiste Desvaux, Shahar Fineberg, Valentine Leÿs, Mathieu Rigo, Karla Isolda dos Santos Buss, Ana de Staal. **Scientific revision:** Ana de Staal, Jean-Baptiste Desveaux.

Brazilian target language team: Bartholomeu de Aguiar Vieira, Claudia Berliner, Lucas Charafeddine Bulamah, Gustavo Dean-Gomes, Wilson Franco, Pedro Hikiji Neves, Pedro Marky Sobral, Roberto de Oliveira, Ludmilla Tassano Pitrowsky, Luiz Eduardo de Vasconcelos Moreira. **Scientific revision:** Daniel Kupermann.

Brazilian edition coordination: Daniel Kupermann.

About the editors and contributors

Christopher Bollas is a psychoanalyst, honorary fellow of the Institute for Psychoanalytic Training and Research (IPTAR) in New York, the British Psychoanalytic Society (BPS), and the Los Angeles Institute and Society for Psychoanalytic Studies (LAISPS). Inspired by the contributions of Winnicott and Bion, he remains however a fiercely independent thinker who has been described by André Green as "autonomous". He is the author of an important body of work, with books such as *The Shadow of the Object* (1987) and *The Infinite Question* (2009). Ithaque has undertaken the translation of some of his titles, having published to date: *Le Moment freudien* (2011), *Hystérie* (2017), *Sens et la mélancolie* (2018), and *Avant la chute … Psychoanalyse de l'effondrement psychique* (to be published in 2021). A British-American national, he lives and works in Santa Barbara and London.

Patricia Cardoso de Mello is a training psychoanalyst at the Sociedade Brasileira de Psicanálise de São Paulo. Her clinical practice includes children and adults. She has been working with autistic children and their families for almost thirty years. She holds master's and PhD degrees in fundamental psychopathology and psychoanalysis from the University of Paris-VII (France). She lives and works in São Paulo.

Bernard Chervet is a psychiatrist, psychoanalyst, and training member of the Paris Psychoanalytical Society (SPP), where he was president from 2011 to 2015. He is on the board of the International Psychoanalytical Association (IPA); director of the Congress for French-speaking Psychoanalysts (CPLF); founder of SPP Editions; author of more than 230 publications; and general editor of more than ten books. He was the winner of the Bouvet Prize in 2018 and rapporteur at the CPLF in 2009 on the theme of "*L'après-coup*", and contributed to its entry (2019) in the IPA Encyclopaedic Dictionary. He lives in Paris and Lyon, France.

Joshua Durban is a training and supervising child and adult psychoanalyst and teacher at the Israeli Psychoanalytic Society and Institute, Jerusalem, and faculty member of Sackler School of Medicine, Tel Aviv University, The Psychotherapy Program. He works in private psychoanalytic practice in Tel Aviv with autism spectrum disorder (ASD) and psychotic children and adults. He is the founder of the Israeli Psychoanalytic Inter-Disciplinary Forum for the study of ASD.

Antonino Ferro, MD, is a training and supervising analyst (SPI, APsaA, IPA). Former president of the Italian Psychoanalytic Society (2013–2017), he received the Sigourney Award in 2007. He has authored and co-authored many books, including *Torments of the Soul, Avoiding Emotions, Living Emotions, Psychoanalysis and Dreams,* and *A Short Introduction to Psychoanalysis* (with Giuseppe Civitarese). He works in private practice in Pavia and Milan, Italy.

Serge Frisch is a training and supervising analyst and past president of the Belgium Psychoanalytic Society, a training and supervising analyst at the German Psychoanalytic Society, past president of the European Psychoanalytic Federation (EPF-FEP), and a member of the board of directors of the International Psychoanalytical Association.

Steven Jaron trained as a psychoanalyst with the Psychoanalytic Society for Research and Training (SPRF), in Paris, France. He is on the staff of the Quinze-Vingts National Ophthalmological Hospital and works in private practice in Paris. He holds a PhD in French and comparative literature from Columbia University and is the author of *Edmond Jabès: The Hazard of Exile* (Legenda, 2003) and *Zoran Music: Voir jusqu'au coeur des choses* (L'Echoppe, 2008). His essays have also appeared in *Libres cahiers pour la psychanalyse* and in *Bacon and the Mind: Art, Neuroscience and Psychology* (Thames and Hudson, 2019).

Daniel Kupermann is a psychoanalyst and a professor at the Institute of Psychology, University of São Paulo. He is currently the president of the Sándor Ferenczi Brazilian Research Group and a member of the board of the International Sándor Ferenczi Network. He has authored articles published in French, English, Spanish, Italian, and Portuguese, and books published in Brazil. He lives and works in São Paulo.

Howard B. Levine is a member of APSA, PINE, the Contemporary Freudian Society, on the faculty of the NYU Post-Doc Contemporary Freudian track, on the editorial boards of the *International Journal of Psychoanalysis* and *Psychoanalytic Inquiry*, editor-in-chief of the *Routledge Wilfred Bion Studies Book Series*, and in private practice in Brookline, Massachusetts. He has authored many articles, book chapters, and reviews on psychoanalytic process and technique and the treatment of primitive personality disorders. His co-edited books include *On Freud's Screen Memories* (Karnac, 2014); *The Wilfred Bion Tradition* (Karnac, 2016); and *André Green Revisited: Representation and the Work of the Negative* (Karnac, 2018). He is the author of *Transformations de l'irreprésentable* (Ithaque, 2019) and the forthcoming *Affect, Representation and Language: Between the Silence and the Cry* (Routledge).

François Lévy is a psychoanalyst, associate (full) member of the Société de psychanalyse freudienne (SPF), current vice-president of the Société de Psychanalyse Freudienne, and former secretary of the editorial board of the French psychoanalytical journal *Les Lettres de la SPF*. He is the author of many articles, of the French preface to the *Clinical Seminars* of Wilfred R. Bion, and of *La Psychanalyse avec Wilfred R. Bion*, a work rigorously presenting the thought and work of Bion, which has been translated into several languages. For more than twenty years he has been the leader of a teaching seminar on the work of Bion, a true place for reflection and exchange. He lives and works in Paris, France.

Riccardo Lombardi is a training and supervising analyst of the Italian Psychoanalytic Society (SPI) and the author of several papers on the body–mind relationship, time, psychosis, and other severe mental disturbances, published in leading psychoanalytic journals. He is the author of the books *Formless Infinity: Clinical Explorations of Matte Blanco and Bion* (Routledge, 2014) and *Body–Mind Dissociation in Psychoanalysis* (Routledge, 2017). He has a full-time private practice in Rome.

Alberto Rocha Barros is a philosopher, editor, and senior candidate in psychoanalysis at the Brazilian Psychoanalytical Society of São Paulo.

Elias Rocha Barros is a training and supervising analyst at the Brazilian Psychoanalytical Society of São Paulo, fellow of the British Psychoanalytical Society and of the British Institute of Psychoanalysis. He is a past editor for the *International Journal of Psychoanalysis*, Latin American chair of the Task Force for the International Encyclopedia of Psychoanalysis (IPA), and recipient of the 1999 Sigourney award.

Michael Rustin is a professor of sociology at the University of East London, a visiting professor at the Tavistock Clinic, and an associate of the British Psychoanalytical Society. He has written widely on interconnections between psychoanalysis, society, and politics, in books including *The Good Society and the Inner World* (1991) and *Reason and Unreason* (2001). His most recent books include *Social Defences against Anxiety: Explorations in a Paradigm* (edited with David Armstrong, 2015); *Reading Klein* (with Margaret Rustin, 2017), *Researching the Unconscious: Principles of Psychoanalytic Method* (2019), and *New Discoveries in Child Psychotherapy: Findings from Qualitative Research* (edited with Margaret Rustin, 2019). He is an editor of *Soundings, a Journal of Politics and Culture*.

Ana de Staal is a psychoanalyst, member of the Freudian Psychoanalysis Society (SPF), and psychosomatist. Former editor-in-chief at the review

Chimères, founded by Gilles Deleuze and Félix Guattari, she now runs Éditions d'Ithaque in France. She has translated and published the French editions of most of W. R. Bion's seminars, as well as the works of important authors of contemporary psychoanalysis such as Thomas Ogden, Antonino Ferro, Christopher Bollas, Martin Bergmann, and André Green. She works in private practice in Paris.

Jean-Jacques Tyszler is a psychiatrist and psychoanalyst, medical director in Paris of the Psycho-Pedagogical Medical Centre (CMPP) of the Mutuelle générale de l'Éducation nationale—the French national education health insurance fund (MGEN). A former president of the International Lacanian Association (ALI), he is a member of the European Foundation for Psychoanalysis, of the Psychoanalytic School of St-Anne Hospital, and of the School of Ville-Evrard Hospital, where he directs training in the psychoanalytical approach in psychiatry. He is the author of numerous articles, publishing in English, French, and Portuguese. He lives and works in Paris, France.

Editors' note

> "We like to think that our ideas are our property, but unless we can make our contribution available to the rest of the group there is no chance of mobilising the *collective wisdom* of the group which could lead to further progress and development"
>
> —W. R. Bion, *Bion in New York and São Paulo,* p. 26.

The idea, not to say the necessity, of organising a book on the effects of the pandemic on psychoanalytical practice appeared to us around April 2020. We were still in full lockdown, stunned by what was happening.

For many of us, the rapid and quasi-imposed passage from the couch to the screen had raised legitimate questions about the impact of these unprecedented events on our practice. Not that the question of remote psychoanalysis was a new subject. Some of us were already practising it occasionally, during supervisions for example, or in order to continue working with an expatriate patient. For the past ten years or so, a number of books had been published on the subject, regularly and from a wide variety of angles.[1]

---

[1] For instance: Jill Savage Scharff (2013–2018), *Psychoanalysis Online, Mental Health, Teletherapy and Training, vols. 1–4,* New York & Abingdon, Routledge; Alessandra

With the pandemic, however, we found ourselves in a very new situation, not only because of its compelling and universal nature (we were all more or less obliged to close our consulting rooms and rearrange our sessions, or even stop them), but also because it seemed to have the potential to influence our practice more radically. Indeed, to what extent could the setting, this container of psychic reality without which the psychoanalytical process has no frame within which to take place,[2] bear the weight of such a brutal, untimely, and traumatic reality? It seemed obvious that it would not be impervious to it, and perhaps it was better that it should not be. But then …?

When we first began to gather some authors around this reflection, we addressed to them an initial argument:

> With the closure of our practices due to the pandemic, many of us have been "transposing" on screen not only the classical analytical setting but also specific psychotherapeutic ones (psychosomatic consultation, for example). This experience, both trying and fascinating, seems to provide us today with enough elements for a first reflection on the resilience of the analytical framework, which has been subjected to various types of extensions and loads since the middle of the 20th century. To what extent is psychoanalysis dependent on its concrete setting? Are the foundations of the framework truly non-negotiable, non-adaptable? On the contrary, is this system susceptible to transposition? But at what price? What happens in the analytical situation when the field of vision is framed by the eye of a camera? What about the analysand's journey to the consulting room (the daydream on the way, considered by some as an integral part of the session)? What happens to the "atmosphere" of the treatment, dear to Theodor Reik? How to situate the body, the presence/absence in telephone and video sessions? …

Lemma (2017), *The Digital Age on the Couch: Psychoanalytic Practice and New Media*, New York & Abingdon, Routledge; Frédéric Tordo et Elisabeth Darchis (Ed.) (2017), *La cure analytique à distance, Le skype sur le divan*, préfacé par Serge Tisseron, Paris, Harmattan.

[2] Bleger, J. (1967). Psycho-analysis of the psycho-analytic frame, *International Journal of Psychoanalysis*, 48(4): 511–519.

As the reader will see, the responses to this argument have been very diverse, often going beyond the initial problem of the frame. Some wanted to think more broadly (and psychoanalytically) about the political and social context of the event, others about its theoretical or institutional implications, and still others chose to account for the specificity of remote clinical experience.

At the time we embarked on this project, our desire was to take a first look at the question, and, faced with the pandemic that was assaulting bodies and minds everywhere at once, we wanted to break down language barriers and differences between schools, by calling on analysts from all over the world and with the most diverse sensibilities: from Freudians to Lacanians, from Ferenczians to Bionians to Kleinians. We welcomed all inspirations, not in the name of an obligatory and probably infertile eclecticism, but in the spirit of the *collective wisdom* that Bion talked about.

Also, this internationalist and decompartmentalised will, so to speak, was obviously at the antipodes of a desire for exhaustiveness or doctrinairism. We wanted neither a manual of technical attitudes to follow, nor a pseudo-consensual (and therefore necessarily pretentious) discourse on what should become the standard of practice in Covidian life. Our intention was above all to signify that psychoanalysis lives and thinks within its times—certainly, taking the time to elaborate its profound modifications, but always in full accord with what constitutes its very essence and purpose: the development of our capacity to think about life and death without negotiating away our debt to our humanity. And precisely, by accepting everyone's contributions with the greatest openness of mind, we have simply tried to photograph at a moment "t"—between August and December 2020—the way in which each of us was trying to confront the death brought about by the pandemic by reflecting on its more immediate impact on our patients, our practice, and ourselves. For it is not possible to get to the heart of the traumatic event itself when we are synchronically living it; therefore, this book is only one step in a long reflection that has just begun.

At the time this project was launched, we were certain that things would "get back to normal" a few months later, perhaps by the fall of 2020, and that our customary routines would start again. As the months went by, we realised the obvious—nothing could be less certain … At the time of this writing, hospitals are still not letting up, the second wave is officially declared everywhere, a third wave is expected, general fatigue is growing, and even the strongest among us are starting to feel the pinch. We realise that, from the highest levels of government decision-making to the most modest levels of intervention, responses are being developed, not to say tinkered with, day after day, without anyone being able to imagine with any certainty a kind of future. There is something of a "figuration deficit" that starts to contaminate people, at the same time as the coronavirus.

The relentless work of biologists in search of vaccines could be a metaphor for our own situation today: we too are in the midst of a research, and it will take time also for us, to better observe and then theorise about the damage caused by the pandemic on our patients, on our practice, on our way of working through and understanding psychoanalysis. The pandemic has made death too visible, too obvious, at the same time as it has buried everything that has always helped us to "live" with the death—our family and social ties, our celebrations, our funeral rites, our artistic and cultural production, our parks and our travels …; it has placed us, dumbfounded, before the bluish light of the screens, making evident our need for meaning, for sublimation, for an inhabited internal world, and for an external world open to connections and possible futures.

We hope that these contributions may give the reader, as it has given to us, some food for thought and consolation.

Ana de Staal and Howard Levine

Part I

The background scene/ the context

CHAPTER 1

Civilisation and the discontented*

Christopher Bollas
London, England

I

The populist movements in the United States, Brazil, the United Kingdom, Hungary, the Philippines, and elsewhere reveal how democratic processes are vulnerable when an otherwise rational large group—such as a nation—abandons its ordinary structures of government as significant numbers of the population succumb to psychologically disturbed processes of thought and action.

Whilst we know quite a lot about our thought processes and behaviour in small to medium-sized groups, we have not given enough thought to mental processes in the large group that we term a nation. I shall be considering how we can begin to think of our ongoing psychology as a nation,[1] especially when we become disturbed, as is the case now. I shall focus mainly on one example, the United States, and in particular on its group psychology in 2020.

---

* Copyright © Christopher Bollas, 2021.
[1] I shall use the term "nation" instead of "nation state" as this is most commonly used today.

As the president fuelled white nationalism and the far right, drumming up support from his fan base, the word "virus" became a signifier that bifurcated to identify two seemingly unrelated phenomena: the transmission of a biological virus and the transmission of false news. Covid entered the American body and killed people, while Trump created a social virus, a malignant mutation of previously adequate social structures, as he spread psychically destructive communications that were meant to enter the American body politic or mind. The convergence of both viral forms of communication created a mentally confusing pathogen. As they travelled around the country, both were psychically invasive, breeding fear on a scale that the American community had not experienced before.

In this situation, there was what psychoanalysts term an "overdetermination" of meanings. Covid, presidential madness, police killings, mass unemployment, and civil unrest merged into one malignant condensation to produce an unthinkable mental reality. The matrix I have described, though a psychological phenomenon in many ways, is not a dream. It is an event in the real: a social nightmare driven by a psychotic social reality. As Franz Fanon wrote, we can "be overdetermined from the outside" (2008, p. 95).

As Americans witnessed the dismantling of institutions that had been tasked with protecting the lands and environment (such as the EPA—the Environmental Protection Agency) we saw social implosion: the collapse of structures crucial to large group functioning. The implosion returned the nation to a feudal world in which millions of people were meant to "follow the leader", a process I shall discuss further.

But let us begin by thinking about some aspects of group psychology.

Our first group is our family of origin, an ad hoc oligarchic assembly run by the adults with the children as subordinates. As we internalise the unthought known[2] assumptions of our family group, we form axioms that will influence, if not govern, our behaviour for the rest of our lives.

In the good enough family we experience and absorb the two "L"s: love and law. We love and are loved by mother, father, and others, but

---

[2] Readers unfamiliar with my work and some of the terms I use—"unthought known", "maternal order", etc.—and who wish to have a better understanding of them are advised to read Sarah Nettleton's *The Metapsychology of Christopher Bollas: An Introduction* (London, Routledge, 2017).

not because we have earned this; we are simply loved, as if this were the fundamental predicate of existence. Along with love we are taught law. From the beginning, mother has her clear set rules of behaviour, communicated through interactions that constitute unspoken laws (which I term the "maternal order"), but later we learn social laws communicated through language (in what I term the "paternal order", following Lacan's theory of the symbolic order) that are required for our future participation in all other groups.

If all goes well, then unconditional love gives way, gradually but unremittingly, to conditional love. The experience of love, loving, and being loved does not disappear, but its limitation can be disturbing.

Our next significant group will be our school where we are tutored in group relations by teachers who stress the importance of good behaviour in the group. New forms of love and law are passed on and further integrated into the assumptions of group life. We need to be loved and to be in love, but we also need the law and it needs us.

Babies offer the mother a taste of their food and they react to her states of mind; they are naturally empathic. This is emphasised by teachers and others and leads in turn to the development of another psychic capacity: the ethical sense—the ability to consider the internal world or circumstances of the other. The empathic and ethical senses evolve naturally from love and the law. We are beginning to become generatively structured.

As Daniel Stern (1985) emphasised, children find new objects extremely interesting. Usually, after what Winnicott termed a "period of hesitation", they will reach for new objects to explore including other people. Small children will embrace strangers because the other is interesting. This leads to the growth of a capacity beyond empathy which we may term "otherness".[3] This involves a part of our mental life structured to receive others and to enjoy difference.

Childhood is termed the *formative years* for good reason. Our personality as form will be shaped by our integration of qualities that will prove essential to our belief in our self, our dedication to others, and our contribution to our world throughout our lives. The structures that comprise love, law, empathy, the ethical sense, and otherness are crucial

---

[3] Krishnamurti (2003) referred to "otherness" throughout his work and while we use the term differently there are also points of convergence.

to our becoming civilised social beings. These capacities enable creative participation in the various groups in our life: our family of origin, the family we may later generate, our workplace, and participation in our community.

In *Civilization and Its Discontents*, Freud (1930a) argued that the formation of the superego mitigates the strength of our instincts—aggression and sexuality. Since we cannot simply satisfy any passing urge that might bring us pleasure, we exchange that pleasure for another, intrasubjective relation. One part of our personality (the superego) loves and admires another part (the ego) for giving up rapacious instincts, or at least for modifying them. This internal love relation is in part what makes us feel good about ourselves as it leads to a sense of conscience and to conscientious behaviour. Mental health professionals have been understandably reluctant to provide a clinical commentary on the disturbed figures involved in national politics. Ordinarily, for a professional to diagnose an individual he or she would meet the subject in person and undertake a detailed assessment. However, there can be exceptions to this private evaluation when an individual openly demonstrates a highly disturbed state of mind in public, via radio, television, or social media. If the subject provides enough "material" in this way, then it is possible for a clinician to make a diagnosis, not about personality but about process. So whilst I would not identify a *politician* as borderline or paranoid, it can be appropriate to identify a *thought process* in this way, provided one spells out one's reasons for holding such a view.

People involved in extremist politics—on the far right or the far left—often take their positions either from an actively distressed state of mind or from an ideology that "holds" a disturbance within itself, allowing its advocate to be calm or even serene. That is, an ideology can be quite mad—in effect containing a group's psychotic thinking—leaving its advocates otherwise rather calm.

II

The threat to democracy in 2020 in the United States and elsewhere emerged from psychotic group processes that had been cultivated by the alt-right for decades. (Needless to say, were the threat coming from the far left, we would be examining their psychology.)

All groups and all individuals will move in and out of toxic states of mind. Both the neurotic and the psychotic processes are part of normal life. The neurotic process involves conflict between the contents of the mind. The psychotic process involves conflict between the parts of the mind, for example between our conscience and our impulses.

In neurotic group states, members will hold and express different parts of a complex ideational dynamic, switching roles as issues are passed around amongst them. In psychotic group states, people deal with ideational complexity by getting rid of those parts of the mind that would ordinarily handle distressing thoughts.

The neurotic process slows us down, forces us to think and rethink ideas that pop up into consciousness, and it can depress us, because although we know that reasoning is valuable, we discover there is no final mental resting point from which we can serenely survey the landscape of the mind and feel all is well. The ordinary self understands that a common source of distress is mental life itself. We need help in unravelling the tangles of ideation and affect, historical fact and imagined past, and the vectors of wishful thinking and the promise of pleasure versus the sense of reality which compromises the fulfilment of the wish.

The psychotic process, on the other hand, attempts to eliminate intrapsychic conflict—the conflict between parts of the self. This is accomplished by denying mental conflicts and splitting the personality so that the unwanted parts of mental life are banished from consciousness by being projected into the other. Hatred of the cast-off parts of the self produces globalised fear that the other, who has been the victim of this mental violence, will seek revenge, which leads to a paranoid retreat into enclaves of supporters in order to gain support and offset isolation.

When Trump, for example, claimed that Mexicans and Central Americans who were huddled on the American border were "criminals" and "sexual predators" he projected his criminal and sexual disturbances into Latinos and others. When he urged the nation to build a wall—a great big wall—he projected the psychological wall he had long constructed inside himself that protected him from perceiving his responsibility for his transgressions.

We all engage in moments of both neurotic and psychotic thinking. The extreme right wing frame of mind should therefore be viewed, less as a personality disorder, more as a way of thinking that any of us could find ourselves stepping into. In our everyday lives, we enter and leave psychotic processes of thought without batting an eyelid.

III

During the Covid crisis in the United States, the failure to deal with the crisis in a timely and efficient manner derived in large part from half a century of increasingly effective opposition towards the federal government. From before the Constitutional Convention, after the Civil War, and ever since, a significant number of Americans have always been opposed to federal government. American libertarianism is an anarchist philosophy. This view of government competed with the conservative Republicans in the second half of the twentieth century and displaced them in the twenty-first century.

At the same time, the Christian core of American politics was moving to the right. The nearly agnostic dispassion of American theologians, following Reinhold Neibhur and Paul Tillich, shied away from monotheism's primal and archaic mythologies about the "founding gods", focusing instead on the ethical standards that had been promoted by Christians for centuries. The evangelical movement offered an approach very different from that of the quietist, more academic reflections of the pastoral tradition of progressive Christianity. They offered a highly emotional group process, giving figurative rebirth to people who had found their faith.

Their concept of being "born again" shoved the biological mother into the hinterland. At the same time they violently judged biological mothers-to-be for terminating their pregnancies. As millions of Americans became born again, we might think it bemusing that, in this unconscious attack on the birth mother, they were implicitly sanctioning their own form of abortion. In place of the actual mother and family, now there was a group of smiling people who would support all these children of faith without having gone through the labour of birth.

Eventually faith-based thinking displaced Christian reason. For many who had been raised in austere puritan households, the joyful Pentecostal groups singing and dancing their religiosity must have come as a relief. Freed from overt puritan strictures, you could *feel* the cure of Christianity within you.

At this same time, American capitalism, which had been brought under the auspices of government during the presidencies of FDR and Eisenhower, was gradually cut loose from governmental regulation, most decisively under Reagan. Both evangelical Christianity and the neoliberal capitalists—those who advocated unregulated capitalism—based themselves on faith. Certitudes displaced reasoned argument. "Let market forces decide our strategies" fits very well with "Let this be in God's hands".

As I discussed in *Meaning and Melancholia* (Bollas, 2018), by the early 1960s there was a growing antipathy towards the federal government; indeed, towards the very idea of being governed. Reagan's "trickle down" America meant that the country would in effect be ruled by the economy, not the government. Indeed, it seemed best to reduce the federal government to the point of near disappearance.

The cry to deregulate the government was built on invested suspicion. Regulation was seen as an attempt to take over the country in order to suppress the people. But, as is often true of such thought processes, the object of fear (government takeover) expressed the group's own ambition to take over the country and eliminate all other views. Which is what they set out to do, and successfully so.

The historical trend towards deregulation of government does not simply gratify the drive to accumulate wealth. It expresses a wish to walk away from government. An unregulated country is the wish of the unregulated self.

And what about the law?

The cynical appointment of William Barr as attorney general empowered a man of the religious right (a Catholic zealot) and promoted opposition to the laws of the land. When troops dispersed those assembling peacefully outside the White House in order to enable the president to walk from there to St. John's Episcopal Church on 1 June 2020, a president literally tramped over the constitutional right of assembly and violated the separation of Church and state. This undoing of American governmental structure illustrated the lawlessness of this group process. The president did not disguise his exploitation of religious groups and faith-based thinking for his own political advantage. It happened before our very eyes, in the large group we term a nation.

As he paraded one corporate executive after another at his daily health briefings in March and April of 2020, Trump outsourced government responsibility to the corporate world. This was done with a panache that rivalled Mussolini's charm as he turned Italy into a corporate nation.

When the secretary of the treasury, Steven Mnuchin, dispensed 2.2 trillion dollars to stimulate the economy, billions went to corporate America. Not to be accounted for, this bailout confirmed the United States as a nation moving towards national socialism. The American people were watching major transformations in the structure of their country.

These developments—by Trump, Barr, Mnuchin and others—were action-thoughts. Psychoanalysis identifies the way a person acts as a form of thinking, and in considering a national group process it is important to see how the implementation of policy constitutes a way of thinking about the world.

IV

An unregulated country breeds unregulated selves.

In June 2020 certain governors suspended social distancing in the United States (a mistake repeated in many other countries). The result? A resurgence in Covid.

Oddly, and we will return to this, "freedom" led to hospitalisations and death, while "restrictions" enabled people to go about their lives without malignant consequence.

Many people were furious at any government regulation of their right to do as they liked. Refusing to mask, they thronged to the beaches, to the bars and restaurants, and they partied. True to "id capitalism"[4]— only here, it was not "profits before people" but "pleasure before people". What the self wanted it got.

For most people, the ethical mental structures that are part of our formative years play an important part in life. We can all at times employ psychotic mechanisms, but unless a person is a psychopath, the positive impulses derived from relational love, law, ethical sense, empathy, and otherness will serve as a resource to mitigate those malignant states

---

[4] A term I use in *Meaning and Melancholia* (Bollas, 2018) to describe unregulated capitalism driven by the greed of those investors and captains of industry that put profit before people.

of mind that would otherwise destroy what we may now refer to as "a person of conscience". In this context, I mean a person grounded in psychic qualities, who makes use of them in their life, and who recognises that these formative structures can be destroyed.

When Americans (and people in other nations) defied social distancing and social isolation, knowing that their beach parties meant they could carry Covid home and infect others, this offered a sort of poll—a demography—of the group state of mind.

Face masks might be recommended but they were not declared a matter of law. This anarchic view—that the people should decide and not the state—divided the nation into those who wore masks and those who did not. The Confederate flag may have come down, but the mask-free face was firmly in evidence.

With this successful attack on the regulatory benefit of government, we saw social anarchy and Covid deaths in huge numbers. There emerged a form of psychopathy: an unconscious strategy for gaining immediate gratification without considering the consequence. This became the new normal, and it could only take place through annihilation of the conscientious self. It is this killing that has most profoundly disheartened those millions of people who do have a conscience, who care about social democracy and human rights, and who want to get on with improving their world.

Anarcho-capitalism, however, strips people of crucial human qualities. As the self loses these capacities, over time a depressive cynicism arises to provide a new ethos. Some might call it "realism". Whatever the rationalisation for the abandonment of the structures that form conscience, the outcome will be a denuded self. As we lose our humanity we are reduced to primitive axioms of living.

With the ejection of conscience, the self is finally unregulated. Now it is each person for themselves. The American Dream originated in the simple wish of immigrant Americans to raise a family and to give their children the education they themselves had not received. In other words, it was the wish to live a good enough life. Gradually, however, this ethical aim had morphed into a dream that went Las Vegas. By the dawn of the twenty-first century the American Dream had become a route towards heartless gluttony. And this frame of mind contributed to the psychology underwriting neoliberalism.

V

Expressing his right wing fanaticism, Trump displaced the perception of reality with an "anything goes" approach to reporting the "truth". For him there was no difference between fact-based news and fantasy-based assertions. He could make any claim and live without fear of consequence because no one can prove a negative. (We cannot prove that Obama's evidence of American citizenship is not an invention by con artists.) Living in the luxury of this negatively based logic, the right established that they could create any narrative they wished. And their ability to do this was psychologically contagious; it was an invitation to everyone to abandon the chore of dealing with reality and instead to bathe in the delights of fantasy.

It is not difficult to see how through this form of thought the right wing "groomed" many in the Christian community, and other mono-theists. Belief in God is, of course, "faith based". Once the news became structured in the same way, those who created and transmitted it became gods of their own narrative, easily acquiring many followers. After all, if we can be born again, why can't the news? What is wrong with giving the uninspiring facts of life a new birth through an entirely different birth-of-thought process?

A group can be influenced by a number of factors that will alter its axioms or culture. Although a large group may remain calm and efficient for a long period of time, in the right circumstances its psychology can suddenly become volcanic. Known assumptions (group mental struc-tures) can be annihilated with little thought given to them, especially if the group is in a psychotic frame of mind.

A psychotic process always involves the destruction of important mental functions, such as the capacity to perceive reality, to form sound judgements, to filtrate strong feelings, and to be socially adaptive. As the psychotic process splits the self, this involves the loss of otherwise valued parts of mental life—the ethical sense, the capacity for empathy, for oth-erness, and so forth. When we begin to eradicate aspects that we know to be crucial to the humane side of the human being, an odd thing happens in the psychotic process. We experience the loss of these parts of the self as evidence of our having been invaded and diminished by an enemy.

The president's lying has been deplored by many in the country but it is rarely understood as being on a psychotic spectrum. As Trump constantly invents and reinvents reality, with no concern for the factual basis of what he says, the cumulative effect of this constant revision of the perception of reality is that people's sense of what might be true and what might be false falls away in a fog of fantasies. This degradation has created a psychotic atmosphere: it has made it very hard for both supporters and opponents to think, to talk openly, and to come to some stabilised judgement about what is real.

As he creates reality for us, this president offers himself as the leader who will save his people from the chaotic spell his multiple personalities have created. Though hardly a Christian, he has cannily grasped how the faith-based mind works. He has figured out how the predicate of certain Christian myths can be stretched into modern times so that having faith in something becomes far more significant than judgement based on fact.

For some this simply affirms that he is a god: a being who exists above the lives of ordinary mortals, who can see way beyond what we perceive, who knows all there is to know. If you walk like a saviour, talk like a saviour, are persecuted as if you were a saviour (CNN: the Pontius Pilate channel), and are the most powerful person in the world, then what more is there to say? For millions of Americans, what Trump says is gospel.

As Americans are sucked into the president's mental process, politics becomes the art of assembling people behind false realities generated by a psychotic mythopoesis.

Conspiracy theories are pseudo complexities meant to displace the genuine mental challenges of modern life. Turning away from engaging with complexities in the real world, the far right wing mind instead fabricates reality precisely because it immediately puts the self in control of what seems to be an astonishingly complex state of affairs. A conspiracy theory is a delusion. A delusion is a narratively organised (and thus coherent) hallucination.

VI

So what can be done about the situation in which Americans and citizens of many other nations now find themselves?

In order to be part of a national group—one crucially dependent on our participation—people make a compromise. The group that we refer to as a nation is very large, and it is also an abstraction; it is difficult for citizens to be personally involved, to feel that they have a clear idea of how to take part in the group, and to know what the national group idiom is.

It is very hard for those whom we elect to represent us to truly represent the nation's interests, even if they try to do so. In the United States, decades of disparaging Congress—"the do-nothing Congress"—indicates a fatigue about life in a democracy that has eroded people's belief, both in government and in themselves.

Whether it be Congress, the executive, or the judicial branches, Americans have a cynical view of their institutions. Harsh judgements may be warranted, but what if the true cause of this demise is structural? What if part of the problem is the lack of any structure within government that is able to process social distress? And however important economic, political, and existential issues may be, what if American loss of trust in government has a psychological basis? What if they do not trust their psychology to govern?

If we think positively, then we can take heart from the millions of people around the world who are protesting against climate change, social injustice, abuse of power, and malignant capitalism. We do have models of action. We can remind ourselves of how the world community isolated South Africa in protest against apartheid, how external pressure on a government liberated those within a nation state to gain sufficient freedom to fight corruption and turn their country in the right direction.

This model points to the efficacy of "outside help". For a psychoanalyst this incorporates the concept of "triangulation". When two opposing forces are locked in battle, the presence of a third can create another thinking space, one not subject to the malign influences of power groups that have corrupted a nation. We can see, for example, how this changed politics in Northern Ireland.

But this "first responder" approach to national and international affairs—outside help that shows up in an emergency—is inadequate to deal with the complex needs of today's world. In the twentieth century, we saw the formation of the League of Nations (1920), the United Nations (1948), and the European Union (1993). These were serious initiatives that gave nationals a third space, and in doing so they emphasised the potential of the international community.

We all live in a world punctuated—and sometimes occupied—by racism, misogyny, and the other social pathogens. But in spite of our worst characteristics we also live in a world of continuing social improvements. What we learn from the breakdown of governments is that if we abandon institutions intended to hold us to account, then we can regress to primitive and even lethal forms of behaviour. In the absence of a robustly functioning WHO, UN, World Court, and so forth, it is possible for our sociopathic selves to capitalise on any opportunity with little regard for the consequences.

To progress, however, we must be in a position to assess reality. Those vested in representative government must include many skilled in identifying and encountering pathogenic states of mind in the ordinary political process.

In psychoanalytic psychology we try our best to objectify unconscious issues so that they can be considered by consciousness. One of the most common psychotic processes is negative hallucination: not seeing an object or situation that is right in front of us. The so-called "elephant in the room". Negative hallucination is one way of paring down the complexity of governance. In fact all governments—parliament or congress and its constituents—are fully aware of how and in what ways they are engaged in corrupt behaviour. But if they do not want to have their actions and behaviours examined, they will elect to keep the unpleasant outside consciousness, outsourced to an "underworld". They will not encourage psychologists to discuss the unspoken for.

Negatively hallucinating important realities—our part in the arms trade, for example—means that we abandon mental contact with those parts of reality that actually require our diligent attention. To be inattentive may make life easier, but some part of us knows that we have done so at the expense of our social responsibility. As we dumb ourselves down, acquiring a cultivated ignorance, we know that disconnection from disturbing mental contents (catastrophic climate change, the plight of people fleeing genocide) does not simply rid us of unpleasant thoughts, it eventually compromises our ability to think about reality. This retreat from our mental obligations—this mental diminishment—can leave us empty, looking for some god to do the thinking for us. A god like Trump.

Although negative hallucination is ordinarily unconscious we are all aware at times of turning a blind eye to things we know will be upsetting.

Unfortunately, however, when we choose to eliminate evident forms of social injustice, negating the troubling and eventually becoming blind to it, we authorise personal corruption. We fail to see an injustice that is right before us, or else we see it but we anaesthetise our emotional response. Then it is easy to collude with malign practice in the company that employs us, or engage in persecuting those at home or abroad.

In the larger group it is easy to become sociopathic when the demands on our empathy can feel impossible. If we paid attention to all the injustices present in society it would be extremely mentally painful. Indeed, no one could possibly think about these every day, as the individual mind cannot contain the group mind. Those who are highly empathic may connect more than most to the pain suffered by so many, but this can lead to unbearable mental distress. Such receptivity is mentally hazardous. We negate reality because to think about it may be overwhelming.

Although there are clear stirrings of conscience in the United States—as evidenced in the Black Lives Matter movement or the increasingly outspoken opposition to the hideous accumulation of wealth by a tiny minority—the far-right opposition to encompassing the complexity of the large group blocks the efficacy of social conscience. From April 2020, Trump dismissed five inspectors general: for Intelligence, Transportation, Defense, Health and Human Services, and the State Department. In ridding the government of those who hold government to account, he lobotomised the nation's ability to exercise conscientious governance. There was to be no oversight now, no accountability.

Hatred of government began to escalate in the 1950s, with the John Birch Society and then increased in the post Goldwater conservative era. The wealth of the middle class of the Eisenhower era waned and the time was right for some to sow discontent within the nation. As Jill Lepore points out in *These Truths*, Nixon's decision to employ dirty tricks against his democratic opponents instituted a process intended to distort the truth and to mess with our sense of reality. Kevin Phillips, one of his advisors, stated that the aim of Nixon's strategy was to make people hate one another. Indeed, Vice President Spiro Agnew wrote: "Dividing the American people has been my main contribution to the national political scene ... I not only plead guilty to this charge, but I am somewhat flattered by it" (Lepore, 2018, p. 639).

How can we understand the emergence of openly expressed hatred of fellow members of a democracy? Why try to undermine one's own nation?

A large group is vulnerable to destructive, hate-driven politics in which the aim is to disable government itself. It is less about opposing particular policies (although that will be so) than it is about making government impossible. By disabling government, the alignment between corporate, market, and capital forces is freed to oil the rails for sociopaths to gain greater power and wealth.

As I have argued, disabling government helps its advocates because complex, inbuilt frustration (such as that of modern American democracy) is nullified through the development of a new mind, one that is unburdened of having to consider issues—wealth inequality, sexism, racism—that require thinking. Whereas in better times democracies depend upon a form of language in which argument is signifier based (what is said means something and leads on logically to other meaningful signified thoughts), in the constriction of democracy imposed by the right, signs replace signifiers. Rather than using language to think with, now it is enough to weaponise and simplify language. "Liberal" means evil. "Pro life" is a sign of goodness even though many in that movement favour the murder of members of the Pro Choice movement.

If we want to tackle this situation, we must confront its psychological dimension. Nations—and international relations—are experienced by all of us as too complex. Right wing thinkers deal with this by negative and positive hallucination. They do not see what they do not like seeing and they invent what does not exist. Left wing thinkers deal with it by atomising the complexity into small segments of smaller group interests: identity politics. The left will pick up favourite passing issues, talk about them, commune together around them, but they do not face the task of making large group democracy functional.

Sometime in the late nineteenth century it was becoming unconsciously clear to people all over Europe that the nation state was a polo ground for sociopathic norms. The socio-generative internal mental structures (conscience, empathy, and so on) that had functioned in smaller social groups such as a village or town were becoming loosened, and a new type of personality emerged. This was the "necessary" sociopath, who was enabled to navigate, thrive, and gain power when the large group operated from within a psychotic process.

I distinguish between a psychopath and a sociopath—a complex topic—which I only mention in brief to help our considerations here. A psychopath is a severely compromised person with no effective conscience, little ego control over his impulses, and not interpersonally appealing. A sociopath is highly skilled in manipulating people and occasions to gain personal advantage at almost any cost. This person is a charmer, able to imitate conscientiousness and empathy, but all positive attributes are learned behaviours easily discarded if need be. This person is a ruthless opportunist who can however bring people together, can initiate change, and see things through, but he operates under the law of quid pro quo: any favour done by him licenses his expectation that the other will return the favour. Thus over time, the sociopath can build up a very large power base of those indebted to him.

One question arising from the populist "mind" is whether this is an answer to the impossibility of governance in the large democratic nation. Are nations simply one step too far away from the individual self's ability to be a genuine participant in such a group process?

Perhaps the American Revolution seemed promising because the founding fathers remained as transitional figures between the formation of the national government and its functions over the decades following the constitution. The first five presidents (Washington, John Adams, Jefferson, Madison, and Monroe) had been involved in the constitutional conventions that formed the government. They were in office from 1789 to 1825: a crucial period of thirty-six years in which through governance they implemented their theory of governing. The next generation of presidents—another period of thirty-six years—involved no less than ten presidents. It was a new generation and in particular one removed from the custodial link between the concept of the country (constitution) and governance. And with the Civil War the United States not only enacted deep divisions, it also stands as a monument to the hazards of trying to pass on democracy to those who have not given it much thought.

Indeed, the Civil War expressed many things, but did it also signal to its population that people could not sustain conscientious thinking in such a large group? In 1774 the population was 2.5 million. In 1861, it was 31 million.

Figures in democratically elected governments are meant to be *links* between the individual and the nation or political body, but how can they be if the constituents are in the tens of thousands? Or, in the case of the EU, did the nationals regard their MEPs (Members of the European Parliament) as representing them?

I use the term "links" both in the ordinary sense—in this case to connect people with their government—and in Wilfred Bion's sense of a psychic connection. The founding fathers linked their theory of government to its practice and in doing so realised preconceptions about government that could eventually be conceptualised. That might lead to constitutional change or acts of Congress, but importantly many of these people were psychologically connected to their obligations and tasks.

However, as politicians diminished the ethical responsibility of their national governments (cf. deregulation)—including the sustained marginalisation of the UN, World Court, and other bodies—instead of facilitating greater citizen involvement in these large groups, the institutions of nation states and the UN were increasingly removed from the populations.

In effect, leaders abandoned the responsibility to ensure representative presence in these increasingly large groups. In doing so, they unwittingly diminished our understanding of how these groups functioned and excluded citizen involvement in these larger entities.

Part of the problem we face in the modern world is the possibility that the nation state is too large a group for the conscientious self and is more suited for the sociopathic sides of ourselves. These large groups not only invite sociopathy, they may need our ability to negatively hallucinate our crimes in order to mobilise the modern state.

If so, then this is a profound psychological crisis. Blaming economic forces, or corruption, or whatnot for the decline of democracy misses the point. In a small or medium sized group it can work. In the mass society, democracy will be occupied by sociopaths, unless we hold people to account for their actions on the national or international stage.

Indeed, the rotating door of politics—like that of CEOs in the corporate realm—means that sociopaths who have wreaked havoc on a nation will come and go—through election or simply resignation—without having to bear responsibility for their actions.

It is the unaccountability of leaders to the large group for their actions that leaves us inside the sociopathic vacuum: one that sucks the ethical life out of selves as they become deeply embedded in known national and international crimes.

This essay has focused on the disturbing convergence of psychotic processes and sociopathy that are, right now, imperilling large countries and the relation between nations. This might be a matter for judicial review but my argument is based on the fact that those processes are also mental health issues and we need to consider how to reform our democracies in order to preserve the necessity of freedom of thought and speech. A ground-up protest movement will not, in my view, generate enough sustained support for reforms to take place. Instead, there needs to be considerate public discussion of a few key transformations.

We need to discuss and engage the psychopathologies of a large group.

For example, when public officials knowingly lie to their constituents we might think of this as ordinary politics, or within the ballpark of spinning the truth to suit one's own policies, and so forth. We should be able to distinguish that sort of falsehood formation from a different reality—serial lying—when a person or a group knowingly produces false information in order to prevent the public from perceiving the truth.

The reason for such accountability proposed here is not on ethical grounds (although one could make that argument) but on the grounds of mental health. Pushing back against serial lying that disables a population from perceiving, assessing, and judging reality is a mental health issue!

Without standards of accountability we cannot possibly navigate the psychological, sociological, and political challenges of the future. As I have argued, however, we cannot expect accounts to be met if we remain in the hinterland of a psychological understanding of group behaviour.

It is beyond time for democratic nations to return to political theory and science, to include people skilled in group relations that will help groups identify, understand, and resolve psychotic and sociopathic processes of thought. The task would be to free the group to come to more considered and sane solutions.

To echo the greatest political psychologist of the twentieth century—Erich Fromm—it is time we renew the quest for a sane society.

Christopher Bollas
August 2020

References

Bollas, C. (2018). *Meaning and Melancholia*. London: Routledge.

Fanon, F. (2008). *Black Skin, White Masks*. New York: Grove.

Freud, S. (1930a). *Civilization and Its Discontents. S. E., 21*. London: Hogarth.

Krishnamurti, J. (2003). *Krishnamurti's Notebook*. New York: Krishnamurti Publications of America.

Lepore, J. (2018). *These Truths: A History of the United States*. New York: W. W. Norton.

Nettleton, S. (2017). *The Metapsychology of Christopher Bollas: An Introduction*. London: Routledge.

Stern, D. N. (1985). *The Interpersonal World of the Infant: A View from Psychoanalysis and Developmental Psychology*. New York: Basic Books.

CHAPTER 2

The coronavirus pandemic and its meanings*

Michael Rustin
London, England

I should say to begin with that although I believe there are significant aspects of the coronavirus pandemic which can be illuminated through the ideas of psychoanalysis, I believe there also many aspects of it which need to be explained in other ways. So before I reflect on how a psychoanalytic paradigm can engage with this ongoing tragedy, I would like to sketch out an understanding of its wider social and political dimensions.

Rather surprisingly a theoretical model which illuminates the current situation is one which was set out by Leon Trotsky in his history of the Russian revolution (1932), in which he explained its historical character. This was his "Theory of Uneven and Combined Development". His argument was that what had made the revolution possible was the presence in an essentially backward Russian society of some exceptionally "modern" and developed sectors. Among these were a flourishing industrial capitalism, an organised working class, and an advanced

---

*A version of this chapter appears in *Revista Brasileira de Psicanálise* Volume 54, Numero 2, 2020, whose editors first invited me to write this as a paper. It is reprinted with permission.

intelligentsia, of which the Bolsheviks and other communists, socialists, and anarchists comprised one element. But what condemned the revolution to extreme difficulties, in his view, was the fact that this "modern" segment existed within a system which consisted of semi-feudal means of agricultural production (serfdom had only been abolished in 1861), an illiterate peasantry, widespread religiosity and superstition, and an autocratic and brutal form of government by the Tsarist state. This was, even when it was published in 1932, a prescient analysis of the situation which the revolutionaries had faced, and which led to the eventual failure of their modernising project and the catastrophes which took place as it proceeded.[1]

How can this theoretical model of change help to explain a crisis as completely different from political and social revolution as the current global pandemic? The explanation lies in the conjunctions of the effects of some highly advanced and some "early" and backward aspects of social and economic development, which are both relevant to these very different phenomena. It seems likely that the coronavirus had its biological origins in food markets in Wuhan, China in which trade in live animals, captured from the wild and slaughtered without preventive hygiene in the markets, was combined with the sale of domestic animals and many other products. It was possible in those conditions (as with earlier epidemics such as SARS) for a virus to cross species, perhaps with intermediate wild animal vectors such as bats. This is the "pre-modern" element of the situation.[2]

Superimposed on this close contact in food markets between the organs and diseases of wild animal species and their human traders (which I describe as a "pre-modern" form of commerce) has been the highly modern speed of transmission of this disease. This has been due to the rapid flow of human beings across the globe that happens in our communications environment. This has been described by one sociologist of globalisation as a "space of flows", a concept developed within the

---

[1] Justin Rosenberg, professor of international relations at the University of Sussex, has revisited the theoretical model of uneven and combined development to explain contemporary geopolitical developments (Rosenberg, 2013).

[2] Unfortunately it seems that for political reasons some in China may now be disputing what seems to be the most likely explanation of the virus's origins.

elaboration of the theory of globalisation by many scholars (e.g. Beck, 2000; Castells, 1998; Giddens, 1991; Harvey, 1989; Massey, 2002; Urry, 2007) in recent decades. Many component features of globalisation were predicted within this model, including the rise of global trade, vast and almost instantaneous flows of finance capital, and the central role of information technology among its features. And, as its resistances or negative "feedbacks", the emergence of "fundamentalist" resistances to modernisation, large flows of refugees, and global terrorism.

A consequence of this situation of combined under- and overdevelopment has been the exposure of the entire world's population, in the space of just twelve months to the Covid-19 virus, which health and social systems in most though not all nations have so far been unable to suppress.

There are other aspects of "uneven development" relevant to the pandemic. Its impact is disclosing large differences in the vulnerability of populations to the virus, and in the capacities of social systems to contain it. These differences are in part a function of relative material wealth, as has always been the case with the incidence of epidemics. It is much more feasible for privileged social groups to isolate themselves, or flee to relative seclusion, than it is for the poor. (It was common in cities in Renaissance Europe for elites to take refuge in rural retreats in this way.[3]) These differences are also a consequence of the quality and amount of resources invested in public health systems—the availability of doctors, hospital beds, testing and tracing facilities, reliable data, etc. But levels of material wealth—average per capita income—are by no means the only significant cause of variance in the harms caused by the virus. It appears that differences in the ideologies and power structures underlying social systems are also critical in shaping its effects.

It is striking, for example, that European nations have for the most part achieved better outcomes than are being achieved in the United States in the management of Covid-19. Within Western Europe, the United Kingdom however has done somewhat worse than its European equivalents, after a period when Spain and parts of northern Italy were

---

[3] Boccaccio's fourteenth-century collection of stories, the *Decameron*, was framed as having been told by a group of noble persons sheltered outside Florence from the Black Death.

overwhelmed by the first impact of the virus. China and other nations in South-East Asia have however been substantially more effective in their action to contain its effects than most other areas of the world.

It seems that differences in the moral foundations and beliefs within social systems make a difference to societies' response to the virus. It is evident that in some societies the value assigned to the protection of lives, *all* lives, outweighs all other purposes, and shapes the priority given to the suppression of the virus. But in some other societies, or among their ruling elites, this has not been the case. Some nations and their governments appear to have been willing to tolerate an incidence of infection and mortality from the virus, which they conceive presumably as an unalterable "fact of nature", to a degree which others are not. They have usually set the growth of their economies and the liberty of individuals as priorities against the role of governments in protecting lives. Many societies believe that they can eliminate the virus entirely, or at least for all practical purposes, while others seem prepared to tolerate infection rates in their tens of thousands, in order that economic life can continue with least damage.[4] A further explanation of this difference lies in the fact that some societies have the willingness and capacity to offset the economic harms done to individuals when markets are suppressed, by collective measures of compensation, or employment-creation, while for others this is ideologically repugnant. The defining difference between these normative systems seems to lie in the value they assign to individuals' freedom, compared with the value they assign to the health and well-being of all persons, to which they hold that some individuals' freedom needs sometimes to be subordinated. Such differences in fundamental concepts of "social solidarity" are also of course revealed in other areas of social life.

These differences do not map in any simple way onto a political spectrum of left and right, although they do sometimes coincide. Some Asian nations which are far from socialist, such as Taiwan, Japan, and

---

[4] Members of Independent SAGE, a group of scientists separate from the UK government's SAGE (Scientific Advisory Group for Emergencies) have argued that this is a false choice, and that those nations which have suppressed the virus most effectively have also suffered least economic damage from it. Such a comparison can be made between Germany and the United Kingdom.

South Korea, have adopted socially protective positions in their response to the coronavirus, as has China, which is ruled by a Communist party but has a substantially capitalist economy.

Many specific kinds of social fracture have emerged in those societies where a commitment to universal protection and well-being, in response to the virus, has been lacking. In the United Kingdom, two sub-populations are revealed to have been especially vulnerable to the virus. One of these was the elderly and infirm population of care homes, where the incidence of infection and death has been very high—some estimates state that this was 20,000 out of 45,000 deaths in the UK by early July 2020.

Another were black and ethnic minority populations, who have also been afflicted in disproportionate numbers. Black and ethnic minority staff in the British National Health Service have been exceptionally vulnerable victims of the virus, for reasons which are not yet wholly understood. More broadly, the severity of the impact of Covid-19 in Britain is correlated with indices of social and economic well-being and deprivation. Through such factors as more densely occupied housing and inescapable obligations to work outside the home, the poorer members of society have suffered most from the virus (Dorling, 2020).

There has to be recourse to explanations in terms of unconscious processes of denial of social realities and of people's needs, and of the projections of vulnerability and of value between social groups, fully to account for these phenomena. The disproportionate impact of the virus on black and ethnic minority populations has become linked to the concerns of the Black Lives Matter movement, as evidence has appeared during this period of police mistreatment of black people, following the murder by police of George Floyd on May 25, 2020 in Minneapolis. There have been angry reactions to these events, which in the USA have led to sometimes violent counter-reactions on the streets, creating the polarised and also sometimes violent political environment in which the American presidential election has just been fought.

Psychodynamic aspects of the crisis

So far I have mainly discussed explanations of the current crisis which lie in the domain of social structures and processes, rather than the spheres which are of specific interest to psychoanalysts. The reason for this is my belief that the principal explanations of this crisis have to be sought in the dynamics of societies, rather than primarily in the psychological dispositions of individual actors. However, unconscious processes have an existence in social groups and communities as well as in individuals. I contend that fears, anxieties, and enactments in and by individuals in situations like the present one, although real, are largely shaped by the social environments in which they are formed, although as I have said these social environments have an unconscious dimension. It is differences between societies which cause and most fully explain what happens to the individuals within them, rather than it being the case that differences between individuals cause and most explain what happens to societies.

The dispositions and personalities of figures such as Trump, Bolsanaro, and Johnson of course have significant consequences for their societies (and for all of us). Nevertheless their attributes and characteristic kinds of action are best understood as the effects of their social milieus rather than as their cause. Freud (and those like Adorno (1951) who developed a Freudian analysis of Fascism) saw "leaders" as produced by the socio-psychological needs and collective transferences of their followers, rather than as the primary causes of their behaviours. The dynamic interactions between Donald Trump and the mass rallies which he has continuously used to re-energise his own feelings of resentment and rage are a contemporary example of this interactive process.

But one should ask, what does a psychoanalytic perspective add to our understanding of a crisis and conjuncture of the present kind? Is there a conception of unconscious mental processes, as these functions are shared at collective levels of mind, which adds illumination, and needs to be incorporated within the framework of a socio-political analysis? Here is the broader problem of how one might bring about a theoretical integration of psychoanalytical and sociological understandings, which is a topic I have explored elsewhere (Rustin, 2016).

I believe the psychoanalytical concept most valuable in the understanding of the present crisis is Bion's idea of "containment" (1975) and what arises from its presence or absence, its strength or its weakness. What the present crisis, with its overlapping and intersecting dimensions, is bringing about is the collapse of many "containing" structures, and the habits of mind and capabilities which depend on them. What is "contained", in the psychoanalytic view, by containing structures are anxieties, both recognised and unrecognised, and both conscious and unconscious (which are not quite the same thing.) What emerges when containment is lacking are many often extreme defences against anxiety, such as splitting and denial, the projection of feared threats and evils into others, and a reversion to paranoid-schizoid and narcissistic states of mind. Melanie Klein and Wilfred Bion both believed that the capacity for reflection and thought, and for holding together in the mind the awareness of dispositions both to love and to hate, had their preconditions in a person's emotional and mental development. Klein thought of this as the attainment of "depressive" capabilities, or the "depressive position" (Rustin & Rustin, 2017; Segal, 1973). Bion thought of it as the presence of a secure relation between "container and contained". Such experiences of containment take place in the first instance in the earliest months and years of life, in the context of the intimate family. That is, in a relationship between infant and mother, but also between mother and father, father and infant, and between members of a larger family group, including siblings. This is the primary location or incubator of the capacity to form and maintain relationships, which once formed usually become extended beyond the sphere of the family into a wider environment of communities and workplaces. And also into establishing relationships, which have both an internal and an external dimension, with other kinds of "objects" which can have symbolic as well as emotional meanings, such as vocations, places, forms of art or science, and cultural or social "goods". Early experiences of containment are the micro-settings within which the capacities for life in society are developed and made possible.

Such micro-settings depend for their existence on wider environmental contexts of security and well-being. In well-functioning societies these can often be taken for granted, to a greater or lesser degree, as the good enough contexts for lives to be lived and for personal development to take place, and even adventures into the unknown to be embarked upon. What happens when grave multiple crises such as those of the present occur is that such surrounding contexts, or conditions of existence, become deeply threatened and disrupted. In relation to the Covid-19 disease itself, we see trust in others, and also in governments, being eroded, as dangers and risks to individuals and families grow. We now see many governments becoming concerned that the reserves of public trust and the compliance on which practical means of containing this disease depend (e.g. quarantines, the use of face masks, social distancing, vaccination, caution in the use of public spaces) will be eroded, if people lose confidence in governments' capabilities and actions. This breakdown of trust is already occurring in many places, and for understandable reasons.

Another level of disruption occurs when particular social groups (e.g. people of colour) come to believe that the society in which they live, and especially those holding power within it, neglects, mistreats, and even brutalises them. Additional anxieties arise when basic material security becomes endangered, for example through economic recession and unemployment. Further kinds of threat are experienced at the level of cultural identity, when it is felt that the symbolic worth of a group's entire "imagined community" is put in jeopardy, for example through denigration by others, or by the perceived capture of power and privilege by competitors. Arlie Hochschild's book, *Strangers in Their Own Land* (2016), showed the origins of the resentment of Republican voters in the American South in their feeling that they had been excluded from the opportunities offered by the "American dream" by the privileging of rival groups in society, located in their minds mainly in northern cities. Fintan O'Toole (2018) has described the emotional core of the Brexit campaign in England as made up of a combination of triumphalist omnipotence and masochistic victimhood and self-pity. Resentment towards "others" who are perceived to be in the ascendant, and the building of animosity towards such groups, are a principal resource of nationalists and populists like Trump for sustaining, often by demagogic means, their bases of political support.

The crisis of "uneven and combined development" which I have characterised has both revealed and intensified many kinds of structural inequalities within and between nations. This crisis is giving rise to understandable and indeed justifiable demands for their redress. Some in this situation find themselves taking up highly radical and even utopian positions in asserting what now ought to be done. Some believe that the entire social system should be dismantled and started afresh, difficult as it is to give a specific meaning to this idea. What we know, however, is that demands made of society from those lacking recognition and power are liable to provoke countervailing demands and reactions from those who currently possess it. Redistributions and adjustments of power and privilege to resolve opposed and competing claims are usually difficult to achieve. Conflicts arising from such struggles can give rise to the risk of organised violence and social breakdown, as we have seen in the past. Strategies for reform and for redress of inequalities and injustices need in my view to take account of the probability of such counter-reactions, and to find ways of limiting their severity and destructiveness.

I am inclined to believe that in the present crisis the restoration of a measure of "containing" government, which can begin to tackle and resolve immediately critical problems (like those caused by the coronavirus and by global warming) is a prerequisite for bringing about the many fundamental changes which the general condition of "combined and uneven development" makes desirable and necessary. It seems likely that President-elect Biden will now try to bring this about in the United States.

However, it should be noted that a concern with states of "containment" is not the only psychoanalytic preoccupation with a social condition which might have relevance. In an astute observation about Freud's own writings, the sociologist Zigmunt Bauman (2009) noted that the main anxieties which preoccupy a society were subject to change, even between social epochs. Freud's main preoccupation, Bauman wrote, was with the excessive repression of desires, and with the constraints imposed in his time on thought and action, especially in the sexual sphere. This was before the liberating effects of his own teaching on this cultural climate, which has been significant, took effect.[5] Excessive repression was also a concern of Melanie Klein, as we see in her focus on the destructive effects on personalities of a persecutory superego. But in modern times, in Bauman's view, the pendulum has swung far in the opposite direction, such that a dominant social anxiety now arises in regard to what are perceived to be excessive freedoms of sexual

---

[5] Ernest Gellner, who had previously (1985) been a severe critic of Freud, wrote later in his work (1995) of the great debt which society owed to Freud, in the effect of his writing in diminishing social repression, and in thereby making possible wider experiences of pleasure and enjoyment.

expression and action. Thus we have almost phobic anxieties about the sexual safety of children, and about whether sexual initiatives in interpersonal life are to be experienced as aggressive or abusive, or are merely to be recognised as overtures and approaches without which no sexual relationship could ever come about. (Of course they can be either of these.) In the broader sphere, the additional scope for expression and communication, for example through "trolling", which has been enabled by the expansion of social media, gives rise to anxieties about abuses of free expression. Intemperate abuse, and sometimes violent threats, are reported to be common features of communications to public figures through these media, debasing and degrading the entire climate through which ideas and opinions can be exchanged, and no doubt deterring many people from taking any part in them. It seems that the forms of regulation which have to some degree constrained violent and antisocial kinds of communication through conventional printed media can often be completely evaded in the use of social media. At the present time moves towards the restraint of such unrestrained kinds of social media is desirable, even urgent. Some pushback against this situation is in fact now taking place, in the demands on "platforms" such as Facebook and Twitter that they exercise greater surveillance over what appears on them. It is in this cultural climate that I believe a psychoanalytic focus on the "containing" end of the spectrum between freedom and control has relevance. Times differ, and what is psychoanalytically indicated as being desirable and appropriate for such times may differ also.

A more benign aspect of the "uneven and combined development" which I have suggested has been the context of the pandemic has now emerged (as was indeed anticipated from early on) in the discovery and impending mass manufacture and distribution of vaccines against the disease. If, as now seems likely, this proceeds according to plans, it will amount to a remarkable achievement of science, and of public health systems which make its discoveries available for human use. Institutions and practices of "modernity" (of course they are partially different ones) which made possible the global spread of the virus within the span of a year, seem now likely to alleviate and perhaps even suppress its effects within a similar period of time.

It is probable that the social inequities and ideological divisions which have shaped the social impact of the virus will continue to be present in the distribution of its vaccine remedies, both within nations and between them. Some nations will commit themselves to universal free access to vaccines, others will allow inequalities of financial access to health care to influence access to vaccines. In some nations, such as the USA, it appears that antipathy to and suspicion of governments is such that even vaccination is perceived as an affront to individual liberty, with obvious consequences for public health. But there are influential voices such as that of the World Health Organization which are committed to ensuring the equitable access of the vaccine between rich and poor countries, broadly the North and South, and it seems these voices will have some effect.

Some of those with power, such as those in Trump's administration, have been seeking to call a halt to the processes of globalisation and its instruments, and thereby to hold on to the advantages they believe they already possess. That ideological position has just suffered a major defeat in the American presidential election, and it seems likely that some good consequences will now follow from this. My own view is that the solution to the harmful effects which globalisation has undoubtedly had lies not in arresting or reversing its development, but rather in making these in some of their aspects more universal and comprehensive in their extent. This would aim at a form of combined and even, rather than uneven, development. I've elsewhere imagined this as a "progressive modernisation" (Rustin, 2019).

This is to imagine a world order in which, for example:

- The goals of good public health and the means to secure this become universal.
- The arrest of global warming becomes a common human task. Just as the sciences have provided the key to solving the problems set by the pandemic so it is clear that their role is also central to overcoming the problems of climate change. The achievements of science in the domain of public health should now be a source of hope in regard to this greater crisis.
- The predicted problems of unmanageable flows of refugees from impoverished and war-torn countries are dealt with not through constructing barriers and "beautiful walls", but by enabling problems of poverty and disorder to be addressed in the regions from which refugees come.

- Goals of economic development are set for the entire world, and not merely for individual nations.
- The emergence of governments capable of "containing" the anxieties of their citizens, rather than of arousing and provoking them through their manifest irresponsibility and divisiveness, is a necessary condition of positive development.[6]

It is only of course competent and well-supported governments, working together with each other, which could bring such a benign process about, in cooperation with other social, economic, and cultural actors. It might seem an impossible prospect, though not necessarily so when one sees what Europe accomplished in the years after the Second World War, or indeed what the Chinese have been accomplishing, in regard to poverty and living standards, within their own national boundary.

Such goals are not far from those which have been advanced by many international agencies, and by visionary theorists of human development and "flourishing" such as Martha Nussbaum and Amartya Sen (1993) and which became embodied in the United Nations Human Development Index and Annual Reports.

And after all, what other alternatives are there to global catastrophe?

Michael Rustin
November 2020

References

Adorno, T. (1951). Freudian theory and the pattern of Fascist propaganda. Reprinted in: A. Arato & E. Gebhardt (Eds.), *The Essential Frankfurt School Reader* (pp. 118–137). Oxford: Blackwell, 1978.

---

[6] I have surmised that dysfunctional and untrustworthy governments in the USA and the UK have unconsciously diffused and transmitted their disturbed states of mind to much lower levels of leadership in their society, even within specific institutions. It follows that greater responsibility and reflective capacities at higher levels, such as we may now see at least in the USA, may also transmit themselves downwards, and indeed sideways. This is a hypothesis which may now become subject to test.

Bauman, Z. (2009). Freudian civilisation revisited: or Whatever happened to the reality principle? *Journal of Anthropological Psychology*, *21*, Department of Psychology, Aarhus University: 1–9. https://psy.au.dk/fileadmin/Psykologi/ Forskning/Forskningsenheder/Journal_of_Anthropological_Psychology/ Volume_21/target.pdf (last accessed December 21, 2020).

Beck, U. (2000). *What Is Globalisation?* Cambridge: Polity.

Bion, W. R. (1975). *Attention and Interpretation*. London: Tavistock.

Castells, M. (1998). *The Information Age: Economy Society and Culture, Vols 1, 2, and 3*. Oxford: Blackwell.

Dorling, D. (2020, November 29). Want to understand the Covid map? Look at where we live and how we work. *Guardian*. https://theguardian.com/ commentisfree/2020/nov/29/want-to-understand-the-covid-map-look-at-where-we-live-and-how-we-work (last accessed December 21, 2020).

Gellner, E. (1985). *The Psychoanalytic Movement*. London: Paladin.

Gellner, E. (1995). Freud's Social Contract. In: *Anthropology and Politics* (pp. 62–93). Oxford: Blackwell.

Giddens, A. (1991). *The Consequences of Modernity*. Cambridge: Polity.

Harvey, D. (1989). *The Condition of Modernity*. Oxford: Blackwell.

Hochschild, A. R. (2016). *Strangers in Their Own Land: Anger and Mourning on the American Right*. New York: New Press.

Massey, D. (2002). Globalisation: what does it mean for geography? *Geography*, *87*(4): 293–296. https://think-global.org.uk/wp-content/uploads/dea/docu- ments/dej_9_2_massey.pdf (last accessed December 21, 2020).

Nussbaum, M., & Sen, A. (Eds.) (1993). *The Quality of Life*. Oxford: Oxford University Press.

O'Toole, F. (2018). *Heroic Failure: Brexit and the Politics of Pain*. London: Apollo.

Rosenberg, J. (2013). The "philosophical premises" of uneven and combined development. *Review of International Studies*, *39*(3) 569–597.

Rustin, M. E., & Rustin, M. J. (2017). *Reading Klein*. London: Routledge.

Rustin, M. J. (2016). Sociology and psychoanalysis. In: A. Elliott & J. Prager (Eds.), *The Routledge Handbook of Psychoanalysis in the Social Sciences and Humanities* (pp. 259–277). London: Routledge.

Rustin, M. J. (2019). Is there an alternative to reactionary modernisation? *Soundings*, *71*: 116–127.

Segal, H. (1973). *Introduction to the Work of Melanie Klein*. London: Karnac, 1988.

Trotsky, L. (1932). *The Russian Revolution*. New York: Simon & Schuster.

Urry, J. (2007). *Mobilities*. Cambridge: Polity.

Part II

Living and thinking
in pandemic times

CHAPTER 3

The shattering of a denial as food for thought

Bernard Chervet
Paris and Lyon, France

O ur reflexivity, or the fact that we recognise the implications of our unconscious psychic life in our thoughts and acts, is solicited as soon as we feel feelings of loss and lack, regardless of their origin; and even more so, when these feelings are linked to a symptom or caused by disturbances in our environment signifying the loss of friends and family and of our daily points of reference, our habits. We can deduce from this that we had attributed to that now missing part of external reality a function that should have been governed by a superego derived from personal elaboration, rather than by a borrowed superego that arises through delegation. That part of reality made up also a part of us therefore.

This exteriorised delegation of part of our narcissistic functions is at the core of child development, as well as at the core of the analytical cure due to the transference of authority and the transference of aspirations in reference to an ideal. The parent and the analyst, in as much as they are *fellow human beings* who are physically as well as psychologically close to us, that is, close in actuality and close also to that towards which the subject will strive, represent the ideal mental functioning that we are supposed to attain. They are the object of a transposition of the psychological potentialities to be laid in place. In the best-case scenario, such a transposition may have helped the subject to transform her anxiety into a fear of danger, by drawing on the support of a tangible and perceivable object.

As early as 1895, Freud names this transpositional *other* the *Nebenmensch*, and recognises its three qualities: being the object of satisfaction, being the object of hostility, and being a helping force (Freud, 1950a, p. 330). In 1921, when he had begun contemplating the impact of the tendency to extinguish impulses through the repetition compulsion, fate neuroses, and the negative therapeutic reaction, he again refers to this *other* and specifies that the other intervenes "as a model, as an object, as a helper and as an opponent" (1921c, p. 69).

This anaclitic transposition onto an exterior, of potential psychic functions pending their full realisation, eases our psychic work by momentarily adopting the solutions brought by another, and at the same time makes us very dependent on this external element. This is how the *cultural superego* is formed from prefabricated solutions found within the family, groups, and culture. The main function of this collective cultural superego is to alleviate the suffering that emanates from the traumatic core present in the heart of each and every one of us, by providing us with worldviews (*Weltanschauungen*), with saturating definitions of truth, of reality, of research, of science, of life.

Psychological thinking emerges from loss and from the ambivalence experienced during the mourning process occasioned by such losses. In 1915, in the midst of WWI, Freud elaborated the psychology of the conflict of feelings as experienced at the death of a beloved person who is at the same time hated and felt to be a stranger.

Contextualisation

All psychoanalysts around the world have had to experience such changes and losses in their daily practice as a result of the disruption created by the Covid-19 pandemic caused by the SARS-CoV-2 coronavirus.

A conflict of feelings towards our practice emerged. It was already there, albeit often ignored. We had to come up with and employ new methods of working.

This adaptation required of us a supplementary psychic effort, which led to the exacerbation of our feelings of ambivalence. Some patients and analysts preferred suspending treatment. There was also a tendency to transform sessions into mundane conversations and to give up on maintaining the asymmetry conducive to transference. Indeed, transference shifted to psychoanalysis itself, which became steeped with nostalgia, or on the contrary, with disappointment and anger.

Since contagion did not develop at the same rate around the world, we must contextualise the following remarks along a timeline. In France, the concerns for public health due to the virus first appeared in early March 2020, and by mid-March our practice was interrupted. The lockdown lasted two and a half months and our practice resumed in mid-May under the sign of such terms as *distancing* and *prevention measures*. The disruptions to daily life, and the consequent modifications to our practice, have been with us for six months and counting, while the number of deaths and hospitalised patients has decreased significantly and is currently very low. On the other hand, since the number of tests has increased, so has the number of positive tests. The vast majority of cases are asymptomatic. But since the beginning of this pandemic we have observed a very particular use of statistics. Only those that increase may be cited. What they represent becomes secondary, if not equivalent to the numbers themselves.

This contributes to maintaining a harmful traumatic pressure and source of conflict that results in the displacement of the tension thus created. Such use of statistics has made it possible to escalate social distancing, preventive measures, and the wearing of the mask. Far from being precautionary recommendations calling for citizens to assume their civic responsibility in halting the spread of the virus, these instructions have become mandatory prescriptions and their non-observance is subject to coercive measures.

The pandemic reminds us of what has long been known: "An epidemic is a social phenomenon with some medical aspects" (Virchow, 1995) (Rudolf Virchow, 1821–1902, German physician and politician).

Psychoanalytically speaking, numbers are used by the psyche to divert experiences of lack. The apotropaic effect of Medusa's head on the perception of castration consists in distracting one's attention from the presence of a lack by offering up a multitude of images, thus drawing awareness away from the lack and its experiences. This anti-traumatic measure can be used by anyone, but mass psychology employs it most readily.

This use of Covid statistics, to intentionally saturate a desperate population with diverting and traumatising affects, must be subjected to interpretation. It is possible to imagine that this saturation—all the more guaranteed when it makes use of highly unpleasant affects—serves to conceal other sources of lack, some of them less palpable, such as a widespread malaise in our Western civilisation following a century of very notable progress and the present-day limits of its capacities to evolve. Climatic concerns related to the depletion of our planet's resources due to exploitative theories of economic and industrial growth (based on the consumption of resources) in our Western civilisation are certainly more difficult to address than the diffuse yet nevertheless more discernible alarm caused by the virus. The fact that this virus is new (and requires a certain amount of time before a specific remedy may be found for it) facilitates its use as a displacement of these more fundamental concerns about the future of our civilisation, to which we also have no answer.

There is no doubt that our era, dominated by the notions of disinformation, alternative facts, and "post-truth" (elected Oxford Dictionaries Word of the Year in 2016), is conducive to disarray, conflicting contradictions, and peremptory declarations. This transference onto the word makes it possible to confuse facts and speech acts (i.e. opinions) with facts and acts that refer to things. Insofar as they are related via words, facts and acts may be considered equivalent, whereas from the point of view of their reference to things, they are not equivalent at all. A need for confusion dominates this beginning of the twenty-first century, which expresses the desire to create the world using words.

Initially, the factors of the Covid-19 disturbance may have appeared to have had a purely external origin: a virus coming from elsewhere. The awakened traumatic dimension called for an immediate response, with recourse to classic anti-traumatic means such as clinging to the sensory perception of tangible external realities capable of providing psychic content, and hence the anxious, repetitive, and even haunting and macabre appetite for messages concerning the virus, the disease, and the death toll. But there was also curiosity and the need to know about this virus, about infectious diseases, about their treatment, etc., as well as a more personal recollection of contagious childhood diseases, of family and group responses (school evictions) from our early childhood. We also appealed to history, that of the devastations caused by the great epidemics and pandemics of the past. We have had to recognise that there is a specific kind of amnesia regarding pandemics, and a denial as concerns their possible reappearance in the West. The old ones are part of the historical literature on plagues. More recent ones, of 1957 or 1969, have been forgotten. If the 1918–20 pandemic, the Spanish flu, has turned into myth, it now belongs to a collective memory heritage that remains imprecise as to the actual number of deaths it caused. The comparison with the flu following WWI (which saw 8 to 10 million deaths) is totally neglected, as is that with the annual seasonal flu (about 600,000 deaths). The Spanish flu caused at least 50 million deaths (WHO cites 100 million), 2.5% of the population at the time (about 2 billion, while today we are close to 8 billion); 2.5% of today's population would mean 200 million dead. The Asian flu of 1957 caused 2 million deaths, the Hong Kong flu of 1969 caused 1 million (between 32,000 and 40,000 in France). Who remembers that?

Similarly, for psychoanalysts, the mourning that Freud had certainly experienced, albeit modestly, for his daughter Sophie, who was swept away by the plague within five days in January 1920, is also ignored, or taken into account in an effort to personalise certain theoretical developments. A false determination is attributed to it concerning the introduction of the death drive into psychoanalytic theory. When Fritz Wittels, Freud's first biographer, called Freud's attention to this construction, the latter replied (1923) that he would certainly have made the same connection, but that *Beyond the Pleasure Principle* had been delivered to the printers in September 1919, at a time when Sophie was in "flourishing health". And he adds, by way of warning against the application of psychoanalysis to an author's biography: "What seems true is not always the truth" (Freud, 1924g, p. 287). In several personal letters Freud talks about his suffering and the absence of causality to blame: "I have no one to blame, and I know there is no place where one can lodge a complaint" (Letter to Ferenczi, February 4, 1920).

This sentence clearly expresses the extent to which the events that correlate with intrapsychic trauma provoke the search for aetiology, for causality, for an explanatory theory, a need to attribute responsibility to another or to oneself, a need to blame and to blame oneself; all this against a background of powerlessness.

After this first ambivalence in recognising the virus's existence and how dangerous it was, all means of protection and refuge were called upon, in addition to the search for causality, be it even in the form of the accusation of this or that wrongdoer. But there was also the call for a saviour, in this case in the guise of the medical and scientific knowledge that we attribute to the "specialists supposed to know". They were denied any chance of progressive understanding. They *had* to know.

The initial traumatic fright was joined by a causal theorising that accompanied the distressing experiences of our deprived narcissism. Since childhood, infantile sexuality theories meet this need for causality by deploying a dramatised scene of removal. The fantasy of castration by the father is thereby invoked, which leads to the advent of the father figure.

This traumatic disturbance has reminded us that our practice is embedded ordinarily in a social and political context whose implications are not apparent during normal times. This sometimes facilitates our proximity to the ideal psychoanalytical method, but more often than not forces us to work at a distance from this ideal model. The latter is in fact theoretical and serves as a reference in reflecting upon analytical practice.

True reflection was made possible once the existence of a private and collective denial (whose existence had preceded the traumatic external event concerning the threat to the general population's health) was recognised. A current denial can be used to maintain a past denial, or some other preoccupation that we are far less equipped to deal with. The shattering of the denial concerning epidemics has revealed and potentiated an internal traumatic quality awakened by the external threat of a contagious disease. The intrapsychic noise caused by this shattering was used to keep other denials in place. From that point onward, the contagion proved to be double, infectious and psychological, calling upon the logic of mass psychology at the origin of active mass amnesia in Western countries.

The ensuing reflection concerns both our individual psychology and the mass psychology present in our psychic life.

When contagion reared its head, it was first minimised, then met with preventive measures, and finally lockdown. Cities, streets, squares,

stations, everywhere emptied out. Bistros, restaurants, stores, librar-
ies, theatres, all meeting and cultural venues were closed. A feeling of
uncanny strangeness reigned, along with a haunting questioning: where
have all the people, cars, movements, noises gone? An anxiety-provoking
silent immobility had fallen over the world.

Then, feelings of ignorance, paradox, contradiction, and persecution,
even of nonsense, appeared. The traumatic experiences were constantly
being re-energised. The traumatic neurosis continued its low-frequency
course. The feeling of an *endlessness* began to set in, along with resignation and anger. The threat was impossible to outline; the feeling of pestilence, of possible contamination via proximity fuelled agoraphobia and
misanthropy towards one's neighbour. Puritanism awakened beyond
what the risks of the disease had called for. Closeness and physical contact were banned. Proximity and promiscuity became synonymous.

At the same time, the need to share, the need for solidarity, the concern for others, and a spirit of generosity brought about unexpected
mutual aid. The invention of a new way of living and working went
hand-in-hand with the hope of reinstating life as it had been before, and
of quickly putting an end to this external scourge. But the psyche had
been shaken as concerns its comforts, its habits, and its denials. Psychic
work is now underway; and even if attempts to reinstate denial accompany it, there is also an effort to gradually replace emergency anti-traumatic responses with a liberating mentalization of our object cathexis.

The disarray associated with ignorance and diffuse threats has long
provoked well-known reactions, but the context of social media has
exacerbated them. Aristotle once said: "The ignorant asserts, the learned
doubts, the wise reflects"; then Darwin: "Ignorance more frequently
engenders self-confidence than does knowledge."

In the twenty-first century, this principle has been called ultracrepi-
darianism, or the Dunning–Kruger effect. Those least qualified or competent to give an opinion are the ones who overestimate their competence
and the value of their opinion since they lack the means to evaluate it!

The context of uncertainty and our lack of anticipation have solicited
most particularly the castration complex as regards each person's feeling
of guilt, with its two-stage mechanism that consists of the *threat* (what is
heard) and of the *perceived reality* (what is seen); and hence the solutions
emanating from mass psychology, with the expounding of opinions of

all kinds and the search for causal theories whose saturating effect gives a sense of stable conviction and belief. Intense polemics that take no heed of rational arguments have reinforced this need to combat disarray.

Other generic solutions have appeared, such as the introduction of new words, neologisms (deconfinement, presential, distantial), or the modification of the meaning of words (social distancing in order not to say physical distancing) in the hopes of subduing this *traumatic other*. Yet more solutions have been sought, such as the appeal to the fantasy factor, with the need to find dramatic scenarios onto which we can transpose our concerns. The sale of works that metaphorise contagious diseases has skyrocketed. Such is the case of *The Plague* by Camus, which uses the metaphors of plague and rats to render the atmosphere of war and the advent of the Nazis. But science fiction books, fantasy literature, and even horror literature have also re-emerged. Echoes exist with the tales of the Brothers Grimm, the fantasy tales of Poe and Hoffmann, Gothic novels (Mary Shelley's *Frankenstein*), short stories and horror films (Stocker's *Dracula*), science fiction, works of premonitory value (Huxley, Orwell), and many other works that evoke dystopic worlds.

For psychoanalysts, the evocation of some psychic contagion vectored through a plague-ridden bestiary cannot but evoke Sophocles's *Oedipus Rex* and the punitive logic that follows the transgressions of psychic laws; not to mention Freud's own reference to the plague, a metaphor he used for psychoanalysis en route to contaminate the USA!

In the name of the unconscious guilt active in everyone, the viral contagion was readily interpreted somewhat animistically through the lens of the castration complex and its ineluctable destiny, namely castration. Instead of the return of an ancestor's wandering soul, we get intergenerational suspicion. The disease plays the role of the vengeful Erinyes.[1]

Social discourse bears many signs that evoke the relationship between psyche and drives, and calls for psychoanalytical interpretations that are rejected by mass logic.

This transposition of disarray into works of metaphorisation, through the traumatic characteristic that is ever in play in them, aids us in the task of mentalization. This detour through literature and works of art helps us

---

[1] Editors' note: In Greek mythology, the Erinyes (Furies) punished evildoers and those who had sworn false oaths.

to deal with the true endogenous origin of this traumatic quality, which initially lay hidden under external trauma and our appeal to causal theories.

Analytical practice

It is this intrapsychic and environmental context that has brutally projected itself onto our practice, with the immediate consequence of leaving our consulting rooms empty of the concrete, in-the-flesh presence of our patients, causing us to seek out means of remote work. We have continued sitting beside our empty couches, favouring the distal sound path. Fortunately, current technologies have been useful as such.

Several questions about our practice as analysts arise from the preceding reflections. What transferential reminiscences are awakened due to such changes in setting? How does the fundamental rule continue to aid in the process of mentalization, that is, the analytical method, while taking into account these changes? What does this change tell us about that which may have been hidden in the previous setting, disguised as a cultural superego shared collectively by us analysts? What are the effects of the new conditions that involve the phobia of proximity, the ban on touch, and the prescription of physical distance? How does the reduction of this physical presence to a distal sound, as well as the elimination of the sensory solicitations of concretely present bodies in a session, influence the psyche's use of thought and perception in order to treat the drive's tendencies to extinction, and to transform them into the promotion of desire? Is there no risk of mentalization being limited to enunciation, to the exclusion of renunciation and mourning?

This remote work has thus been imposed on us, which prevents an unequivocal comparison to the technique of remote analysis. It is thus necessary to differentiate between remote analysis as a method that stems from a choice made at the very beginning of analysis, and the remote sessions imposed by the aforementioned context, when there is no other possibility of working in our offices as we await the day when in-person sessions resume.

Amalgamation and confusion took hold of certain distinctions that seemed we thought were straightforward: in-out, individual-collective, singular-mass. They turned out to be less certain than we had wished to believe.

The analyst–analysand asymmetry wavered in the face of shared affect and common threat, the couch–chair setup became an uncertain landmark, but above all the representation–perception pair proved to be much more involved in our daily practice than we had previously thought. Suddenly, the oft-masked idealisation of analysis appeared patently before us, through a positive transference involving idealisation, as well as through its obverse, the hatred of transference in the name of the unreliability, if not the betrayal, of the promises made during analysis.

The analyst faces another major difficulty, in that she must take into account during the session a difference in speeds: between the speed of the epidemic and the ensuing race to disseminate contradictory information that cancels itself out as soon as it is issued; and the speed of the psychic work, which requires a latency interval in order to process the *après-coup* effect as governed by the laws of the psyche. The importance of the two-stage dynamics of this process must be respected by the analyst.

The situation of traumatic neurosis now confronts analysts all the more urgently. We are faced with the obligation to formulate interpretations of the desire to subdue this daily traumatic experience into latency: to forget it, to be able to rest from continually awakened fears, to return to the previous world, to sleep and to dream of another world, that of an afterwards free of the traumatic characteristic, a world of denial. The situation of denial which preceded its traumatic shattering becomes an object of desire.

It is in this transferential context that the analyst has found himself confronted with his duty not to defect in the face of this type of transference, and to persist in the work that he himself had been advocating. This conflict between invulnerability via idealisation and the restoration of the analytical situation to its familiar dynamics brings to mind childhood reminiscences, such as when a child thinks of the effective, definitive loss of his parents. The parents become mortal. This thought is accompanied by an affect of moral pain, that differs from oedipal thoughts of murder, which are underpinned by hatred. It is also at this time that the child creates his family romance in order to maintain this idealisation. So as not to give it up, he changes parents.

In order to grasp the contribution that all these upheavals have made to our reflection, in order to compare the newly imposed practice with the so-called habitual one, and to be able to reflect on the reverberation and *après-coup* effects that these disturbances have had on it, we must go through the main features of the theory of psychoanalytical practice.

Session, setting, and frame

The analytical method is based on a tripod: free association and evenly-suspended attention, both induced by the fundamental rule (Chervet & Donnet, 2014). This consists of a *setting* with its accompanying variants, and a *frame* made up of the thinking processes of both patient and analyst in the promotion of free association and evenly suspended attention, both induced by the fundamental rule as formulated by Freud in 1938: "complete candour on the one side and strict discretion on the other" (1940a, p. 174). The aforementioned transferential delegation also operates on the setting, which temporarily takes the place of a frame of thought. Setting and frame overlap at times. Hence the traumatic awakening when the setting is suddenly called into question, the patient being caught off guard. What was denied suddenly comes back from outside, through content related to a denial, in a way that is not always easy to identify.

This function of the setting (to serve as a temporary frame) appears abruptly when a denial is eliminated, whereas ideally this function should be gradually replaced by psychic work rooted in the preconscious and in psychic auto-eroticisms. The brutal release of denial is the equivalent of a wild interpretation.

A searching effect is induced by this return from the outside, in the form of a *danger-other* whose behaviour proves to be unexpected, random, and uncontrollable. This provokes a reminiscence of the *infantile search* which produces the infantile sexual theories. Scared, thought starts theorising even before experiencing pain. The search for causality makes use of the transposition of intrapsychic events to perceived external reality, and attributes the traumatic effect to it in the form of the notion of danger.

Through the formal regression in language that takes place during free association, the patient is able to come into proximity with his unconscious, and hence with his incidental thoughts, dreams, and incidental speech specific to the sessions. Evenly suspended attention also favours proximity with the unconscious, but remains linked to the theory of psychic functioning, a link thanks to which interpretations and constructions are able to emerge.

These two modalities of thought could only have been theorised after the integration of passivity into analytical practice. Their deployment in each member of the analytical couple depends on their respective disposition for passivity. The *"letting it come"* is essential, as is the *"letting it go"* through the incidental internal movements and the words of the other. These belong to the *regressive psychic activities of passivity*, as do dream, play, and eroticism, which constitute the points of reference required for the elaboration of a theory of analytical practice.

Session, dream, game

Without going back to the origins of the analytical method, to Mesmer's magnetism baquet, Charcot's hypnosis, Bernheim's suggestion, Breuer's retrogression, hand pressure, but also the Christian practice of confession and the exercises of various initiatory journeys, let us recall that this theorisation was initially inspired by the doctrine of the dream. Free association reveals itself in dreams to be a formal regression in language and a fulfilment of unconscious wishes realised under the guise of conscious becoming. It is also an interpretation, an invitation for realisation by means of the hypercathexis of language. It is a waking renunciation of the pleasure principle to which hallucinatory realisation belongs. It thus allows us to become aware.

Then it was children's play that made its contribution to the theory of practice. The repetition specific to free association and to the game of "Fort-Da" played during a session aims to instal in the patient the psychic processes required for separation and loss. Interpretation helps to complete the construction of the psychic processes that the awareness inherent to the resolution of the Oedipus complex and of future grief requires.

These first two points of reference, the dream and the game, transmit the model of a psychic functioning organised according to the process of the après-coup, and hence in two stages (Chervet, 2009). Dream and play are scenes within this two-stage in-between time, during which unconscious psychic work is carried out. The sessions aim at the same goal by means of language. Dreams use images and play uses material objects on which unconscious psychic processes are transposed, thus conferring an animistic value to the objects of play.

In this way, unconscious desires are realised during the session and thought processes are constructed in the service of the pleasure principle, while all the while remaining at a distance from unpleasant experiences. But repetition may turn into a repetition compulsion, hence the need to recognise that other factors are actively present during sessions.

Clinical work on war neuroses, post-traumatic neuroses, and repetitive dreams as experienced by soldiers returning from war (especially soldiers who had not been physically wounded), as well as the resistance observed during treatment that took the form of a reductive compulsion and a clinging to perception, was at the origin of *Beyond the Pleasure Principle*.

These clinical elements add to the theory of practice in that they compel theory to take into account another characteristic of drives, namely their tendency to restore previous states all the way back to the inorganic, the lifeless. Drives thus carry a traumatic quality by virtue of their *extinctive regressivity*. This can be awakened by external events and sensory perceptions, but it also manifests itself spontaneously internally through all sorts of sensations and discomforts, fearful affects, experiences of threat, anguish, distress, lack, pain. The true source is internal, but the treatment of its extinctive tendency requires a transposition onto external scenes, to which the traumatic origin may be attributed. This transposition takes place under the sign of the *inscription imperative*. This is how all the banal phobias of childhood that oppose the extinctive tendency are constructed: through a link with sensory perceptions and perceptive traces. Primary psychic restraint is thus established through the development of feelings and representations. This period of restraint constitutes the first stage of mentalization. It includes the body and its emotional and erogenous experiences. A tension of restraint is established, which is at the basis of primary masochism, from which thought and desire develop. It is the masochism of renunciation; restraint renounces extinction.

Physical presence and sensual regression

The erotic scene may serve as a point of reference in the attempt to grasp the implication of this new quality of drives in analytical practice. The erotic scene goes through a type of regression that goes so far as to experience extinction. The dream is opposed to it on account of its images, and free association on account of its use of language. The erotic scene carries out regressive psychic work by means of the sensual regression which is characteristic of its preliminaries. Erogenous sensuality regresses all the way back to organ-based sexuality. During this sensual regression, there is a conflict between the tendency to reduce tension and the tendency to seek out the elevation of desire beyond all tension, through the union of the two sensual regressions which potentiate each other. This conflict is resolved by the enjoyment–orgasm pair. The tendency to extinction is active both in reduction and in assertion; it is expressed by refraction, which is the limit of regression. The refractory quality (Chervet, 2020) is as close as possible to extinction, but signifies the latter's boundary, its latch, and is a base from which desire and erogenous sensitivity can be reborn. Regression to the refractory is restraint's outermost limit, which allows the process of libidinal co-excitation to unfold and to lead to the libidinal regeneration of a desire that is now open to the world (Chervet, 2011).

This is also what happens in session, simply through regression in language. The sensual regression experienced on the couch is influenced by the physical presence of bodies, and by the frustration that stems from the abstinence specific to analysis. This sensual regression influences both the content of the patient's associative discourse and also associativity itself, its style, being as it is a source of associativity. The various parts of the body, with their varying erogenous sensations, act as such sources of associativity. Scenes are enunciated in sessions which do not have to be performed otherwise than by the means of their enunciation, which in turn sets their limits. Psychoanalysis thus allows a modification of the erogeneity of a patient's body, and thus of his sexual life outside the session. This situation repeats the emergence of sensuality in childhood and the following resolution of the Oedipus complex, which takes place in proximity and in contact with one's parents. The murder at the basis of oedipal mourning cannot be performed *in absentia*.

By consolidating enunciation in language with the consciousness (making conscious, becoming conscious, becoming aware) of transgressive attractions that lead to extinction, session work intervenes in the process of libidinal co-excitation that can only succeed if the principle of renunciation is active via the superego and the kind of cathexis specific to it, namely hypercathexis. The libidinal regeneration produced by the process of libidinal co-excitation depends entirely on the efficiency of the hypercathexis. This is how the session, through its use of language, facilitates the fulfilment both of dreams and of play and eroticism.

Of course, the extinctive attraction will try to impose itself, disguised as what we call symptoms and resistances within the dream, the game, the erotic scene, and the analytical situation; hence the modalities of psychic work specific to each of these scenes which complement and reinforce each other; hence also all the lapses, temptations, and eventual transgressions. By imposing the enunciation of these scenes during the sessions, the fundamental rule relays the message that they all have their place outside the session, but that their enunciation in session helps in enabling the genesis and liberation of an emergent desire.

Session, collective cultural superego, and language

Earlier, we were reminded of the fact that infectious contagion is easily related to the phenomenon of psychic contagion and to mass psychology, leading us to reflect on the impact that the collective superego has on our sessions. The intimacy that enables session work derives from the tension between a singular intimacy, which takes into account transgressive attractions and temptations from the point of view of the psyche, and an intimacy that conforms to the group mentalities that protagonists inherit through their various unconscious identifications. The regression in session enables the actualisation of these different varieties of intimacy. The shattering of mass denial reveals just how much the collective cultural superego weighs on psychoanalysis. It is surreptitiously conducive to the alienations, ideologies, and systems of denial active within psychoanalytic institutions and schools.

The link between the extinctive tendency of drives and the organisation of solutions specific to mass psychology has also shaped the course of theory. It was just after writing *Beyond the Pleasure Principle* (Freud,

1920g) that Freud wrote *Group Psychology and the Analysis of the Ego* (1921c). Collective group psychology is a reaction to endogenous traumatic experiences.

Even language has been influenced during the pandemic. New terms were created where others had been readily available. These terms were immediately adopted by the entire population, including our patients, attesting to the need to accommodate some new collective cultural superego also within analytic sessions, for the analytical cultural superego was felt to be wavering. We then come to realise that we were using in our pre-pandemic practice terms that were also carrying a collective superego. As a matter of fact, language is by definition conducive to such a collective cultural superego, seeing as since it is different in nature from the extinctive tendency, it expresses the need for inscription even when it tells of the attractions of extinction. By its very nature, language maintains the denial of this tendency of the drives.

Session, denial, and psychosis

These four scenes—dream, game, eroticism, session—share a common feature: they are all regressive psychic activities whose optimal realisation requires both passivity and language cathexis. All these activities are initiated by denying that part of sensory reality which does not give rise to traces and representations: the reality of lack. This denial serves to limit the awakening of the extinctive tendency that the perception of external dangers solicits, and to better take into account the internal origin of anxieties, with the hopes of modifying them. This aspect is very clear in the difference of the sexes, which articulates two differences, that of the male–female couple, and that of the other couple, of the equipped–deprived.

These four activities are thus related to psychosis. They are moments of normal, temporary, reversible, and indeed useful psychosis.

Through the denial of sensory reality, the first stage of session work sets up a saturation of the consciousness of both analyst and analysand, in an effort to keep apart their endogenous experiences of lack and to consolidate the psychic work performed by latency. This allows for a second stage, where this part of denied reality, the sensory perception of the lack, is confronted (Chervet, 2017).

Such reversible denial is based on certain aspects of the environment that enable these scenes, including more or less strict isolation and more or less flexible stability. Rendering social ties—and thus also part of the second stage of session work—latent is one criterion. And in all cases, this kind of psychic work is part of the two-stage *après-coup* process.

Through a hallucinatory mechanism, the dream fabricates identities of perception that allow us to establish the existence of only one world. Children's play also seeks to create a neo-world. The sensual regression of eroticism also leads to the saturating exacerbation of organ sex. Lovers are out of this world.

All these regressive activities aim at facilitating our work on latency, at the heart of which is the process of co-excitation and libidinal regeneration. It is a question of manipulating extinctive tendencies in order to inscribe the drives within the psyche, while at the same time allowing these inscriptions to retain a sensitivity to regressive aspirations and to aspirations oriented outwards, towards the objects of the world. These regressive attractions are expressed in two ways: by a tendency to reduce the painful tensions created by renunciation, and by another tendency, to overcome those tensions through the assertion of an ideal. In the best of cases, this conflict is resolved through the encouragement of a libidinal cathexis thereby generated and thus liberated. The session reveals the object through the object-desire, which bears the renunciations that had participated in its advent.

Other theoretical reverberations

Trauma theory

The pandemic that we are experiencing requires us to re-examine other staples of theory, in particular the theory of trauma that Freud had modified 100 years ago in *Beyond the Pleasure Principle*. There he presents the concept of the death drive, but above all envisages a new definition of all drives based on a previously ignored quality, namely their regressive tendency to restore a previous state back in time, all the way back to the inorganic, the lifeless. This led to a revision of all previous metapsychology. The latter is not invalidated, but among its significance changes is that we discover that its function was to conceal the endogenous origin of the traumatic event.

Beyond the Pleasure Principle internalises the traumatic quality, which until then had been understood as the effect of traumas coming from an external reality, from the sensory perception of the reality of lack, either directly at the time of absences, losses, and disappearances, or indirectly when stimuli prove to be too much for the capacity of the psyche to integrate them. The perceived lack is then that of a psyche deprived of adequate means.

The traumatic thus turns out to stem from a certain characteristic of drives, namely their extinctive regressivity (cf. Chervet, 2014). This change of point of view provoked disarray among the analysts of the time and continues to be the object of criticism and even disavowal.

The pandemic has raised the theoretical stakes concerning perception, its use during sessions, the difference between perceptions of tangible realities that give rise to traces and those of lack that do not, the impact of the missing trace, and changes in the play between perception and representation in the various contexts.

Amnesia and erasure

The question of amnesia in association with the tendency towards extinction raises the theoretical problem of the conservation of traces of the past within the unconscious. The possibility of an erasure of traces, or of their non-inscription, becomes a theoretical question that Freud had previously solved, around 1900, by asserting that time had no effect on their preservation. A new internal conflict then appeared within the psyche, the conflict of erasure, that manifests itself through the repetition compulsion. The unconscious as timeless memory is no longer a primary given, but rather it must be established in the psyche just like the pleasure principle. The role of infantile amnesia is to create a conservative psychic space, a living memory, a reshuffling memory that is opposed to the tendencies to erase.

In the same way, a confusion between the death drive and death has crept into many psychoanalytical writings; as well as a similar confusion between the life drive and life. Freud, however, never ceased to assert that life is the result of two tendencies that he termed the life drive and the death drive, which are only partly regulated between them (homeostasis), but which above all are both subject to the psychic inscription imperative, the superego. The *inclination to conflict* described by Freud (1937c) situates this elementary conflict between the extinctive tendencies of drive and the inscription imperative linked to the superego, thus between effacement and inscription. The fear of such amnesia has often been expressed in regard to the last world wars and to the oblivion of the murders committed by men against other men. Many voices have been raised against this tendency to forget, in defence of the duty of remembrance, especially with regard to WWII, the Holocaust, and the Shoah. In the West, the denial shifted to epidemics and pandemics with a tendency to forget previous ones, resulting in a lack of anticipation, comparison, and perspective.

Perceptions, representations, differences, and the missing trace

The modifications imposed on the analysis apparatus lead us to reflect upon the functions, the allocation, and the distribution of perceptions and representations during a session. We pay little attention to these factors due to the stability of the setting, meaning that changes in the normal conditions of our sessions allow us to draw attention to them.

Being deprived of the usual multiplicity of perceptions in the office, and focusing on sound perception alone, lead to changes in perception and representation for the analyst and the analysand alike.

The patient imagines his analyst sat in his chair in his office, even if he is also able to imagine his analyst somewhere else, in a location unknown to him. He therefore uses the representations of his analyst as constructed during normal sessions, but is deprived of the direct perceptions of the practice and of the analyst.

As for the analyst, he or she is obliged to imagine his or her patient without the crutch of perception-based representations. He concocts imaginary representations concerning the conditions in which the patient has settled for his sessions. He is deprived of the carnal presence of his patient. The couch is empty.

For both, the influence of their carnal presence and the abstinence required by the analytical rule is modified. The issues of exclusion concerning the presence-absence of the other, the "primitive scene" issues concerning the availability of the other, all these must be treated differently.

The stakes of this disappearance of proximal perception are expressed by the clinical manifestations that conceal it. The libidinal co-excitation linked to the lack of being perceived can induce an eroticisation of this lack. The regression to the infantile and to auto-eroticisms is at the origin of "hotline" telephone services. But the extinctive aspirations take hold also of the telephone and of the voice via the mechanism of the castration complex. The telephone becomes black again. Phobias appear more or less disabling. Jean Cocteau offers us some words: "Mirrors are the doors through which death comes and goes" (1927, *Les mariés de la tour Eiffel*). For us, it is the telephoned words that are charged with threats and with fear. The sounds of the voice are the doors through which castration comes and goes and returns.

The representations resulting from perceptions that leave traces facilitate some of our psychological work thanks to their malleability, but they do not replace what direct perception permits and requires. Perceptions without traces do indeed exist, precisely those which are of use to people who have been through traumatic experiences. Lack, absence, and disappearance cannot be represented as such. The appeal to a causal theory is opposed to the extinctive tendency, by the staging of representable scenarios that turn lack into the result of a removal. Feelings and experiences are thus linked to representations within such representable scenes.

A representable object is thus used in order to render lack as a missing object. This is how the gender distinction is approached. The inherent lack present upon perceiving the distinction between members of the equipped–deprived pair invokes the fantasied sexual theory of castration by the father. The other distinction, between the masculine and the feminine, both of them tangible via representation and via sensuality respectively, serves as a reply to the first distinction of equipped–deprived, which leaves no trace.

The psyche uses perceptions capable of producing representations in order to respond to the traumatic quality which, by definition, does not give rise to any specific trace but is expressed by experiences and affects. The recognition of this anti-traumatic function of the perception of tangible realities is one of the major advances of *Beyond the Pleasure Principle*, further developed in *The Ego and the Id*. But it must be complemented by the realisation that all perception awakens the extinctive quality of drives through the perception of difference. This is also very readily transposed to the sensory perceptions of lack. This correlation between the attraction to extinction and the sensory perception of lack is at the origin of the traumatic effect. A trace is missing. The lack of the carnal presence makes it difficult to carry out the anti-traumatic transference of attraction to perception, as well as the psychic work on the missing trace, work that uses representations constructed from perceptions of tangible realities to respond to the tendency to extinction inherent in the desire to live.

Bernard Chervet
August 2020

Translated from French by Shahar Fineberg

References

Chervet, B. (2009). L'après coup; la tentative d'inscrire ce qui tend à disparaître. *Revue Française de Psychanalyse, 73*(5): 1361–1441.

Chervet, B. (2011). "Faire l'amour," la régression sensuelle et les loquets du corps. *Revue Française de Psychosomatique, 2*(40): 9–19.

Chervet, B. (2014). Pulsions avez-vous une vie ? *Revue Française de Psychosomatique, 1*(45): 103–128.

Chervet, B. (2017). La saturation de la conscience dans les rêves, les séances, les sciences. *Revue Française de Psychanalyse, 81*(4): 1177–1194.

Chervet, B. (2020). Le rêve et l'épreuve du réfractaire. *Revue Française de Psychosomatique, 57*: 11–34.

Chervet, B., & Donnet, J. L. (2014). *Pourquoi la règle? Méthode analytique et règle fondamentale*. Paris: Presses Universitaires de France.

Cocteau, J. (1927). *Les mariés de la tour Eiffel*. Paris: Gallimard.

Freud, S. (1920g). *Beyond the Pleasure Principle*. S. E., *18*: 3–66. London: Hogarth.

Freud, S. (1921c). *Group Psychology and the Analysis of the Ego. S. E., 18*: 67–144. London: Hogarth.

Freud, S. (1924g). Extracts from a letter to Wittels, in Wittels's *Sigmund Freud, London. S. E., 19*: 286. London: Hogarth.

Freud, S. (1937c). Analysis terminable and interminable. *S. E., 23*: 209–254. London: Hogarth.

Freud, S. (1940a). *An Outline of Psycho-Analysis. S. E., 23*: 101–208. London: Hogarth.

Freud, S. (1950a). *A Project for a Scientific Psychology. S. E., 1*: 330–332. London: Hogarth.

Freud, S., & Ferenczi, S. (1920). Letter to Sándor Ferenczi (4 February 1920). In: E. Falzader & E. Brabant (Eds.), *The Correspondence of Sigmund Freud and Sándor Ferenczi, Volume 3: 1920–1933*. P. T. Hoffer (Trans.). Cambridge, MA: Belknap Press, 2000.

Virchow, R. (1995). *Collected Essays on Public Health & Epidemiology*. Sagamore Beach, MA: Science History Publications.

CHAPTER 4

Landscapes of mental life under Covid-19*

Alberto Rocha Barros and Elias Rocha Barros
São Paulo, Brazil

Introduction

Frank Snowden, professor of history and the history of medicine at Yale University, published his massive *Epidemics and Society: From the Black Death to the Present* in October 2019. In it, he argued that "epidemics are a major part of the 'big picture' of historical change and development", in other words, that "infectious diseases (…) are as important to understanding societal development as economic crises, wars, revolutions, and demographic change" (Snowden, 2019a, p. 2). The thesis, stated in those terms, isn't exactly new, since it had been hinted at in books by microbiologists such as Michael Oldstone's *Viruses, Plagues, & History* (1998) and Dorothy Crawford's *Deadly Companions: How Microbes Shaped Our History* (2007). But Snowden's book attempts to examine the impact of pandemics on a broad canvas, ranging from the general cultural landscape of society to intellectual history, from the arts and philosophy to

---

* A previous and quite different version of this chapter is published as a paper: Rocha Barros, A., Rocha Barros, E. M., & Rocha Barros, E. L. (2020). O potencial traumático da pandemia de COVID-19. *Revista Brasileira de Psicanálise*, 54(2): 45–57.

individual lives. And in one of those strange coincidences of timing, professor Snowden's book appeared just slightly *before* the Covid-19 global pandemic hit the world with full force. An illustrated paperback edition of the book, with a new preface touching on Covid-19, was quickly released in 2020. And we can perhaps imagine a second edition coming out sometime in the future: in Covid-19 professor Snowden has a brand new case study, given that the world has not seen such a globally impactful pandemic in 100 years (since the "Spanish flu" pandemic of 1918–20).

One cannot claim that what we are experiencing in 2020 was *unforeseen*. A number of popular books and scientific papers had been ringing alarm bells on the risk of emerging infectious diseases for some years (Khan, 2016; Quammen, 2012; Wolfe, 2011) and a World Health Organization report on the matter was issued in September 2019: the "poignant title of the report was *A World at Risk*" (Global Preparedness Monitoring Board, 2019, p. xi). David Quammen, author of the engaging and informative *Spillover: Animal Infections and the Next Human Pandemic* (2012) wrote an article for *The New Yorker* titled "Why weren't we ready for the coronavirus?". In it he reports:

> I asked [Ali S. Khan, former Director of the Office of Public Health Preparedness and Response] about COVID-19. What went so disastrously wrong? Where was the public-health preparedness that he had overseen at the C.D.C.? Why were most countries—and especially the U.S.—so unready? Was it lack of scientific information, or a lack of money? '*This is about lack of imagination*,' he said. (Quammen, 2020, our italics)

Professor Frank Snowden writes in a similar vein: "When COVID-19 began its global spread, it met with success in part because the sentinels had stood down and the world slept" (Snowden, 2019b, p. xi).

Did the world *sleepwalk* into the Covid-19 pandemic? Was this a *failure of the imagination*? In the aftermath of the 2008 financial crisis, David Tuckett wrote an interesting book on how psychoanalysis might shed light on the unconscious mental processes which could have played a part in that economic debacle (2011). Such efforts might begin to delineate a framework through which psychoanalysis could try to make some sense of societies' tendencies to negate, downplay risks, and brush away (split off) disquieting, distressing, or uncomfortable scenarios. But this is an enterprise for the future, since we still need a great deal of more information to reach a better-informed understanding of what happened with Covid-19.

We are living through a historical experience of major significance and which exerts a great deal of pressure on individual minds and triggers reflections on what the world might look like after the pandemic is brought under control. The worldwide psychological impact of the 2020 pandemic of Covid-19 is still in the process of being assessed by epidemiologists, but noteworthy studies are emerging on population samples from China (Wang et al., 2020), Spain (Ozamiz-Etxebarria et al., 2020), Italy (Mazza et al., 2020), and the UK (Pierce et al., 2020). These studies show increased incidences of anxiety, depression, hypochondria, and general psychological distress, even though there have been dissenting voices suggesting that "the pandemic's mental toll" might be "more ripple than tsunami" (Carey, 2020).

As psychoanalysts we have the advantage of being able to observe in detail and through singular cases how our analysands react to the pandemic through the lens of unconscious mental activity, phantasy, deep emotional experience, and symbolic functioning. We go beyond mere symptomatology and perceive how an event like the Covid-19 pandemic colours many aspects of our lives and those of our patients.

In this chapter we would like to touch upon two topics that we have seen emerge in our practice and in our reflections on the pandemic:

- The *symbolic resonances* of the pandemic in our clinical practice, that is, the ways in which the unconscious mind apprehends and interprets the experience of the pandemic; and the ways in which psychoanalysts can make use of the pandemic as symbol for the analysand's mode of being and functioning.
- The *traumatic potential* of the pandemic, a theme which will allow us to briefly reflect on some theoretical aspects of the notion of "trauma" in contemporary psychoanalysis. A modernised and broader notion of trauma might provide a framework for understanding important aspects of how the pandemic affects us unconsciously.

These themes are not intended in any way to be an exhaustive inventory of the psychoanalytically fertile implications of the experiences associated with Covid-19. They merely represent a sample of subjects that we have been discussing among ourselves and observing in our current practices, a cursory glimpse over landscapes of mental life under the impact of Covid-19.

The symbolic resonances of the Covid-19 pandemic

In 1984, the Brazilian sailor and explorer Amyr Klink set himself a daunting task: he rowed alone across the South Atlantic, in a small rowing boat, from Namibia to Brazil. His solitary adventure was chronicled in his *One Hundred Days Between Sea and Sky*, a book that became a huge bestseller and a modern Brazilian classic (1985).

The compact vessel he used in that crossing now quietly rests in the garden of his house in the beautiful colonial-imperial seaside village of Paraty. After being quarantined for 100 days during the Covid-19 pandemic he decided to do an experiment: he wanted to see what it would feel like to go back into that tiny space (a "habitable cell", as he called it), where he had spent 100 days in 1984, and observe the emotions that might arise. The writer Michel Laub recounts what happened:

> "I almost went mad inside there," says Amyr Klink, who got back out of the boat in less than six hours. Not due to claustrophobia or solitude, problems which Klink does not suffer from, but because of an agonizing sense of 'feeling stuck', a familiar concept to all of us who have also traversed these hundred days during which the world has been deprived of novelty, or worse, has been imbued with an excess of tragic news which has the cumulative effect of producing a sense of numbness or a diffuse anxiety that leaves us groundless to confront it. (2020, p. 30)

What could have happened in psychoanalytic terms? How could this familiar object—the vessel he himself built, an old companion of a great adventure—have suddenly transmuted itself into an agonising and intolerable space? We can only precariously speculate, of course. But we could raise the hypothesis that a symbolic transmutation occurred between the "100 days in 1984" and the "100 days in 2020". The same object, Amyr Klink's rowing boat, was invested with a sense of awe, adventure, and accomplishment in 1984, while being divested of these qualities in the context of 2020, becoming drained of liveliness and filled with deadness. Michel Laub writes:

> In the 1984 crossing (…) the events and obstacles that took place—storms, problems with equipment, whales spraying, "moonbows" [rainbows created by moonlight]—pointed to a narrative sense in space and time (…). "I felt like I was construing something, going somewhere, and this is a very gratifying feeling," says Amyr Klink. (2020, p. 30)

Therefore, in 1984, that small-scale boat and the potentially psychologically distressing challenge of a solitary crossing of the Atlantic were being assimilated by Amyr Klink's mind under the sign of vitality, movement, narrative progression, and creativity ("I was construing something, going somewhere"). We can imagine that within the framework of a vitalised and meaningful experience (the cautious and planned adventure of crossing the Atlantic in a rowing boat), Amyr Klink's mind could reinterpret the narrow and boxed-up space of his boat not as something claustrophobia-inducing but perhaps as almost a "second skin", a protective enclosure, a kind of comforting armour for a perilous exploit.

The mental landscape in 2020 is quite different. The experience of the pandemic oozes toxic and disquieting meanings, a "diffuse anxiety", and shifts the way through which Amyr Klink's mind apprehends and represents the confines of his boat. The vessel is no longer a symbol of things moving forwards but becomes a powerful symbol of all that is imprisoning, anxiety-inducing, paralysing, and difficult to mentally digest and interpret about the Covid-19 pandemic. His boat, a friendly nostalgic memento of a great adventure has been transformed into something persecutory and anguishing: he "almost went mad inside there". It no longer is a symbol of life moving forwards but is changed into a symbol of a sense of "feeling stuck", that is induced by the pandemic and the quarantine.

We find Amyr Klink's anecdote quite revealing about how the experience of life under the Covid-19 pandemic is apprehended and interpreted by our minds. And we would like to present a few clinical vignettes of the kinds of conflicts and struggles we have seen our anal-ysands be confronted with. These are situations which we have seen appear again and again in many of our sessions during the present pan-demic and we feel they speak to certain themes that have arisen over this period. We will be writing of individual situations, but we are not concerned with the particularities of the individual cases as such, but with certain *clusters of phantasies* that are typical of what many different analysands are experiencing. We have selected two groups of emotional experience and phantasies that we have observed:

1. A viscous and stifling sense of paralysis and sameness (Amyr Klink's experience of "feeling stuck")
2. The capacity of Covid-19 to become an apt symbol for persecutory and distressing feelings and phantasies; the pandemic's tendency to impose on the mind a continuous sense of danger and vulnerability.

Mr A is in his mid-thirties and is very intelligent, cultured, and lively. With a less intense workload and more flexible working hours he felt that quarantine was the perfect opportunity to finally getting around to reading Tolstoy's *War and Peace*. Initially all went well, and he would talk about the novel in his sessions and of how much he had always wanted to read it. He even joked that if the quarantine lasted long enough, he would move on to other massive Russian novels or even tackle Proust or Joyce. It felt that he had found a good way to make intellectually stim-ulating use of freed-up time and he seemed not to be succumbing to the pull of the anaesthetising effect that many of our patients seek by binge-watching hours and hours of series and films on online platforms such as Netflix. Mr A had purchased an exceptionally good and reader-friendly edition of Tolstoy's masterpiece, full of notes, glossaries, and lists of characters, and had also bought one or two general introductions to Tolstoy. He was excited about this literary project to counterbalance the potential ennui of social distancing and being stuck at home. This looked like a vitalised way of confronting the situation.

But slowly a creeping sense of unease attached itself to the moments he set aside to read Tolstoy. Surprisingly, he found himself dreading the book and feeling quite anxious whenever he approached it. At one point even the sight of *War and Peace* became almost intolerable to him and he felt that something about it was "driving him out of his mind". In our sessions the unconscious forces at work slowly became clearer. *War and Peace* is a notoriously immense novel running to thousands of pages. He would read for hours, but his bookmark barely shifted along the tome. He felt he wasn't moving forwards and was getting nowhere. It gradually dawned upon him how intensely bored he actually was throughout quarantine, how he felt that life was "moving in slow motion or was even paused in a 'standby mode'", as he put it. And his slow progress through *War and Peace* had become an embodiment of precisely that. The unending novel became a concrete symbol of an unending quarantine.

Many of our patients have been complaining about what one analysand called "the swampiness of the pandemic", a claustrophobic impression of sameness and repetition, a viscous and stifling sense of paralysis, of trudging through swampy and foetid marshlands, contaminated by a "diffuse anxiety" (Laub, 2020) or by a free-floating melancholia. Jonah M. Kessel, a film-maker and visual journalist for *The New York Times*, has coined an apt phrase to describe this mental atmosphere: a "seemingly never-ending pandemic purgatory" (2020).

Some people have spoken of a certain paradox in the sense of how time flows during Covid-19: the weeks and months seem to be flying by, while they also feel that time has stood still, that nothing seems to ever change, that even the news seems to be on a loop. A couple of clients have mentioned the 1993 film *Groundhog Day* (directed by Harold Ramis, where the protagonist is stuck reliving the same day over and over) as an expression of this. And another spoke of a lack of visual variety: his life became reduced to his home and one or two other places, making him feel a choking sense of deprivation of visual stimulus. Whereas he was used to being exposed to many different places and spaces in his usual day to day (bars, restaurants, theatres, museums, meetings, friends' houses, trips, etc.) his life was now reduced to basically his house and the supermarket. At one point, he felt an urgent and agonising need to "flee" from the city for a bit, and go to a friend's country house, not only because he missed social contact, but because he desperately needed a change of scenery.

As analysts, we have noticed a potential danger lurking in the way in which talk of the pandemic might express itself within psychoanalytic sessions. While many of our analysands have adapted to the current circumstances and their analyses have resumed their normal flow, for others the situation has shifted and focus on the pandemic has become a dominating theme. There is a risk here in allowing Covid-19 to reduce an analytic conversation to a mere roll-call of complaints and woes. This is a manifestation of a kind of gravitational pull of the mind towards concreteness and symbolic impoverishment. It is the "Groundhog Day" aspect of the pandemic: a tendency of the atmosphere generated by Covid-19 to make the mind get stuck in the swamplands of repetition and sameness and operate under the sway of concrete thinking. In order to attempt to break this pull or spell, it has proved useful to us to try to understand how the experience of the pandemic has latched on to phantasies and unconscious processes already stirring in the internal worlds of our patients.

With Mr A, for example, his sense of unease while reading *War and Peace* suggested a clue to certain distressing feelings that had remained unacknowledged. If the pandemic had the power to disturb him so much, could there have already been something deep within him festering? An unutterable suspicion that certain aspects of his life were congealed, paralysed, and leading nowhere? Not being able to plough through *War and Peace* allowed for a discussion about advancement in life to manifest itself within his psychoanalysis. He even said that the pandemic, in a sense, was the jolt that he needed for these feelings to arise in himself and become explicit: "Before Covid-19, I could never fully put into words how I felt about where my life was headed, nor could I fully understand our discussions about my general boredom." A chain of associations was explored in our sessions: the book without end in sight was an apt symbol for the unending pandemic, which in turn touched upon a phantasy of living a monotonous and repetitive existence. Covid-19 was the "perfect storm" to enhance these fears and make them become manifest.

A variation of this feeling of being stuck was perceived in Mr B. He is in his early twenties, studies literature and creative writing, and has proved himself a very competent student, earning excellent grades at university. But he is exceedingly sensitive and emotional upheavals affect him intensely. His ability to write creatively is one of the measures through which he gauges how he is doing emotionally. He has perceived the pandemic and social distancing as very "imprisoning": he misses the liveliness of going to classes, seeing people, going out with his friends, flirting with girls, etc. He is also quite shy and quiet and tends to withdraw within himself when cut off from stimulating environments and/or relationships.

After months of quarantine, an ever-growing sadness and a frustrating inability to write, he recalled a "fascinating story" he was once told. Some years ago, a high school teacher had spoken in class of a woman who had simultaneously lost both her parents and inherited their apartment. This woman would only enter the parents' apartment with her eyes closed and would walk around it as if blind. B could not recall the nature of this tale: was it based on fact or fiction? But B insisted that the imagery involved in the story encapsulated how he felt about the "imprisoning" aspect of social isolation to perfection. He *sensed* there was something fertile there but could not formulate it exactly. Apart from the more personal resonances of this narrative, the analyst explored with B why the anecdote could be an apt symbol for how he apprehended the atmosphere of Covid-19. The pandemic was catapulting him into the darkness of a mental confinement (he pictured the apartment as constraining, stifling, and poorly lit). But there was also an *active* aspect to this feeling of imprisonment: he was *choosing* to keep his eyes shut and not look at grief, sadness, and deprivation squarely in the face. Although *factual reality* had become impoverished, limited, "blinding" (he missed the liveliness of normal life), he was also "blinding himself" to contact with *inner reality*, which is where he needed to draw stimulus and richness from. If he just "opened his eyes", he might find that good objects (the dear departed parents) were still "alive" and "active" within him. Understanding that our experience of the world and of life is not merely a passive process but requires vital inner activity as well—our picture of the world and of life is both "given" by factual, objective reality *and* construed by mental and emotional life—is part of the resources we have to finding healthy ways of apprehending and interpreting the pandemic: the confining spaces we have been restricted to must be counteracted by an exploration of the vast plains of our inner landscapes. Understanding this was crucial for this analysand. Mr B's creative blockade has been lifted and he is currently setting the story to writing as a class assignment.

We will turn now to our second cluster of emotional experiences, the phantasies and impressions associated with threat and vulnerability.

Mrs C is in her mid-forties and has always reacted badly to certain places and situations. She deeply dislikes hospitals, which make her extremally anxious, and tries to avoid sad books or movies. A dear friend of hers underwent an important orthopaedic operation in 2019 and moved into C's place to recover. The friend was in much pain and very depressed and Mrs C found this all terribly distressing, almost intolerable. She was born in a small town and moved to the city mostly to get away from the domineering influence of her father, a very strict, controlling, and conservative man, ready to disapprove of much of what she does.

Quarantine and Covid-19 are proving to be very difficult to her. She lives close to a hospital and fears that "the virus could be waiting around the corner to get [her]": living so close to a healthcare facility makes her fantasise that she is smack in the middle of a "danger zone". At the same time, she is very personable, highly social, with many good friends, and has been happily married for fifteen years. She is funny and friendly but decided to go into analysis three years ago because of a lingering and constant sense of risk and unease. Her analyst had repeatedly tried to show her how her mental life seemed to be organised around a phantasy of being porous and easily drenched by the toxic fumes of her inner world or surroundings. She seems to feel deprived of mental barriers to protect her from sad stories, suffering friends, a domineering father, or the obstacles of life: anything and everything has the power to penetrate deeply into her and affect her to the very core. Uncomfortable feelings would colour her entire self and reduce her to a single note of despair. C found this idea very difficult to grasp. She would often misinterpret what was being said by recasting it in overly concrete language.

Initially, her sessions during the Covid-19 pandemic were becoming stale and tiring for her analyst. There was a repetitive hyperfocus on the risks of catching the disease and the measures she put into place in order to avoid this. These conversations seemed to be leading nowhere and her anxiety was constantly growing. But her analyst recalled how C was a fan of the Harry Potter books and movies. She grew up reading and watching them. In the magical world of Harry Potter there is a fantastic beast called a *boggart*. This is a shape-shifting creature that assumes the appearance of the thing that is most frightening to those who encounter it:

> So the boggart sitting in the darkness within has not yet assumed
> a form. He does not yet know what will frighten the person on
> the other side of the door. Nobody knows what a boggart looks

like when he is alone, but when I let him out, he will immediately become whatever each of us most fears. (Rowling, 1999, p. 53)

There is something of this boggart quality to the ways in which some of us internally apprehend and interpret the current pandemic. Covid-19 has the potential of transforming itself into an apt symbol of certain persecutory feelings or distressing phantasies that have been haunting us unconsciously. What is interesting about the boggart is that the form it assumes for each one of us is *a clue* to the structure of our personal fears.

Although Mrs C had initially struggled to fully understand how her way of being seemed organised around a phantasy of being porous and easily contaminated, when the metaphor of the boggart was suggested to her, she responded to it in a very productive way. Covid-19 scared her so much perhaps because the risk of being "contaminated" by the virus was symbolically associated with an underlying phantasy of a "weak immune system", a mental representation of herself as fragile and an easy target for "contaminations" of all kinds. After the boggart metaphor was presented to her, she felt she truly had reached an insight. In a sense, Covid-19 was such an explicit and plastic manifestation of her phantasies that she was finally able to interact with her analyst in a more abstract way, discussing the implications of his interpretations of her inner functioning.

This "boggart aspect" of Covid-19 seems relevant to many of our patients. The nature and substance of our fears and fantasies associated with Covid-19 might shed light on what is particularly distressing to each one of us.

Mr D is also representative of this. In a similar way to Mrs C, he is also terribly afraid of becoming sick, but in his case the organising phantasy is not structured around ideas of contamination and porousness, but around a debilitating fear of death and disease. He has been persecuted by such anxieties for many years and has stated that he sometimes likes to daydream that he "might wake up to discover that the fact of death was but the fancy of a nightmare". Death would be just the delusional construction of a bad dream. Indeed, there are many analysands who have spoken of friends and family members who have been invaded by a sense of real and present danger, who are fearful of becoming seriously ill and dying, and who are taking such measures to protect themselves against risks that prove overwhelming to those around them. There is a tricky grey area that separates rational precautions (a healthy management of risk) from becoming enclosed in an obsessional hypochondria or thanatophobia. Daniel Defoe, in his *A Journal of the Plague Year* (1722)—a book that has apparently reached a new audience during this Covid-19 pandemic (Pepinster, 2020; Theroux, 2020)—characterises this atmosphere of potential impending doom that arises in an epidemic as "a close conversing with Death" (Defoe, 1722, p. 140). And Covid-19 indeed exerts, for some people, a magnetic pull on their many diffuse terrors, becoming a manifest representation of what we like to call "a general assembly of all fears".

Mr D dreams of a world without death but feels that he has awoken to a nightmare of Death Triumphant. Another patient, Mrs E, has become a nuisance to all around her, washing and cleaning everything in obsessive detail and submitting her family and work colleagues to intense "interrogation sessions" about their behaviours and safety measures. This is a distortion of life, a kind of mental Dictatorship of Death and Disease. The problem, of course, is that the boundaries between fact and fantasy have become blurred, for there is indeed a dangerous virus wreaking havoc around the world.

We would like to suggest that both Mr D and Mrs E are examples of situations in which Covid-19 has assumed a structuring function in these patients' minds. The pandemic, to them, is not only a fact of the world at present, one among many, but has become a *principle* of *how the world is* and *how the world works*. There is a permanent sense of threat and of fragility (Defoe's "close conversing with Death") and a continuous feeling that things can change at any moment, at any second one can suddenly fall sick and perish. For Mr D the actor Chadwick Boseman's untimely death on August 28, 2020 was vivid proof of this: Life *belongs* to Death, anyone can die of anything at any instant (Boseman died of colon cancer, not Covid), even The Black Panther is no match for The Grim Reaper! Mr D expressed this vividly by saying that he felt he had become a "merman" living under the waves of a "sea of Covid". This fantasy is, to our eyes, richly expressive of the atmosphere imposed by the pandemic: Covid-19 can be experienced as a deluge that has covered the world as we knew it; we have become beings continually immersed and fully absorbed by the oceanic pressure of Covid-19. Even the idea of becoming a "merman" is interesting in the way it suggests the need for a shift in (mental) physiology: the only way to "breathe" once dragged down by the dark waters of the pandemic is by finding ways to evolve and adapt to the new environment, by exercising creativity and finding symbolic expression to metabolise this stressful experience.

The above vignettes are merely meant as an assemblage of some of the ways that the experience of the pandemic has manifested itself in our consulting rooms. But we would like to turn briefly to a related topic: could Covid-19 be perceived as a traumatic event?

Trauma and the traumatic potential of the Covid-19 pandemic

In the first part of this chapter we have tried to present to our readers some of the ways in which the unconscious mind seems to apprehend and try to make sense of the Covid-19 pandemic. We organised our material in terms of two major *clusters of phantasies*: (1) feelings of "swampiness", of life being in "standby mode" or even paralysed; and (2) an ominous and anxious sense of constant threat, risk, and danger. We were less interested in the specificities of each individual case history as such than in selecting certain recurrent themes and fears that we have seen appear again and again in our practice during this period of life under the impact of Covid-19.

Even though we focused on very personal phantasies, we have seen our patients worrying in important ways about the societal implications of the pandemic as well. People have been deeply concerned about the legacy and long-term impact of what we are experiencing. Will the world ever go back to how we used to know it? Or are we headed towards a post-Covid world, a "new normal" (an idea which is anxiogenic to many)?

And what about the cultural impact of Covid? Brazilian culture, for example, is very warm, friendly, highly social, and physical. Shaking hands, hugging, and kissing are common practice, even among work colleagues. But social distancing requirements have greatly changed this, and people are growing more and more accustomed to preserving physical distance. Could we be witnessing a major shift within Brazilian social culture? Some of our patients are commenting how, by not seeing friends for over 150 days, they are uneasily becoming aware that a hunger for social interaction is slowly dying down in them. They *do* want to go back to socialising, but perhaps with less intensity than before. It isn't easy to contemplate the risk that Covid-19 might so fundamentally affect Brazilian sociability for a period of time.

There is also the impact of Covid-19 as a constant topic in day-to-day conversations and worries. Many conversational interactions have become dominated or peppered by the pandemic. And there has been a wholly understandable onslaught of news reports, updates, webinars, meetings, and other kinds of social interactions where the *leitmotiv* is Covid, Covid, Covid, Covid. This can be claustrophobic, exhausting, scary, overwhelming, imprisoning. When will talk and dialogue resume its normal flow and be freed from the tyranny of this disease?

And how will we process the experience of the pandemic as a whole? For many people, 2020 was a "wasted year", a period that was dominated by fear, anxiety, and time lost that can never be regained. Older patients, in their seventies and eighties, speak of having been depleted of precious time, of the sorrow of having had to strictly isolate themselves from their sons, daughters, and grandchildren. They feel angry and deeply frustrated for missing out on at least a year of their lives and are fearful that they won't have enough time left to make up for this loss. Younger patients who are finishing school or are just entering university are paying a heavy toll as well: this is a period in life where there is a deep craving and need for social interaction and exploration, and mentally processing the pandemic has been terribly hard for them as well. What was supposed to be a vividly colourful and exciting time in their lives has become a dull, dud, and dead year.

It may very well be the case that life will quickly resume its old ways after Covid-19 comes under control, but the fact of the matter is that our patients have been currently voicing these concerns about the future and many are struggling to emotionally process the pandemic. Between the more intimate and inner personal concerns we listed earlier in the chapter and these wider social anxieties, is there a unifying theme? We do not want to reduce the richness and diversity of mental unease triggered by Covid-19 to just one common denominator, but perhaps the psychoanalytic concept of *trauma* might possibly shed light on some of the processes that are taking place.

Our current thinking about trauma has been greatly influenced by recent literature on the subject (Levine, 2014; Scarfone, 2017; Viñar, 2017). Authors such as Howard Levine and Marcelo Viñar have pointed out how tricky it is to pin down what exactly the word "trauma" refers to in the field of psychoanalysis. For example, Howard Levine writes:

> The concept of *trauma* (…) continues to occupy a problematic place in psychoanalysis. (…). Shifts in meaning and usage of the word continued after Freud, and, in 1967, Anna Freud observed that, as a technical term in psychoanalysis, *trauma* was in danger of being emptied of meaning through overuse and overextension. (2014, p. 214)

In a similar vein, Marcelo Viñar writes:

> The notion of trauma has acquired such a broad extension and range, both in the diversity of its causes and the magnitude or intensity of its effects, that it becomes necessary to acknowledge its heterogenous character, in order to restore its accuracy, and to prevent it from becoming a wild card that transforms a problem requiring reflection into a Tower of Babel. (2017, p. 40)

Both these authors underline how there is a certain fluctuation and variation in our conceptualisation of trauma:

> … trauma, *per se*, is not a monolithic entity. (…). It, therefore, is confusing—perhaps even impossible—to try to talk generically about *trauma* or categorically about any given trauma or class of traumatic events, as if or with the implication that one was speaking about unitary phenomena with specifiable, generalizable characteristics. (Levine, 2014, pp. 215–216)
>
> [T]he vastness of the issue of trauma compels us to fragment it into chapters or themes that can be encompassed and approached from a reasonably congruent perspective. (Viñar, 2017, pp. 40–41)

Wittgenstein's idea that the semantic range of certain words and concepts is loosely held together by a mere "family resemblance" might be useful here (1953, paragraphs 65–67). It is not always possible or desirable to dissolve concepts into their elemental parts or fundamental constituents.

The reach of certain notions is sometimes highly varied with zones of vagueness and ambiguity (Baker & Hacker, 1980, pp. 189–208). Craving for a fixed reference or for a rigid and clear-cut definition of trauma might be deeply counterproductive, since "trauma" is a word which can be usefully conceptualised within the framework of a number of qualitatively vastly different phenomena, from "the burning horror of war, genocide, and torture" to "the icy horror or marginalization or exclusion" (Viñar, 2017, p. 45); from a deeply painful event circumscribed in space and time (an abuse, for example), to phantasies, thought processes, and impressions that lie without historical time (a phantasy of being unloved or unwanted, for example).

In the recent literature on trauma, there are a number of formulations that seem to us extremally rich and apt. Marcelo Viñar, for example, writes of how trauma destroys the "metaphorical value of a narrative" (2005, p. 324), how trauma launches us into a wilderness where words fail (this is the title of his 2005 paper). In this sense, "trauma" is associated with an acute experience of not being able to put memories and emotions into a narrative form, of not finding words that capture these feelings, of metaphorical resources becoming depleted, of being consumed, perhaps, by a sense of *meaninglessness* rather than meaningfulness in emotional language and emotional experience.

Viñar also uses the metaphor of a rupture or cavity in psychic life to capture the nature of the effects of trauma: "... catastrophic experience is a hole in the representational continuity inherent to psychic life" (2017, p. 42), "[T]he experience of fright [i.e. trauma] (...) does not generate teaching or experience, but representational emptiness" (p. 43). Dominique Scarfone gravitates towards similar imagery:

> In the most general sense, *trauma* is a tear, a breach (...). Trauma, therefore, does not describe simply a loss of continuity in the surface of the body or of the mind; rather, it initiates various degrees of disorganization within what the surface both contains and keeps *operational*. (2017, p. 23)

Howard Levine writes:

> That which earns the designation *trauma* is that which outstrips and disrupts the psyche's capacity for representation or

mentalization. That which cannot be represented or mentalized—thought about or contained within the mind—cannot enter into one's subjectivity or the reflective view of one's personal history. Absent the potential for mental representation, these events and phenomena are historical only from an external, third-person perspective. Until they are mentalized, they remain locked within an ahistorical, repetitive process as potentials for action, somatization and projection. (2014, p. 219)

Levine touches on two important points here. In the first place, he draws attention to how trauma negates historicity and isolates the traumatised person in an ahistorical present. This makes us think of Mr D's interest in comic books and superhero films. In the Superman mythos, the worst criminals from Krypton were typically banished to *The Phantom Zone*, a parallel universe where they would lead a ghost-like existence. Nothing ever happened in the Phantom Zone, there was no sense either of space or place or time or body. In some iterations, inmates were locked in with their sadness and their fears and drowned in an everlasting nothingness and emptiness. Perhaps a trauma has something of this capacity to suck us into an alternative inner world, which is ahistorical, repetitive, and brimming with formlessness, pain, and anxiety.

In the second place, Levine touches on the issue of *unrepresented* or *unrepresentable states of mind* (Levine, Reed, & Scarfone, 2013) as related to trauma. This seems to us to be one of the issues that lies at the core of the problem of trauma. One of the co-authors of this chapter has extensively tried to conceptualise the psychical apparatus as a system that strives to provide symbolic meaning for experience and to structure the formlessness of raw experience into symbolic forms that are plastic and capable of establishing networks among themselves (Rocha Barros, 2000, 2013; Rocha Barros & Rocha Barros, 2011, 2015, 2016). Perhaps, one of the main features of traumatic processes is that the mind is both overwhelmed by an onslaught of excitation/experience/stimulation that is difficult to digest *and* suffers a collapse in its capacity to find representational forms for these experiences. The mind must find ways *not only* to *merely represent* traumatic experience, which in itself it sometimes cannot do when a traumatic process is ongoing, *but also* find symbolic forms for representing experience that are sufficiently vivid, malleable, and richly figurative so as to be able to lay the experience to rest in wider contexts of meaning.

Perhaps we can now list a few of the characteristics of traumatic experiences, be they specific events or ongoing processes, be they the smallest traumas of everyday life, or the extreme traumas of horrible situations:

- Traumas represent a failure or a crack in language, in the possibility of capturing experience in words or in a narrative structure that can shape them and make them thinkable.
- Traumas suck us out from time and catapult us into an ahistorical world of repetition. Historicity is destroyed and sameness and an eternal traumatising present become the mental way of functioning.
- Traumas represent a fracture or rupture in the fabric of mental life, a fissure that is unable to heal itself or weave itself back together.
- Traumas are a decline, collapse, or deficiency in the mind's capacity to digest and metabolise experience, that is, absorbing and retaining what is nourishing and constructive while ejecting and eliminating what is wasteful or toxic. In trauma the process is reversed: nutrients are expelled, and toxins retained.
- Traumas represent a closing up of the mind's capacity for symbolisation. The possibility of creating more plastic and interconnecting forms of metaphorically and symbolically registering experience, producing associative networks of symbolism, is congealed or deadened.

We feel that many of these aspects were operational in the phantasies from the clinical vignettes we have presented and in the wider social fears and anxieties we have noticed surfacing with Covid-19. Perhaps by reshaping some of the ways we conceptualise trauma within psychoanalysis, we will have access to a powerful tool that might help us address alterations in the mental landscape induced by Covid-19.

And an appreciation of trauma, paying respect to more traditional conceptualisations but also incorporating new reflections, could shed light on some strategies for helping patients who are trying to come to terms with Covid-19. Perhaps this pandemic might help psychoanalysis to rethink certain aspects of its conceptual toolkit.

When Mr D spoke of feeling that he was living undersea in a kind of Water World of Covid-19, he is perhaps providing us with an interesting metaphor for the general traumatic aspect of the pandemic for many of us. We are immersed in a "Water World" *constituted* by Covid: our nourishment is drenched in it, we inhale and exhale it, our physiology has been changed by it (we have become Covid-mermen), and it exerts an enormous amount of pressure on us (our ears are almost popping due to the depths we have sunk into). A trauma can become a whole system, a whole way of being and functioning. Understanding the Covid-19 pandemic as potentially traumatic under the framework we suggested, also points directions to how psychoanalysts might understand and address the issues that we face.

During the New York City polio outbreak of 1916, a local doctor famously declared: "As to the lessons we have learned during this epidemic—we have learned very little that is new about the disease, but much that is old about ourselves" (Tilney, 1916, p. 469).

Alberto Rocha Barros and Elias Rocha Barros
September 2020

References

Baker, G. P., & Hacker, P. M. S. (1980). *Wittgenstein: Meaning and Understanding (Essays on the Philosophical Investigations)*. Chicago, IL: University of Chicago Press.

Carey, B. (2020, June 21). The pandemic's mental toll: more ripple than tsunami. *The New York Times*, Mind.

Crawford, D. H. (2007). *Deadly Companions: How Microbes Shaped Our History*. Oxford: Oxford University Press.

Defoe, D. (1722). *A Journal of the Plague Year*. (A Norton Critical Edition). New York: W. W. Norton, 1992.

Global Preparedness Monitoring Board (2019). *A World at Risk: Annual Report on Global Preparedness for Health Emergencies*. Geneva: World Health Organization.

Kessel, J. M. (2020, September 1). How to stop the next pandemic. *The New York Times*.

Khan, A. S. (2016). *The Next Pandemic: On the Front Lines Against Humankind's Gravest Dangers*. New York: PublicAffairs.

Klink, A. (1985). *One Hundred Days Between Sea and Sky*. London: Bloomsbury, 2002.

Laub, M. (2020). A quarentena de Amyr Klink: cem dias entre os tubarões e o tédio". *Valor. Eu & Fim de Semana*, June 26: 30–31.

Levine, H. B. (2014). Psychoanalysis and trauma. *Psychoanalytic Inquiry, 34*: 214–224.

Levine, H. B., Reed, G., & Scarfone, D. (Eds.) (2013). *Unrepresented States of Mind and the Construction of Meaning: Clinical and Theoretical Contributions*. London: Karnac.

Mazza, C., Ricci, E., Biondi, S., Colasanti, M., Ferracuti, S., Napoli, C., & Roma, P. (2020). A nationwide survey of psychological distress among Italian people during the COVID-19 pandemic: immediate psychological responses and associated factors. *International Journal of Environmental Research and Public Health, 17*(9): 3165.

Oldstone, M. A. (1998). *Viruses, Plagues, and History: Past, Present, and Future.* Oxford: Oxford University Press. New revised edition, 2020.

Ozamiz-Etxebarria, N., Dosil-Santamaria, M., Picaza-Gorrochategui, M., & Idoiaga-Mondragon, N. (2020). Stress, anxiety, and depression levels in the initial stage of the COVID-19 outbreak in a population in northern Spain. *CSP: Cadernos de Saúde Pública (Reports in Public Health), 36*(4): e00054020.

Pepinster, C. (2020, March 21). Daniel Defoe's *Journal of the Plague Year* being reprinted after selling out. *The Telegraph*.

Pierce, M., Hope, H., Ford, T., Hatch, S., Hotopf, M., John, A., Kontopantelis, E., Webb, R., Wessely, S., McManus, S., & Abel, K. M. (2020). Mental health before and during the COVID-19 pandemic: a longitudinal probability sample survey of the UK population. *The Lancet: Psychiatry, 7*(10): 883–892.

Quammen, D. (2012). *Spillover: Animal Infections and the Next Human Pandemic*. New York: W. W. Norton.

Quammen, D. (2020, May 11). Why weren't we ready for the coronavirus? *The New Yorker*.

Rocha Barros, E. M. (2000). Affect and pictographic image: the constitution of meaning in mental life, *International Journal of Psychoanalysis, 81*(6): 1087–1099.

Rocha Barros, E. M. (2013). Dream, figurability and symbolic transformation. *Psychoanalysis in Europe (The EPF Bulletin)*, Bulletin 67: 107–120.

Rocha Barros, E. M., & Rocha Barros, E. L. (2011). Reflections on the clinical implications of symbolism. *International Journal of Psychoanalysis*, *92*(4): 879–901.

Rocha Barros, E. M., & Rocha Barros, E. L. (2015). Symbolism, emotions and mental growth. In: J. Barossa, C. Bronstein, & C. Pajaczkowska (Eds.), *The New Klein–Lacan: Dialogues* (pp. 235–254). London: Karnac.

Rocha Barros, E. M., & Rocha Barros, E. L. (2016). The function of evocation in the working-through of the countertransference; projective identification, reverie, and the expressive function of the mind—reflections inspired by Bion's work. In: H. B. Levine & G. Civitarese (Eds.), *The W. R. Bion Tradition: Lines of Development, Evolution of Theory and Practice over the Decades* (pp. 141–154). London: Karnac.

Rowling, J. K. (1999). *Harry Potter and the Prisoner of Azkaban*. London: Bloomsbury.

Scarfone, D. (2017). Ten short essays on how trauma is inextricably woven into psychic life. *Psychoanalytic Quarterly*, *86*(1): 21–43.

Snowden, F. M. (2019a). *Epidemics and Society: From the Black Death to the Present*. New Haven, CT: Yale University Press.

Snowden, F. M. (2019b). *Epidemics and Society: From the Black Death to the Present*. Illustrated paperback edition with a new preface. New Haven, CT: Yale University Press, 2020.

Theroux, M. (2020, May 1). The end of coronavirus: what plague literature tells us about our future. *The Guardian*.

Tilney, F. C. (1916). Discussion of symposium on poliomyelitis. *Long Island Medical Journal*, *10* (November): 465–471.

Tuckett, D. (2011). *Minding the Markets: An Emotional View of Financial Instability*. Basingstoke, UK: Palgrave Macmillan.

Viñar, M. N. (2005). The specificity of torture as trauma: the human wilderness when words fail. *International Journal of Psychoanalysis*, *86*(2): 311–333.

Viñar, M. N. (2017). The enigma of extreme traumatism: trauma, exclusion and their impact on subjectivity. *American Journal of Psychoanalysis*, *77*(1): 40–51.

Wang, C., Pan, R., Wan, X., Tan, Y., Xu, L., Ho, C. S., & Ho, R. C. (2020). Immediate psychological responses and associated factors during the initial stage of the 2019 coronavirus disease (COVID-19) epidemic among the general population in China. *International Journal of Environmental Research and Public Health, 17*(5): 1729.

Wittgenstein, L. (1953). *Philosophical Investigations*. The German text, with an English translation by G. E. M. Anscombe, P. M. S. Hacker, & J. Schulte. Revised 4th edition by P. M. S. Hacker and Joachim Schulte. Hoboken, NJ: Wiley-Blackwell, 2009.

Wolfe, N. (2011). *The Viral Storm: The Dawn of a New Pandemic Age*. London: Allen Lane.

CHAPTER 5

Catastrophe and its vicissitudes: denial and the vitalising effect of "good air"*

Daniel Kupermann
São Paulo, Brazil

> *La vie est ailleurs*
> —Sorbonne, 1968

"I can't breathe": catastrophe, regressions, progressions

Since the great original catastrophe that fell upon the planet and that led to the emergence of sexual beings—the drying up of the seas described by Sándor Ferenczi (1924) in "Thalassa"—breathing has never not been a problem. This is something that the several illnesses that intrigue psychosomatic scholars insist on reminding us. Nevertheless, the Covid-19 pandemic seems to have refreshed our memory to the fact that we are no more than fish, more or less adapted to the aerial space, dependents on the flow and circulation of oxygen in the environment that we live in. "I can't breathe" becomes, therefore, a metaphor and a cruel reality when

---

*This chapter was based on my participation in a series of discussions promoted by *Grupo Brasileiro de Pesquisas Sándor Ferenczi*, a debate shared with Dr Virgínia Ungar on July 18, 2020, available at https://youtube/hwq8VKIAX8U.

we evoke the protests that took over the world since May as a result of the cowardly murder by asphyxiation of George Floyd, a new version of Eric Garner's death in July 2014. Both were victims of the oppression and social and political segregation in which we find ourselves entangled due to the excesses of neoliberalism.

The first Hungarian edition of *Thalassa* (sea in Greek) was called *Katasztrófa* (cf. Sabourin, 1985). On this essay on genitality—which Freud (1933c) considered "the boldest application of psycho-analysis that was ever attempted"—Ferenczi proposes a conception of how adaptation occurs in catastrophes, which may be useful when thinking about the psychic destinations of the pandemic that we are going through. According to the "bioanalysis" proposed by Ferenczi (1924), catastrophes are events that put both a creative potential as well as destruction into play, demanding on the one hand resignation, and on the other, adaptation. Adaptation is paradoxically conservative, sustained by the desire to restore the ways of satisfaction previously experienced, what Ferenczi called the "Thalassic regressive desire", and progressive, in tune with the newly emerging sense of reality. So, too, catastrophe, usually thought of as a destructuring traumatic event can, at the same time, hold out the potential of also being a structuring one, in the sense that it creates new modalities of libidinal satisfaction and fruition of life.

Therefore, sea creatures will adapt to the aerial environment, fulfilling the desire to return to the ocean abandoned in primitive times, which denounces Ferenczi's Lamarckian filiation (also Freud's)—that there would be no evolution without internal motivation (cf. Freud, 1915). From the bioanalytical conception derives the idea that restoring the lost humidity (and unity) would first occur by means of penetrating the body of the other, which would have originated—after a war of all against all—the difference of the sexes, the mating, the fertilisation inside the mother's body, the pregnancy in amniotic fluid. Therefore, the *grief* for the drying of the sea is accompanied by the *grit* to return to the lost humidity and for the advent of powerful curative processes.

From the inspiring "scientific phantasy"[1] presented in *Thalassa*, we maintain the idea that, upon facing catastrophe, we react in regressive movements, which can be benign—in the sense that they stimulate adaptive progression—or malignant, in the sense of disavowal (*Verleugnung*)

---

[1] Citation by Freud (1933c).

of the new reality that is about to come: the "new normal". Whatever their destinations, catastrophes demand a great deal of psychic work, which perhaps explains the fatigue, and even the torpor ("laziness"),[2] which so many analysts and analysands have mentioned since the beginning of the pandemic (I will come back to this point later on).

Based on the above considerations, I will propose reflections on the destinations of our pandemic catastrophe, taking the Brazilian example as a *princeps* case, but also considering that the situation in Brazil can illustrate some universal psychic mechanisms that have shown up all over the world in the last few months. While I put forward my argument, I invite the reader to accompany me on a few vitalising trips: first to the United Kingdom, then we will join Freud on his stroll through the Dolomites during World War I, we will then return to contemporary Brazil, and we will end our journey in the Hungarian Alps accompanying Ferenczi on his idyllic stroll. Fasten your seatbelts ... but not too tight. We need to breathe.

"It will pass": transience, melancholy, and revolt

"Please believe these days will pass." That was the message on colourful billboards and signs in major cities in the UK during the beginning of the pandemic. It is a creation of artist Mark Titchner, who declared the project was made to "boost morale" of citizens and help them cope with the grief associated with the loss of loved ones or with the postponement of libidinal satisfactions imposed by social distancing.[3] In Brazil, there were also ads put out by the government in the same spirit, and several compositions of the popular song that has in its chorus "*vai passar*" ("it will pass"). Considering that there is no postponement in the unconscious—and that this would be the job of working-through and sublimation—we can question the meaning of these frequently explored mottoes in government ads in so many countries. What will pass? How will it pass, and how to wait? And what won't or shouldn't pass? What grief and grit will we inherit from the pandemic?

---

[2] Editors' note: The author is alluding to Lafargue's (1883) essay, "The right to be lazy". See below.

[3] https://creativereview.co.uk/mark-titchner-please-believe-these-days-will-pass-build-hollywood/.

The theme of "the passenger" gave Freud the opportunity to write one of his most beautiful texts: "On Transience", published in 1916, exactly during the catastrophe caused by World War I. In it, Freud (1916a) describes a summer stroll through the Dolomites in the company of a young poet (Rilke, as we know) and a "taciturn" friend (Lou Andreas-Salomé). In spite of the exuberance of the landscape—and the purity of the air, we must point out—the poet confesses that he finds no joy in it, since he is disturbed by the idea that in a short time all this beauty will disappear, outweighed by the cold and snow. It is the romantic version of the well-known adage, "winter is coming" (for those who have watched *Game of Thrones*). The transience of beauty, and not only natural beauty, but also that which is created by Man is, for the poet, the reason for its depreciation.

By poring over the gloomy humour of the poet, Freud is, as you can imagine, taking his first steps towards his renowned essay dedicated to mourning and melancholia (1917e). The poet and his companion darken the brightness of summer by bringing forward the pain of loss of beauty, always ephemeral, therefore jeopardising the enjoyment of the present and the pleasure of the journey. According to Freud, modern mankind can have two common reactions to that which is transient, to that which passes: a painful fatigue that is close to the melancholic humour, and a "revolt against the reality of facts"; in other words, denial. For the narcissistic subject, attached to his possessions as if they were to define the value of his ego, the loss of the object is dramatic, and death inconceivable.

Alternatively, Freud seems to want to convey a tragic perspective of existence, for which transience should make the present more valuable, bringing joy to the finite experience of fruition. He insists that even a flower that blossoms for a single night should not seem less beautiful because of the brevity of its existence. Finally, on the last lines of the essay, Freud (1916a, p. 306) assumes the obvious metaphor and mentions the destruction caused by the war—which had already caused so much suffering in Europe—stating with rare optimism: "We shall build up again all that war has destroyed, and perhaps on firmer ground and more lastingly than before." The winter, too, shall pass.

According to Freudian metapsychology, waiting and postponement are part of the process of the constitution of subjectivity. This is due to the work of the ego ideal, able to stimulate sublimatory processes. Delay allows the subject to invest in existential projects, that is, to divert the sexual libido from its original target and channel it to socially valued purposes, a move that implies the ability to create new objects of satisfaction (Freud, 1914c). Yet one of the most visible effects of the pandemic was exactly an increase of despair and scepticism towards the future, something observed most keenly among teenagers and young adults.

This dystopian scenario provoked by the pandemic catastrophe exacerbates its destructive feature and tends to be lived by the subject only as resignation. And when resigning gratification, the primary tendency of the psychic apparatus is, as Balint (1968) pointed out, towards malignant regression, to ways of previous satisfactions, characterised by the inertia imposed by the idea of omnipotence. Perhaps this is because our inborn memory indicates that, in fact, nothing will go back to what it was before.

The three denials: the case of Brazil

After six months of the pandemic and having surpassed the staggering mark of 130,000 deaths in the country (I write this in mid-September), a nuanced reflection of the different types of denial discourses that characterise the government's reaction to the pandemic—as well as the reaction of sectors of civil society—is imposed on us. Statements from President Bolsonaro are engraved in our memory which, in other social-political contexts, would be considered impeachable offences. On March 15, at the beginning of the pandemic in Brazil, a claim that we were succumbing to "neurosis". Two days later, facing protective sanitary measures imposed by several governors, a statement was released saying that the virus had caused "hysteria" in the country. On March 20, the coronavirus was compared to a "little flu". On March 29, when we surpassed 4,000 cases and 100 deaths, the wise observation was made that "We will all eventually die." In the following month, when we surpassed 2,500 cases, he refused to speak on the subject: "I'm not a gravedigger." Finally, on April 28, when questioned about the 5,000 deaths, the insurmountable, "So what? Sorry. What do you want me to do? My name is Messias [Messiah in Portuguese], but I don't perform miracles."[4]

---

[4] The Brazilian president's full name is Jair Messias Bolsonaro. His election was strongly linked to the influence of the Evangelical community. These statements can be found

Sad is the republic in which we feel shame (our own and vicarious, in this case) of supreme authority. Critical is the fact that, apart from all the shame—and humiliation to which we were and are submitted in a period that in itself causes a great deal of suffering—statements made by authorities have concrete effects on how citizens think, feel, and act. Consequently, it influences the conduct of protection adopted by a large portion of the population and, therefore, the increase or decrease in cases and deaths.

Considering the Brazilian scenario, it can be said that not only one form of denial is at play when dealing with the Covid-19 pandemic, but rather three: "delusional denial", "hypocritical denial", and "pragmatic denial". It is important, in any analysis of clinical–political consequences of the pandemic, to observe the differences—often subtle—among them. Denial—in regard to subjective singularities—is a psychic defence (Freud, 1925h, 1927e). However, in the context of a pandemic, it is also a political act that reflects on the surroundings—especially among the most vulnerable population—as severe physical and mental health issues, for which social and political treatment is necessary. And in this case, psychoanalysis can contribute to mapping the forces at play in its production.

Delusional denial is founded on the defence activated in situations in which one finds oneself in a state of complete impotence and vulnerability. When faced with traumatic helplessness, one reverts to malignant omnipotence, which is expressed by the mantle of arrogance. The delusional denier thinks himself to be more powerful facing risks and wiser about the facts than he actually is. And his omniscience feeds conspiracy theories as described by Freud's "psychology of the masses" (1921c)—for example, the accusation made by the former education minister saying that the new coronavirus had been a creation fostered by the Chinese Communist Party—or miracle cures for the uncertainties that afflict him. This only shows the subject's escape from reality to a wishful rather than realistic vision of the world. Bolsonaro's insistence—after testing positive—on appearing in the media raising a box of hydroxychloroquine as if he were the captain of the Brazilian national team raising the

---

at   https://noticias.uol.com.br/saude/ultimas-noticias/redacao/2020/05/01/todos-nos-vamos-morrer-um-dia-as-frases-de-bolsonaro-durante-a-pandemia.htm.

World Cup trophy can illustrate this process. The obscene gesture has an even more obvious motivation: delusional denial has great appeal for a significant portion of the population who yearn to believe that their anguish is no more than nonsense. Something that gives this type of denial great potential to deceive frightened and faithless masses (cf. Freud, 1927c).

Alternatively, hypocritical denial has as one of its main sources an exacerbated and even perverse version of what Freud (1921c) called "narcissism of small differences". Its other source, split from the first, resides in what Ferenczi called "hypocrisy", the insensitivity of the subject towards the other's suffering, which is reduced to an object of the subject's drive satisfaction (Ferenczi, 1932, 1933). This is the denial present in a great portion of the more privileged classes of society (politicians, businessmen, merchants) who know that there will always be the possibility of comfortable social distancing for them (often in large beach/country houses away from large city centres), medical care, hospital beds, and ventilators that work, as opposed to those overpriced, bought-in-a-rush with no public tender by government authorities. There is also something delusional in hypocritical denial, since it is based on the belief in selective invulnerability—apparently guaranteed by expensive health insurances that stifle the Brazilian middle class—which is always fragile in the context of the numbers caused by a pandemic. However, this reasoning also reflects a somewhat cynical calculation based on rationalisation, as described by philosopher Peter Sloterdijk (1988), a calculus that elevates and justifies the distinct values of some lives based on wealth, class, religion, ethnicity, etc., compromising any type of empathy among the different classes that make up our fragile social fabric.[5]

Hypocritical denial is also responsible for the distorted issue put to us by portions of the government and business community in which we are told that we must choose between saving lives—those of the most vulnerable to the coronavirus—and saving the economy, therefore avoiding an even greater number of deaths due to the cost of social recession, such as unemployment, poverty, and hunger. In this case, imposing a type of Sophie's choice that reflects less the reality of facts[6] and more the

---

[5] See also the concept of pseudo-speciation proposed by Erikson (1966).
[6] See Greenstone & Nigam (2020).

intellectual addiction of conservative economists fuelled by the logic of exploitation: people must continue to work so that productive sectors of our society don't lose out on their profits and the government can continue to collect taxes needed to fill its coffers. In contrast, however, we quickly learned that there can be intermediate solutions to not only save lives, but also avoid decreasing economic activity. Not to mention the emergence of solidary initiatives that can help to decrease the hardship of those more in need.[7] Furthermore, as the months went by, healthcare professionals gained knowledge on how to decrease mortality in cases of the new coronavirus. That is to say, preventing untimely deaths does not mean "postponing deaths", but rather saving lives.

Finally, we were also witness to pragmatic denial—present in most segments of the less fortunate population—whose voice says that social distancing is not possible because one needs to work, that masks and hand sanitisers are luxury items, that one lives in small, confined spaces with a large number of other people in communities that don't have basic sanitation and, therefore, social distancing is only possible for those who can afford it. Thus, pragmatic denial is driven by self-sacrificial morals adopted by someone who does not indeed recognise the value of their own life, characterising what Ferenczi (1931, 1933) called "identification with the aggressor". Counterpart to hypocritical denial, it is also defensive, since it has the purpose of shielding the subject from the anguish felt by facing the risks the disease imposes and the threat of death.

Fed by the federal state's "denialist" discourses as described above, all three types of denials are intensified by their morbid mechanisms. By denying the destructive potential of the new coronavirus, the government—represented by the president—makes each citizen question their own perception of reality and the risks that the pandemic brings. This created a true confusion of tongues—both anxiogenic and traumatic—among the different versions issued by the several national and international health organisations on the risks and care necessary to protect oneself. Among the predictable results, there is guilt and shame felt by those who try to practise self-care with the purpose of

---

[7] In Brazil, where maids and cleaners are the sole or primary breadwinners of millions of households, there was a strong movement to keep paying salaries without obliging employees to show up for work.

protecting themselves or those more vulnerable (the elderly and those in high-risk groups), and the premature ceasing of such practices. This, until death which is never wrong separates the wishful, defensive illusion from reality.

The vitalising effect of "good air": compliment to laziness

One of the most powerful clinical–political reflections in Ferenczi's works can be seen in the short essay with the exotic title "The refreshing and curative effect of 'fresh air' and 'good air'", from 1918.[8] Although Ferenczi does not mention Freud's stroll through the Dolomites, it is tempting to think that it is a response to "On Transience". For apart from its temporal proximity, Ferenczi's text refers to environments of forests and mountains. His argument is based on the vitalising and curative effect of "fresh air", or "open air", or "Alpine air". Let's then accompany Ferenczi in his relaxing stroll through the Hungarian Alps, trying to understand his perspective of the existing relation between breathing, life, and psychoanalysis.

Having a dialogue with the medicine of his time, Ferenczi discusses the limits of explanations on the effects—both chemical and physical—of inhaling the fresh air from nature. According to physiologists, good air would favour deep breathing—helped by the dilating of nostrils and the decongestion of sinuses—as opposed to superficial breathing that occurs in closed, overcrowded, mildew-smelling spaces. Deep breathing has known effects on blood circulation and in the functioning of abdominal veins, stimulating the cardiac muscle and visceral organs. However, apart from the physical-chemical aspects, the Hungarian psychoanalyst (and hiker) draws his readers' attention to psychic factors of those who inhale the pure air present in natural landscapes, their "internal disposition", indicating the insufficiency of medical rationale.

Indeed, while physiology adopts the principle of utility as a paradigm which favours the isolated function of each organ or the interrelation

---

[8] There is no known translation of this text into English, only a suggested translation of the Hungarian title found at the bibliography of Ferenczi's writings in *Further Contributions to the Theory and Technique of Psycho-analysis*, compiled by John Rickman (Ferenczi, 2002, p. 457).

of organs for the performance of certain functions, Ferenczi points out the effects of suffering and pleasure to the integral functioning of the organism and of its "vital mechanisms". By indicating that a person who finds themselves working in a closed space "breathes" (in quotes in the original) when he leaves the environment and the exhausting toil, Ferenczi highlights the dimension of relaxation and pleasure in the new situation. And, what shouldn't surprise those who read Freud—inventor of the *Lustprinzip*[9]—he relates the vitalising and curative effects to this relaxation and experience of pleasure. Therefore, in order to understand how the vital mechanisms of the organism work, it would be necessary to conceive a physiology that also considers psychic humour; "a *Lust-Physiologie* to complete the *Nutz-Physiologie*".[10] It is worth sharing the depth of a short passage of the original text:

> Physiology conceives an organism as a simple *machine for work*, whose only concern is to carry out as much useful work as is possible with the least amount of energy, when in fact an organism is also made up of *joy of living* and consequently strives to obtain as much *pleasure* as possible for each organ and for the organism as a whole and when doing so, frequently ignores the economy recommended by the utility principle. (Ferenczi, 1918, p. 307, italics in original, our translation)[11]

It is then clear that Ferenczi's perspective on his stroll through the Alps is significantly different from that taken by Freud's friends, incapable of experiencing the joy of living when in contact with natural landscapes. What prevented Rilke and Salomé from breathing, letting themselves be taken over by the melancholy of transience?

It's inevitable to associate *Nutz-Physiologie*—physiology based on the principle of utility—with hypocritical denial, which sets the priorities of the economy in opposition to the priorities of life, imposing

---

[9] "Pleasure principle".

[10] Physiology of pleasure and physiology of utility.

[11] "La physiologie conçoit l'organisme comme une simple *machine à travailler* dont le seul souci est d'accomplir le maximum de travail utile avec un minimum d'énergie dépensée, alors que l'organisme est fait aussi de *joie de vivre* et s'efforce par conséquent de procurer le plus de *plaisir* possible à chacun des organes et à l'organisme tout entier, négligeant souvent, ce faisant, l'économie recommandée par le principe d'utilité" (Ferenczi, 1918, p. 307).

the rationales of economical pseudo-reasoning so that work is never interrupted. Facing this necropolitical economy based on the principle of utility, Ferenczi seems to indicate a possible resistance inspired by a vitalising contemplation. (It is not surprising that his conception of *Lust-Physiologie* is also an inspiration to a clinical style guided by the principles of relaxation, regression, and play in analysis, but this is a subject for another time.) Therefore, there would be something positive about the fatigue and even the "laziness"[12] that took over a lot of us during these first few months of the pandemic, mentioned by several analysands and colleagues overburdened by the demand of the less free-floating attention of online practice.

In the classic nineteenth-century Marxist literature, *The Right to Be Lazy*, Paul Lafargue (1883)—Marx's son-in-law—developed reflections on how surprised he was that European workers demanded better salaries and even fought against unemployment, when they should have actually been fighting for "laziness"—free time, and idleness— which would provide purpose and joy to their existence.[13] In line with Lafargue, the attitude described by Ferenczi on his stroll in the mountains speaks to a curative dimension of Thalassic regression, and presents another psychoanalytical anthropology, in which the *drive to rest* (*Ruhetrieb*), found in the *Clinical Diary*, demands its place next to the sexual and death drives (Ferenczi, 1932, p. 200). An area not fully explored, not even by his commentators, the drive to rest speaks to a primordial monism responsible for the omnipotence lived by the child in the "introjection phase" to which one returns throughout life, every time a spontaneous and creating gesture is expressed (cf. Kupermann, 2019).

The drive to rest differentiates itself, however, from the Freudian Eros, since its purpose does not coincide with sexual satisfaction and with the pleasure arising from the decrease of psychic excitement. It also does not have the objective of returning to the inanimate, nor has death as its goal, like Thanatos. The affect that would best describe reaching its goal *(Ziel)* is the joy of existence, source for the necessary acceptance

---

[12] See footnote 3 and below.

[13] Ferenczi (1919) would describe workers who suffered from "Sunday neurosis", the tension-filled boredom, guilt, and displeasure in the face of free time and idleness that prevented them from valuing and enjoying the "laziness" that Lafargue (1883) advocated.

to work through one's grief, and also for the power and energy of the grit that keeps the subject desiring and creating. Will this be one of the destinations of the catastrophe caused by the pandemic in our lifestyle? The assertion of our right to fatigue, to "laziness" in its most positive and life-affirming sense, and to have time to breathe and re-experience the joy of living?

Daniel Kupermann
September 2020

Translated from Portuguese by Karla Isolda dos Santos Buss

References

Balint, M. (1968). *The Basic Fault: Therapeutic Aspects of Regression*. London: Tavistock.

Erikson, E. H. (1966). Ontogeny of ritualization in man. *Philosophical Transactions of the Royal Society of London. Series B, Biological Sciences, 251*(772): 337–349. Retrieved November 23, 2020, from http://jstor.org/stable/2416745.

Ferenczi, S. (1918). Effet vivificant et effet curatif de l` "air frais" et du "bon air". In: S. Ferenczi (Ed.), *Psychanalyse II, Œuvres complètes, 1913–1919*. Paris: Payot, 1994.

Ferenczi, S. (1919). Sunday neuroses. In: J. Rickman (Ed.), *Ferenczi, S., Further Contributions to the Theory and Technique of Psycho-analysis*. London: Karnac, 2002.

Ferenczi, S. (1924). Thalassa: a theory of genitality. *Psychoanalytic Quarterly, 2*: 361–364.

Ferenczi, S. (1931). Child-analysis in the analysis of adults. *International Journal of Psycho-Analysis, 12*: 468–482.

Ferenczi, S. (1932). *The Clinical Diary of Sándor Ferenczi*. Cambridge, MA: Harvard University Press, 1995.

Ferenczi, S. (1933). Confusion of the tongues between the adults and the child—the language of tenderness and of passion. *International Journal of Psycho-Analysis, 30*: 225–230.

Ferenczi, S. (2002). *Further Contributions to the Theory and Technique of Psycho-analysis*. J. Rickman (Ed.). London: Karnac.

Freud, S. (1914c). On narcissism. *S. E.*, *14*: 67–102. London: Hogarth.

Freud, S. (1915). *A Phylogenetic Fantasy: Overview of the Transference Neuroses.* I. Grubrich-Simitis (Ed.). London: Harvard University Press, 1987.

Freud, S. (1916a). On transience. *S. E.*, *14*: 303–307. London: Hogarth.

Freud, S. (1917e). Mourning and melancholia. *S. E.*, *14*: 237–258. London: Hogarth.

Freud, S. (1921c). *Group Psychology and the Analysis of the Ego. S. E.*, *18*: 65–144. London: Hogarth.

Freud, S. (1925h). Negation. *International Journal of Psycho-Analysis*, *6*: 367–371.

Freud, S. (1927c). *The Future of an Illusion. S. E.*, *21*: 1–56. London: Hogarth.

Freud, S. (1927e). Fetishism. *International Journal of Psycho-Analysis*, *9*: 161–166.

Freud, S. (1933c). Sándor Ferenczi. *International Journal of Psycho-Analysis*, *14*: 297–299. Also *S. E.*, *27*. London: Hogarth.

Greenstone, M., & Nigam, V. (2020). Does social distancing matter? University of Chicago, Becker Friedman Institute for Economics Working Paper No. 2020-26. Available at SSRN: https://ssrn.com/abstract=3561244 or http://dx.doi.org/10.2139/ssrn.3561244 (last accessed December 21, 2020).

Kupermann, D. (2019). *Por que Ferenczi?* São Paulo, Brazil: Zagodoni.

Lafargue, P. (1883). The right to be lazy. *Lafargue Internet Archive (marxists. org)*, 2000 (last accessed December 21, 2020).

Sabourin, P. (1985). *Ferenczi, paladino et grand vizir secret.* Bégédis, France: Éditions Universitaires.

Sloterdijk, P. (1988). *Critique of Cynical Reason.* Minneapolis, MN: University of Minnesota Press.

Part III

The setting under pressure

CHAPTER 6

Being online: what does it mean for psychoanalysis?

Antonino Ferro
Pavia, Italy

I do not think there is much to be said about working remotely in psychoanalysis, as opposed to the usual setting, in emergency situations such as the ongoing pandemic. Instead, what I do think is worthy of discussion is whether any part of remote working can be transferred into our everyday work after we return to normality. Could it become an alternative way to routinely offer analysis? More precisely, are there any benefits we can derive from this approach that has been forced upon us? Does it offer any new methods and acquired knowledge which could become useful and constructive even in everyday situations?

Remote working has always aroused strong objections and had strict limits imposed upon it, as if people feared that working remotely could distort the true nature of analytic work. The person's physical absence was thought to potentiate the possibility of activating unmanageable emotions or of avoiding and suppressing potentially manageable ones. Before lockdown, the opportunity to work remotely, across long distances, already existed in certain circumstances. This primarily involved the less controversial possibility of conducting supervisions online, but was also resorted to in personal analyses when circumstances such as geographic distance or special needs for confidentiality mitigated against an in-person analysis.

Two seminar papers presented in Italy during the height of lockdown—one by a newly qualified analyst, the other by a highly experienced training analyst—were absolutely opposed to working remotely because both authors felt the method engendered a loss of emotional closeness. Any change in psychoanalysis has always been difficult (we have only to think of the Controversial Discussions of 1943–1944), but it is also true that psychoanalysis has greatly expanded in recent years, in particular regarding work with very small children, the very old, and patients who are seriously ill, where technique has evolved. I believe that the changes necessitated by the Covid pandemic have heralded the arrival and acceptance of working remotely, producing nothing less than a revolution—one that has begun to spark countless debates and discussions, forcing us to see many old assumptions and problems from new and original points of view.

What I say below is not offered as fact but is simply what I have experienced with my own patients online.

Elasticity and invariance: negative capability and play

The first thing I noticed as an unanticipated evolution within myself, working remotely, was a greater freedom in using negative capabilities, or, to quote Keats, the capability of "being in uncertainties, mysteries, doubts, without any irritable reaching after fact and reason" (1817, p. 277). I also encountered a facilitation of the communicative process within the analytic field (being "on line" in every sense) that I believe has to do with an inevitable dimension of playfulness that, in my experience, increases in remote working and that I hope I will be able to transfer to in-person work. Perhaps, for me, this increase in freedom and playfulness reflects a feeling that the non-traditional setting evoked an even greater improvisational atmosphere while the traditional setting carried the connotation of a more institutional dimension. Personally speaking, I feel freer and work better in the analytic situation when I feel less burdened by institutions.

Many people claim that the screen works as a "blocking filter" for emotions, but this is not my experience. I found it enabled a new, free circulation of emotion to open up. After all, is theatre necessarily more involving and emotionally impactful than cinema?

The dimension of verbal play has also gained more space through working remotely, and I believe this is of fundamental importance because it opens the way directly to the dimension of dreams.

Everything that is differently real is a portal to the imaginary, the oneiric, the transformation of concrete sensorial experience and concrete narration into the waking dream. A concrete, realistic field is different from a field that presents itself as playful and oneiric from the outset. This playful dimension also admits the pleasure of analysis where psychoanalysis has always emphasised the importance of pain.

Here, I would like to refer readers to what Ogden (2019) says about epistemological and ontological psychoanalysis, that the former has to do with knowing and understanding while the latter has to do with being and becoming. The oneiric dimension is developed by the aptitude to dreaming that analyst and patient are able to bring to the session.

In a television series called *The Bridge*, which takes place in a city on the border between Mexico and the United States, the main characters are a fierily passionate Mexican policeman and an American detective who has clear and pronounced Asperger's syndrome. I believe that the analyst, and consequently also their patient, must be able to oscillate between emotional involvement and autism-like withdrawal. I believe that working remotely and in person must be two ways that minds can meet in a session, and that constantly oscillating between the two is a guarantee of a dynamic constructivist approach.

One dimension that was always present in the work of Jim Grotstein was playfulness (2007). I am therefore sure he would have laughed at (and then searched for the possible serious value of) the postulate of the existence of not only the alpha function but also, in the mental setting with computers, an alpha-r (remote) function delegated to alphabetising the entire sensory experience related to the functioning of the screen, computer, keys, and Wi-Fi connection, which thus become normal inhabitants of the new setting.

One of the most evident characteristics of psychoanalysis is a certain ossification which has slowed both its progress and its evolution. Usually a lot of resistance is offered to the introduction of the "new". For many analysts, the classical setting begun by Freud is still the most used and esteemed one. In regard to theories, in different ways, and in different geographical areas, there have been varying degrees of openness, as demonstrated by the introduction of new theoretical vertices and assumptions, such as Kleinian and Bionian paradigms, and Bionian field theory.

With respect to rigidity and invariance in the setting, the ability to adapt and to continue to mourn the loss of the traditional situation has begun to prevail, no doubt connected to the degree to which the change has begun to be accepted by analyst and patient. (Let us not forget that the change in setting has not only constituted a loss. For many patients, working online has meant gaining several hours in their weekly schedule.)

With my own patients, I had no difficulty offering sessions online and having them accepted, and I respected the patients' organisation of the setting. Without any prompting from me, almost all of them arranged a couch to lie down on, with a computer open on a side table—they would call and see me at the start of the session, and we would close together at the end. Only a couple of patients overcame the disorientation of the new setting and sat in front of the computer. It was always tacitly understood that, once Covid was under control, we would resume the sessions in my office as usual.

Conclusions

It seems to me that the arrival of the remote working method has completely changed the way we look at analysis. Thanks to this storm that has struck our way of working, we have now caught up to the modern world, instead of continuing in the same ways we have been following for the past 100 years, ossified with little innovation.

Now, with remote analysis, the setting becomes more of an imaginary place (Vallino, 1999) and field theory facilitates this view. Furthermore, it seems to me that remote analysis teaches us that we must become adept at managing disasters and that nothing can be taken for granted. The peaceful repetitiveness of the setting in which the agglutinated nucleus stratifies (Bleger, 1967, p. 47) has been called into question, and I think this cataclysm may help us to be better equipped to contain previously unthinkable thoughts.

The late Sicilian writer Andrea Camilleri, who in some respects has certain points of contact with Pirandello, went blind in the last years of his life, having written a large number of very successful Montalbano novels. He said that, after he lost his sight, when he approached someone, he had a kind of vision of the mental characteristics of that person. His statement intrigued me. Being a novelist and having a great aptitude for creating stories, narratives, and characters, he was able to make up for the lack of physical sight with an imaginative vision which revealed even aspects of how other minds functioned that were not immediately visible. In other words, Camilleri had a constructivist access to the minds of others. Real sight is replaced by oneiric vision.

Camilleri's blindness can be viewed as a sort of extreme lockdown, and it allows us to see how he developed other forms of understanding. In the same way, I have noticed with many of my patients how the loss of certain aspects of their normal life has led them to develop other creative aspects of the mind. In my reflections on remote analytic work, I probably need to consider the nightmare in which they found themselves dreaming: a pandemic (Jarvis, 2020).

Thinking about our ability to adapt to change, I am reminded of the Craig Gillespie film, *Lars and the Real Girl*. The main character in this film has never had a relationship with a girl, something his whole family constantly reproaches him for. One day, after his family issue the umpteenth invitation to dinner, telling him to bring a girlfriend if he has one, he appears with a lifelike doll. His family act as if nothing is wrong; however, they go to a psychiatrist the next day and tell her all about it. The psychiatrist advises them to behave completely normally when Lars appears with his doll companion. The doll has her own food phobias and a series of traits that make her appear more and more human in everyone's eyes. After a while, the giant doll becomes part of the family group. This shows how even the strangest things can be normalised if you look at them without bias. The same holds true for remote analysis.

We have seen it happening in many people's everyday lives in relation to the use of *masks*. Something that would previously have been seen as strange becomes normal at some point, to the extent where anyone not wearing one now attracts strange looks. Habit creates normality.

Lars's girlfriend is humanised, and we do not know if it is because he develops an aptitude for interpersonal contact or because nobody pays attention to the difference anymore. The same thing happens when the setting is conceived as a place of the mind: what is initially strange becomes familiar. For some people, the move from the familiar old setting to the new setting might be similar to having to change house. At first they will feel uncomfortable and disoriented, but it is sometimes surprising how little it can take to accept the new situation. After all, children replace primary objects with transitional objects, making this an important evolutionary step. The ability to process grief and create new islands of safety is a maturing process that allows human beings to adapt to new situations.

We are familiar with Kafka's story *The Metamorphosis*, in which a human being finds himself transformed into a cockroach overnight, but not yet sufficiently familiar with what McEwan (2019) tells us about the transformation of a cockroach into a man. In which direction will it be stranger to go? Towards the formerly known or towards the formerly unknown?

Antonino Ferro
August 2020

Translated from the Italian by Gillian Jarvis

Acknowledgement

I wish to thank G. Jarvis for her invaluable editorial assistance and comments.

References

Bleger, J. (1967). *Symbiosis and Ambiguity: A Psychoanalytical Study.* Hove, UK: Routledge, 2013.

Grotstein, J. S. (2007). *A Beam of Intense Darkness: Wilfred Bion's Legacy to Psychoanalysis.* London: Karnac.

Jarvis, G. (2020). Personal correspondence.

Keats, J. (1817). *Letters.* M. B. Forman (Ed.). Oxford: Oxford University Press, 1952.

McEwan, I. (2019). *The Cockroach.* London: Vintage.

Ogden, T. H. (2019). Ontological psychoanalysis or "what do you want to be when you grow up?" *Psychoanalytic Quarterly, 88*(4): 661–684.

Vallino, D. (1999). Le storie ed il luogo immaginario nella psicoanalisi del bambino. In: A. Ferruta, R. Goisis, R. Jaffé, & N. Loiacono (Eds.), *Il contributo della psicoanalisi alla cura delle patologie gravi in infanzia ed in adolescenza* (pp. 48–62). Rome: Armando Editore.

CHAPTER 7

The burnt compartment. Or: Psychoanalysis without a couch

Ana de Staal
Paris, France

"Act as though, for instance, you were a traveler sitting next to the window of a railway carriage and describing to someone inside the carriage the changing views which you see outside."
—Sigmund Freud, "On Beginning the Treatment" (1913c, p. 135)

"And why should we remain seated by the window, commentating, if, for example, there is a fire? And if the flames reached the train and burned the compartment?"
—Antonino Ferro, *Psychoanalysis and Dreams: Bion, the Field and the Viscera of the Mind* (2014, p. 3)

I

My consultation room is located on the last floor of an old Haussmann building in Paris, in what we refer to here as a *chambre de bonne* (maid's room): small rooms that had originally housed domestic staff, and now serve mostly as lodgings for students or lone workers. Many, such as I myself, use them as offices, studios, consultation rooms. A building will typically have five or six such rooms, nestled under the slanting mansard roof and lining a narrow corridor one after the other. Mine is the second in a row of five. During the time of the events I am about to recount, two young researchers were living in the first room; the third served as an occasional office for a quarrelsome elderly gentleman, a "veteran of the Algerian War" as he tended to mention in either livid or helpless tones, as may be required by the situation at hand; and the remaining two rooms housed a philosophy student and a nurse in training, respectively.

It so happened that on a cold winter night in 2016, towards the end of February, a fire completely ravaged the third room, that of the old military man, and left mine in a pitiful state.

It all began at about half past eight in the evening, when the analysand, Mr L, lying on the couch for the past twenty minutes suddenly interrupted his deliberations on a range of internal object relationships (the central concern of which was the status of the powerless father). He said to me: "Did you hear that?!" Indeed, I had heard a sort of muffled little explosion. But as the wind was wailing outside, and the old window in the corridor tended to burst open at the slightest breeze, I preferred to keep quiet, to wait and see. The following thirty seconds went by under the superficial yet vigilant silence of both the patient and me, before we heard the same noise again, now louder. "Do you mind?" I said to Mr L, and got up to inspect what was going on outside.

What I saw down the corridor froze me in my tracks. A huge lick of yellow and blue flames was bellowing ferociously out of the old man's den. I saw the man through the half-open door doing battle in sweat, in silence, and above all in vain against a mountain of files and suitcases on fire. (I later found out that the suitcases were crammed with the paperwork of the numerous lawsuits he had addressed to various parts of officialdom over the span of half a century.) There was no doubt that the man was battling the demons of his madness; there was also no doubt that we were about to perish along with them.

To my left, then, in the pyre, a mad soldier was drawing us into his nightmare, which had materialised through the magic of a vanquished man's hatred; to my right, lying on the couch, a young computer engineer with volcanic yet restrained emotions was patiently awaiting the return of his analyst. What to do? I still see myself, staring in a daze at a random dot of blue flames, scurrying through the archives of my mind to find the folder marked "Fire Emergency Instructions".

Five or six years prior, I had undertaken the publication of Antonino Ferro's works in France, as well as the revision of some of the French translations of his work. I ended up knowing those texts more or less by heart, and was certain that the file I was searching for was somewhere in those shelves, that is to say, somewhere in the section labelled "The analytical situation—radical thought". Let me explain.

For the past thirty years, and especially during the 2010s, Ferro has ceaselessly been enriching contemporary psychoanalysis[1] in a manner both original and perfectly in line with clinical work, by cultivating some of his predecessors' most fertile hypotheses. His works have thus led to some considerable advances (particularly, in my opinion, concerning the treatment of psychosomatic and borderline patients). He skilfully blends the notions of the "field" (Baranger & Baranger, 1961–1962) and of "maternal reverie" (Bion, 1962), a blend that he then seasons with a long-held and creative dialogue with Thomas Ogden. These ideas, these garnishes—Ferro has a penchant for culinary metaphors—allowed him to "cook up" a kind of session where space/time was protected from any intrusion from external reality and would, in contrast, transform into a telling and properly analytic field, which allows one to perceive not only the weave of affect in play within the analysand's internal world, but also the threads of this emotional stuff, including the spots where it might be tearing. Like a surgeon preparing a sterilised field before an operation, or like a spectator or actor waiting for the lights to go off and for the show to commence, Ferro has created a setting that is sealed off from the external world by the rigorous application of daydreaming qualities to the analytical situation.[2]

---

[1] Ferro's rich bibliography contains about twenty books and over 120 articles translated across a dozen languages. I refer the reader in particular to *Avoiding Emotions, Living Emotions* (Ferro, 2007), a fairly exhaustive book that covers many aspects of his theory of technique. One may also find it useful to read two of his more recent works: *The New Analyst's Guide to the Galaxy. Questions about Contemporary Psychoanalysis* (Ferro & Nicoli, 2017), constituting a dialogue with Luca Nicoli, and *Psychoanalysis and Dreams: Bion, the Field and the Viscera of the Mind* (Ferro, 2014).

[2] The idea in and of itself was not original and is first found in Bion (1962), then, in a very developed manner, in Ogden (1997, 2005, 2008, 2009). Ferro's specificity, very

He writes:

> [...] considering dreams as a continuously operating level in
> the session enables us to work within a virtual space, a field that
> is created by the *encounter between a patient, an analyst and a
> setting* without having to address so-called "external reality"—
> which does not belong to us as analysts in a consulting room with
> a patient. It speaks to us continually of other things; the other
> things are what concern us, notably the development of tools
> for managing, weaving, metabolizing, digesting and giving both
> meaning and depth to these "other things". (Ferro, 2007, p. 57;
> my italics)

And elsewhere:

> [...] blindness to all external reality allows us to see scenes in
> the consulting room that the glare of reality would obliterate. In
> one session, we are the "Russian call-girls"[3] who save the patient
> from depression; in another, "my monster of a husband who's the
> absolute limit, expecting me to make love when I am completely
> worn out" (this after a transference interpretation) [...] (Ferro,
> 2014, pp. 34–35)

---

much inspired by the Kleinian's analysis of *hic et nunc* transference, is in the radical
way in which he makes use of the idea: taking into account the necessary adjustments,
he includes it in a "field" which thereupon functions as a kind of space that generates
dreams and stories, apt to "dissolve emotions into narrations" (Neri, 2009, p. 45). Let
us also add that, as Laura Ambrosiano and Eugenio Gaburri (2009, p. 109) highlight,
the field "does not coincide with the setting in as much as a therapeutic meeting place";
but rather, "indicates trans-personal space-and-time, crossed by energies of which the
interlocutors may just be carriers, [or, sometimes, the *personified embodiments*]". In this
sense, from the point of view of a theoretical archaeology, the Ferroan "field" is related,
in my opinion, more so to the issue of *transference/countertransference* than to that of the
setting. Incidentally, the field must be propped by the frame (as defined by Bleger, 1967)
in order to function. For a discussion of these questions, cf. also the remarks of Claudio
Neri (2009, pp. 50–55).
[3] An example of the "personified embodiments" mentioned in the previous footnote.

The virtually hermetic container that is a Ferroan session functions as a site conducive to a synchronic narrative construction that is able to transform psychic pain and repressed or non-lived emotions into so many stories of one's life—dedramatised stories, of course, but which, importantly, have been nuanced by a new possibility afforded to the patient: to express their history in a sufficiently protected space. They may then safely gain access to a palette of very varied, colourful, subtle, liveable, representable, meaningful and, thereby, depathologised emotions.

Simply put, in the heat of action, it was this specialist of psychic reality whom I sought to consult, in the hopes of finding the emergency procedure to be executed in the event of untimely and violent irruptions of real reality into an ongoing session: I remembered having read somewhere in his works a remark made in passing, but which I shall never be able to retrieve (does it even exist?), even though I am still able today to "hallucinate" it somewhere at the top of a page of one of his books, in the first or second paragraph.[4] I recalled that somewhere in Ferro's spell books it said that, in the event of a fire, earthquake, or other natural disaster, the analyst would nevertheless do well to take into account the reality before him with humility, firstly by demobilising the frame, and then by "teaming up" and "confronting" it, just like during a session, but simply on the new pitch where the game is now taking place. Being prepared and present, ready to face the rapid level change taking place in the reality in which we find ourselves—all of this made me think of the plasticity of the techniques used in the analysis of children, and of the way in which Ferro has made use of them in order to re-inform the analysis of adults.

What Ferro was expressing here, in those three little lines that I had found somewhere within me, was that the "session as reverie" was in no way to be confused with hallucination or a "folie à deux", but rather—in

---

[4] I nevertheless have found this in one of his recent texts: "Reality can only come in when the setting is turned off. If there was an earthquake, it would be foolish to just stand there and try to interpret the shock that the child felt as he broke away from the nipple of the mother—it would be absurd to do such a thing even without an earthquake—but let's imagine there is an earthquake: What do we say to the patient, what do we do? We wait and, if there is a second tremor, we get out. At that time though we turn off the setting, we are no longer analyst and patient, we are two frightened individuals who have to get safely out of that room" (Ferro, 2017, p. 35).

the face of reality—that it constituted a veritable technique. A special-ised technique, difficult to wield, and which produces its best results under rather more ideal circumstances, namely when the frame (how-ever it may have been constructed by the analyst) is, to use Bleger's terms (1967, p. 512), perfectly "dumb". Here, in the extraordinary circum-stances I found myself facing, the undeniable intrusion of the real into our session had jolted the frame and forced the analyst to rethink her strategy without a moment to spare.

I quickly returned to my office, shut the door behind me, and without sitting back down, told the analysand who was still lying there on the couch: "You were right … We will have to end our session now. Come, let's see what we can do. There is something very serious happening next door." The cold wind that was sweeping through the corridor had frozen me; fear crept into my heart and made me tremble. I grabbed my scarf. Mr L, disconcerted, leapt to his feet. We stepped out into the corridor. The flames were still roaring out of the neighbouring room, the old man was red and dripping with sweat, the corridor ceiling was turning black with soot, an acrid smoke began spreading: the plastic lining of the suit-cases had begun to melt. No one downstairs seemed to have taken notice of the event; below, families dined calmly in their spacious apartments, or were watching the news; on our floor, the young renters were not yet home and only the first room, where the two young researchers lived, seemed inhabited.

The analysand turned to me in a look of combined bewilderment and determination:

"What shall we do? And how?" "Let's do what we always do. We share the workload, OK? You call the fire brigade; I'll go knock on doors and alert the neighbours …"

The fire brigade arrived within five minutes, accompanied by a troop of howling sirens and lights. The fire was growing in intensity, but we, together, had accomplished the tasks that the firefighters communi-cated to us over the phone: the analysand had blocked the elevator and dragged the mad old man out of his room (which was far from easy, as the man was in the throes of a full-blown frenzy); we made sure to leave the entrances to the building open for the firemen and their ladders; we knocked on all the doors and made sure that no one was left trapped in the building.

Back in the office, I grabbed my backpack, stuffed into it two packets of clinical notebooks, while the analysand, of his own initiative, was busy rolling up the rug and the sheets that covered the couch, in the hopes of protecting them from the flood of water that would soon be inundating the room; he also drew the curtains and left the windows wide open, thinking that the water cannons would surely pass through from there. Our actions were clear, determined, and coordinated, taking us no longer than four or five minutes. We soon undertook the perilous leap from our innermost existence to the great outdoors, and found ourselves in a street blockaded by the emergency services, the police and the fire brigade. We were surrounded by the inevitable passers-by, who, wrested from their screens, had left their buildings in bunches to witness the spectacle "live at the scene".

The incident, as one may imagine, rattled us all, analyst and analysands alike. It also kicked us out to the curb for a good two weeks, while the mess was being cleaned up. When sessions resumed, the incident had the effect of setting in motion a whole phantasmatic world in some patients, who, not having personally lived through the event, first had to deal with the abrupt suspension of their sessions, and now had before their eyes the traces of destruction that were only fully repaired in the spring.

Thus, for example, about three months after the event, this phantasy of Mrs D, freely associating after some comments on a minuscule crack still visible on the wall: "You know, in my mother's opinion, you were not actually in session with a patient during the night of the fire. You were in the company of a lover … for sure, busy, making love on the couch." This beautiful and intelligent woman, whose life was now cruelly shrivelling under the harsh regard of a hysterical (internal) mother, was exposed throughout her adolescence to her parents' demonstrative and vindictive sexuality in the years preceding their (inevitable) divorce.

The frame, as Bleger (1967) pointed out, is the stable, invisible, dumb part of the analytical situation. It represents the non-process that serves as a backdrop for the analytical process to take place, just as it represents the non-ego whose backdrop allows the ego to construct itself and to evolve through a process of detachment. This point of stability, which we perceive only "when it changes or breaks", includes "the role of the analyst, the set of space (atmosphere) and time factors, and part of the technique (including problems concerning the fixing and keeping of times, fees, interruptions, etc.)" (p. 511).

After the fire, the office walls—the concrete and materially enveloping part of the frame, meant to remain invisible[5]—had made a spectacular eruption onto the stage, revealing now the scar tissue of something from behind the scenes of analytical work, of the reality that lurks behind life, of the mother who is not all-powerful and who will perhaps not always be there, of the mother/child symbiosis that will not last forever.[6] I feared a generalised unleashing of anxieties as sessions resumed, but, with the exception of one or two quite difficult patients, things took a different turn.

The remains of soot, the cracks, the myriad little marks, and vague odours left behind by the flames on the consultation room walls suddenly became apparent, and what's more, gave form and meaning to the intimate sufferings of many a patient, in a dynamic not dissimilar to the self-reparation of the frame. Indeed, these traces would recuperate their invisibility, as if by magic, only once they became vested with the analysand's words, or simply designated through their anxieties or their dreams. Their words plastered the walls, literally. It was as if the analytical frame, for the analysand in session, had to survive at all costs, despite the load of anxiety that each of their "reparative" words had to bear in order to keep it in working order—that is to say, invisible and ever present like a mother, symbiotic, unshakable, regardless of what may happen. For three months, the burnt walls of my office acted, to my great surprise, as a thermometer that I used to evaluate the degree of the introjection of the frame by each of my patients. Some interpretations were offered and progress was made.

As for the analysand with whom I had lived through the fire, we resumed work as soon as possible. A few days following our resumption, he sent me a photo via SMS of the corridor in flames. It was impressive;

---

[5] We have all had the experience where, after three or five years of analysis, a patient suddenly notices a painting or a bookshelf that had always been there: the sign of a partial letting go of the symbiotic link anchored at the core of the process.

[6] "Symbiosis with the mother (immobility of the non-ego) enables the child to develop his ego. The frame has a similar function: it acts as support, as mainstay, but, so far, we have been able to perceive it only when it changes or breaks" (Bleger, 1967, p. 512).

it was still very present in his mind. The day Mr L returned, he entered the room, looked around and smiled, noting proudly that the damage had been limited. But it did not escape my notice that the spell of psychic reality had been broken. Then, without either of us saying a word, we instinctively sat down face to face. He had lived through the story and was no longer in the mood simply to watch the landscape go by through the window of his compartment.

II

> "[We will attempt to] understand how, while knowing that one never says the same thing, one may say *nearly* the same thing.
>
> At this stage, the problem isn't so much the idea of the *same* thing, nor that of the same *thing*, but rather the idea of *nearly*. How far can that *nearly* stretch?"[7]
>
> —Umberto Eco, *Dire quasi la stessa cosa.*
> *Esperienze di traduzione* (2003, p. 8)

Four years later, more or less around the same time as the fire, we were once again kicked out of our couch and chair, but under quite different circumstances: the pandemic had arrived.

In France, we started getting seriously worried about the new coronavirus around mid-February. A month later, on March 16, the government declared a general lockdown. I had been closely following the disease's terrifying progression through Lombardy and was preparing for the worst about a week before lockdown was announced. I had already endeavoured to "shift" my sessions to the screen or to the phone, according to my patients' needs (i.e. having theorised nothing at all, but simply out of ethical concerns: not to abandon my analysands in the midst of treatment, to remain present and accompany them in what we were living through …). By way of consequence, on the day the country came to a halt, my office had already been closed for three days, and all the patients I had in analysis or in therapy, with very few exceptions, already knew that their next session would be carried out remotely.

---

[7] My translation from Italian. Translator's note.

Farewell dear trip to the session, dear Portuguese café on the corner of the street, dear eclairs of the bakery across the road, dear inevitable forgetting of the building codes on a Saturday, dear rickety old elevator covered in the red velour of a bygone century ... Farewell little attic office, the cosy rug, the embroidered cushions, the shrink's bergamot perfume ... Farewell sweet den. Greetings to the Skypes, the FaceTimes, WhatsApps, and Zooms, and all the other glaring spaces of remote communication.

In the transition from couch to screen, we had come to lose a material, concrete—but also very affectively invested—aspect of our habitual working frame. What to expect of the new setting before us, no one knew. Was it fireproof, this time? How do you show up late? What smell did it have? We had to wait and see.

As for the psychoanalytical societies, at first a kind of expectant silence reigned over them. Then, after a few days, messages started circulating, timidly. The various dispositions to adopt—continuing work at the office at all costs, ceasing all work, or resorting to remote sessions—were left to the discretion of each practitioner, but with a penchant towards the use of phones, which the younger analysts made fun of in their message groups, adding not without a dose of irony, "Landline phones, please!" The different societies' communications left a distinct feeling of an ever so slight hint of cautious anachronism. The grand Viennese dame, who had survived the Spanish flu and two World Wars, clearly did not wish to be overpowered by this world, soon to consist of teleportation and holograms. An understandable position. Kudos to whoever is able to tell where indeed we are headed. And now, removed from our couches and our offices, where could psychoanalysis actually take place? How to shift the setting, how to rearrange it, without corrupting our famous "certain ceremonial which concerns the position in which the treatment is carried out" (Freud, 1913c, p. 133), without tearing down the very edifice of psychoanalysis itself?

Some experienced this as a moment of perplexing resistance ("I am suspending sessions, we will wait as long as necessary!"); for others, it was a great leap forward, bordering on denial ("Yes, yes, it works just fine, you'll see. All we need is to step out of the field of vision and charge via bank transfer!"). The simple truth of the matter is that we were not expecting reality to oblige us to come to a decision in such strict and collective fashion on a matter that we had been contemplating since the end of the 1970s ...[8]

We found ourselves with our backs against the wall.

Because ... pandemic or not, discussions of the frame—and the organic link between psychoanalysis and frame—have long been taking place, and no one could argue that the necessary contemporary theorisation of the frame, due to the extension of psychoanalysis to non-neurotic structures, has not already begun in earnest. André Green (1974, 1980, 1997, 2006, 2012), Jean-Luc Donnet (2005), René Roussillon (1984, 2004, 2006, 2007, 2016), to cite but some of the more prominent thinkers on the question, have not only rooted this issue at the core of their elaborations, but have also suggested time and again that this could be the very starting point for renewing psychoanalytical thinking.

In his work "Pour une histoire de la pensée clinique contemporaine" ("Towards a History of Contemporary Clinical Thinking"), Fernando Urribarri (2012) retraces the course of events that led psychoanalytic theory to the gates of "the contemporary", and thereupon to profound re-elaborations of the theory of the frame. This brief yet luminous text summarises the historical evolution as proposed by André Green (1974), starting with the 1975 IPA Congress in London, thus making sense of the way in which "contemporary clinical thought was born of the conceptualization of the frame and of the redefinition of analysability" (Urribarri, 2012, pp. xii–xiv).

Urribarri writes:

> *The Freudian model* concentrates on the intrapsychic conflict from a theoretical point of view, and on transference from a practical point of view. Neuroses serve as its paradigmatic cases. In the *postfreudian model*, on the other hand, theory centers on the relational or intersubjective (with special attention given to object relations and the role of the Other), whereas technique has

---

[8] It seems to us, as noted by Fernando Urribarri (2012, p. xii), that, following the precursory works of Bleger (1967) and of Winnicott (1955), the theory of how to use the frame as a crucial element of analytical technique begins developing in earnest in the 1970s (cf. Green, 1974), before accelerating again in the 2000s, at least in France, in part thanks to Roussillon's valuable contributions.

been reformulated around counter-transference (or the analyst's desire). Here, psychotics and children serve as emblematic cases. The *contemporary project*, in its embryonic form, concentrates on psychic functioning within the frame, in order to account for borderline functioning. It aims to recognize, historicize and over-come the theoretical and clinical impasses that the Freudian and postfreudian models have encountered. (Urribarri, 2012, p. xii)

It is possible to summarise these stages in a simplified table:

The extension of psychoanalysis and of psychoanalytic models since Freud

	Freudian	Postfreudian	Contemporary
Theoretical object	Intrapsychic conflict	Intersubjectivity/ otherness	Psychic functioning
Technical approach	Transference	Countertransference	Frame
Paradigmatic cases	Neuroses	Psychoses	Borderline cases

(Despite the fact that not all analysts are Greenians, and that accounts of the recent history of psychoanalysis may vary, this detour through the eyes of André Green seems useful to us. It provides us with a method, and with a modest basis—formed on past results and on the clinical tools currently available to us—from which we may evaluate the perti-nence of new settings.)[9]

---

[9] Let us note that in Brazil, after an ignorant, racist, misogynist, and bellicose far right took power in the most recent presidential elections (2019), analysts attempted to put into place new settings for psychic accompaniment of those individuals who were most affected by this democratic debacle (blacks, natives, LGBT): these were often the poor-est members of society, and analysts set up fixed hours in mobile mini-offices in the streets, by the metros, at the exit from offices, in public squares, etc. These flying offices were sometimes made up of no more than two foldable stools and a snack (coffee, cake) offered to whoever wished to take a seat. These walk-in consultations were free of charge, but one had to wait patiently in long queues. One of the theoreticians of this "rede-sign of the setting" was Tales Ab'Saber, psychoanalyst, clinical psychologist, and pro-fessor at the Institute of Sedes Sapientiæ in São Paulo. To my knowledge, no detailed account of the experiment has been made yet; the interested reader may nevertheless find easy access to numerous reports on the internet (in Portuguese). See for example:

In other words, these are the stages leading to the *contemporary problematisation of the frame*:

1. Extending both the theory and clinical work of psychoanalysis (beyond the model for neuroses and psychoses)
2. Exploring of the limits of analysability (the issue of symbolisation; the need for an apparatus for thinking the thoughts in session) (Bion, 1962)
3. Taking into account the inclusion of a thirdness (Green, 1990; Ogden, 1994), in the form of the frame, into the analytical pair (symbolisation matrix; the frame as metaphor for the psychic setting)
4. Including psychotherapy in clinical work (expanding analysability; refusal of a "second class" psychoanalysis; improving Bion's technique of a daydream session (Ogden, 1997, 2005, 2008))
5. Rearranging the frame, leading to a "paradigmatic turning point that entails the *potential disarticulation of the definition of psychoanalysis and the use of its original setting*" (Roussillon, 2004; my italics).

As for the question of how far can we go in terms of rearranging the frame: Roussillon, starting in 2016, suggested the following plan:

> We must continue working on theoretical and clinical issues of the technique. [...] the analytical setting of couch-armchair is an "ideal type" for the analysis of frames; that which we have been able to elaborate based on its particularities may serve as a model for approaching other settings. (2016, p. 41)

This answer may seem simple at first glance, but it is a precise one. Indeed, (1) the clinical history of psychoanalysis has forged effective tools over the years that can be considered as "matrices"; (2) the role of a matrix is to allow for new iterations based on an ideal model; (3) the models, whether ideal or idealised, are not reproducible as such, but rather provide us with the possibility of creative transposition—the passage from the couch setting to that of the screen surely requires of

---

https://comciencia.br/escutar-as-ruas-e-desafio-das-clinicas-publicas-de-psicanalise/ (last accessed December 21, 2020).

us more than simple imitation, but rather a healthy dose of adaptation, invention, acceptation of losses and gains, in short, the negotiation of a *nearly*, as Eco might say (2003, p. 9). We will determine the frame's elasticity and ability to extend based on that which favours the reinvention of the rearranged object in such a way so as not to lead to the destruction of the model.

Which is why I would add the imperative not to settle for psychoanalytical kitsch, namely stale and supposedly "identical" reproductions, and to "continue working on theoretical and clinical issues of the technique".

Very well. But then, a psychoanalysis devoid of its couch, on a screen—how exactly does that work? It works, one could say, if we take care not to fall into the trap of premature and definitive verdicts; if we accept persevering in our research, without neglecting the important steps already taken in the history of our discipline, including the debates on psychoanalytic psychotherapy, to cite but one example, which dominated the 2000s.[10] Moments of undeniable progress, these controversies nevertheless shed light on an all too rudimentary rift between a supposedly noble brand of psychoanalysis, whose couch reigns by "*droit divan*"[11] over those graced by the Holy Spirit and its Word, and a plebian psychotherapy, sat in a chair, face to face, for all the rest (those damned, asymbolic souls).

We should therefore take care not to relapse into this false binary under its new iteration of couch/screen. Such equations now seem outdated. In the psychoanalytical train, there is no distinction between first- and second-class compartments; the frame nowadays is based on new theoretical foundations, and the very context and essence of the debate concerning what constitutes (or does not) psychoanalysis (namely, analysability) seem to have radically changed (cf. Urribarri, 2006, pp. 656–666).

---

[10] See the interesting and complete account given by André Green *in Les Voies nouvelles de la thérapie psychanalytique*, a real sum on contemporary practices (2006, chap. II, pp. 61–98); see also Green (2001) and Widlöcher (2008).

[11] A pun on the French *divan* "couch" and *divin* "divine", as in *droit divin* (divine right). Translator's note.

Needless to say, the psychoanalytic process is internal, even though there are some non-process, external, stable, and persistent factors that constitute the necessary (but insufficient) conditions for a process to take (a) place. And yet, the threat we face during these pandemic times is not so much the decomposition of the frame in light of some other setting, but rather the havoc wreaked on our own internal worlds in the context of an exterior (external frame) that has become too unstable, too uncertain, and which, all of a sudden, scoffs at any pretention we may have of maintaining our (already sufficiently complicated) transitional psychic space and its capacity for friction. The intolerance for any form of symbolisation is becoming all the more apparent. It is as if this constant barrage of bad news—pandemic, climate change, the destruction of oceans and forests—is inhibiting our psychic respiratory system, our capacity for reverie. As if we are trapped in a reality turned psychotic.

After the fire in my office, and as opposed to those who had not lived through our adventures (and thereby able to phantasise over them), the analysand who had been brutally ripped out of his symbolisation space quickly showed signs of traumatic fatigue, consisting of a persistent glumness, stomach aches, and inopportune blanks that invariably cut short his train of thought. Despite the rather fortunate ending to the whole affair—no deaths or serious injury, damage limited to just a few square metres—the analysand's associations became impoverished, and his discursive tissue started tearing. He was about to set out on a long journey through a psychic desert.

I sometimes wonder whether we might not be headed towards a similar fate in the wake of this pandemic sequence. A few days ago, a patient, looking quite lethargic on her side of the screen, sighed: "It's starting to get too quiet inside of me … There's like some sort of silence in my heart that's tiring me out …"

This is perhaps at the root of what has been called "pandemic fatigue", that brutal extirpation from the external frames that we were familiar with, from our normal ecosystem; followed by a sudden silence that appears in our hearts, that shrivelling of the internal world that is otherwise nourished by our ties, our social and political activities, our possibility for culture, for spaces of creation.

Our internal world is made up of robust and plastic psychic matter, certainly, but it cannot endure every ordeal; it is not autonomous, self-begotten, self-sufficient; it is symbolic, metaphorical, allegorical even, without ever being insubstantial, ethereal, or monadic; it needs an outside, a horizon, a lively world more or less in working order, in order to live.

A. S.
December 2020

Translated from French by Shahar Fineberg

References

Ambrosiano, L., & Gaburri, E. (2009). Las Meninas. In: A. Ferro & R. Basile (Eds.), *The Analytical Field. A Clinical Concept* (pp. 107–132). London: Karnac, 2009.

Baranger, M., & Baranger, W. (1961–62). The analytic situation as a dynamic field. *International Journal of Psychoanalysis, 89*: 795–826.

Bion, W. R. (1962). *Learning from Experience*. New York: Basic Books.

Bleger, J. (1967). Psycho-Analysis of the Psycho-Analytic Frame. *International Journal of Psychoanalys, 48*: 511–519.

Donnet, J.-L. (2005). *The Analyzing Situation*. London: Karnac, 2009.

Eco, U. (2003). *Dire quasi la stessa cosa. Esperienze di traduzione*. Milan, Italy: Bompiani.

Ferro, A. (2007). *Avoiding Emotions, Living Emotions*. London: Routledge, 2011.

Ferro, A. (2014). *Psychoanalysis and Dreams: Bion, the Field and the Viscera of the Mind*. Abingdon, UK: Taylor & Francis, 2019.

Ferro, A., & Nicoli, L. (2017). *The New Analyst's Guide to the Galaxy. Questions about Contemporary Psychoanalysis*. New York: Routledge.

Freud, S. (1913c). On beginning the treatment. *S. E., 12*: 121–144. London: Hogarth.

Green, A. (1974). The analyst, symbolization and absence in the analytic setting. In: Green, A., *On Private Madness*. London: Hogarth.

Green, A. (1980). The dead mother. In: A. Green, *On Private Madness* (pp. 142–173). London: Karnac, 1997.

Green, A. (1990). On thirdness. In: A. Green, *Psychoanalysis: A Paradigm for Clinical Thinking* (pp. 233–278). London: Free Association Books, 2005.

Green, A. (1997). Le cadre psychanalytique: son intériorisation chez l'analyste et son application dans la pratique. In: Green, A., *La Clinique psychanalytique contemporaine* (pp. 5–29). Paris: Ithaque.

Green, A. (2001). The crisis in psychoanalytic understanding. In: A. Green, *Psychoanalysis: A Paradigm for Clinical Thinking* (pp. 303–316). London: Free Association Books, 2005.

Green, A. (Ed.) (2006). *Les Voies nouvelles de la thérapeutique psychanalytique.* Paris: PUF.

Green, A. (2012). *La Clinique psychanalytique contemporaine.* Paris: Ithaque.

Neri, C. (2009). The enlarged notion of field in psychoanalysis. In: A. Ferro & R. Basile (Eds.), *The Analytical Field. A Clinical Concept* (pp. 45–80). London: Karnac.

Ogden, T. (1994). The analytic third: Working with intersubjective clinical facts. In: *Subjects of Analysis* (pp. 61–86). Northvale, NJ: Jason Aronson. Reprinted in: A. Ferro & R. Basile (Eds.), *The Analytical Field. A Clinical Concept* (pp. 159–188). London: Karnac.

Ogden, T. (1997). *Reverie and Interpretation. Sensing Something Human.* London: Karnac, 1999.

Ogden, T. (2005). *This Art of Psychoanalysis, Dreaming Umdreamt Dreams and Interrupted Cries.* Abingdon, UK: Routledge.

Ogden, T. (2008). On talking as dreaming. *International Journal of Psychoanalysis, 88*(3): 575–589.

Ogden, T. (2009). *Rediscovering Psychanalysis.* New York: Routledge.

Roussillon, R. (1984). Du baquet de Mesmer au "baquet" de Sigmund Freud (Premières réflexions sur la préhistoire du cadre psychanalytique). *Revue française de psychanalyse, 48*(6) Variations du cadre: 1363–1384.

Roussillon, R. (2004). Aménagements du cadre analytique.In: F. Richard & F. Urribarri (Eds.), *Autour de l'œuvre d'André Green. Enjeux pour une psychanalyse contemporaine* (actes du colloque de Cerisy) (pp. 53–65). Paris: PUF, 2005.

Roussillon, R. (2006). Le "langage" du cadre et le transfert sur le cadre. In: P. Denis, B. Chervet, & S. Dreyfus-Asséo (Eds.), *Avancées de la psychanalyse* (pp. 106–117). Paris: PUF, 2008.

Roussillon, R. (2007). *Logiques et archéologiques du cadre psychanalytique.* Paris: PUF.

Roussillon, R. (2016). Le cadre psychanalytique en chantier. *Le Journal des psychologues, 339*: 39–43.

Urribarri, F. (2006). La théorie dans la psychanalyse actuelle. À la recherche d'un nouveau paradigme contemporain. In: A. Green (Ed.), *Les Voies nouvelles de la thérapeutique psychanalytique* (pp. 653–666). Paris: PUF.

Urribarri, F. (2012). Pour une histoire de la pensée clinique contemporaine. In: Green, A., *La Clinique psychanalytique contemporaine* (pp. ix–xxx). Paris: Ithaque.

Widlöcher, D. (Ed.) (2008). *Psychanalyse et psychothérapie*. Toulouse, France: Érès.

Winnicott, D. W. (1955). Metapsychological and clinical aspects of regression within psychoanalytic set-up. *International Journal of Psychoanalysis, 36*(1): 16–26.

CHAPTER 8

Individual distress, institutional distress

Serge Frisch
Luxembourg and Brussels, Belgium

A s a cultural and scientific phenomenon, psychoanalysis is influenced by the world in which it operates. The Covid-19 pandemic has thus had a serious impact on the exercise of psychoanalysis, on relations between analysts, and on their institutional life.

When, over the course of one weekend, lockdown was decided upon by the authorities in my country, Luxembourg, we, including my patients and myself, were caught completely off guard. On Monday morning, we were lost, and had to organise ourselves in view of this new situation. My patients called in to know how we were meant to continue our sessions. At that time, I had no idea whether private practitioners were authorised to receive patients.

From a health perspective, the measures taken by the authorities corresponded to the state of scientific knowledge at the time, but psychoanalytically speaking, we were faced with "acts". An "act" usually leads to a "counter-act" (Haber, 1986). I found myself compelled to react, and proposed that whoever wished to come in person may do so, that I would receive them in my office in accordance with the measures of social distancing. Impulsively, I had also suggested that they may continue their sessions over the phone or via Skype. Today I remain perplexed by the fact that I had proposed such a thing spontaneously, before my patients had even asked for it. I should mention that a fair amount of my analysands live in countries that neighbour our small land of Luxembourg, coming from Germany, Belgium, or France. The authorities had already closed the borders and my patients were no longer authorised to travel. If sessions were to take place with these patients, they would necessarily have to take place remotely.

Like many of my colleagues, I was faced with an unprecedented situation without having had time to think about it or to plan for it. Left to my own devices, I tried to throw together some minimalistic frame and implement it for remote sessions: I would sit at my usual place in the office, at the same time, on the same days as before. The patient would also have to be at home, always in the same room, and if he was in analysis, he would have to orient his webcam in a certain way. I must admit that I was a complete neophyte as far as remote analysis goes, having never before practised it. My surprise was such that never at any moment did I think of *not* proposing Skype to my patients, seeing as I am not in favour of such remote techniques. Even more surprising: why did I, just like many other colleagues, allow myself to be driven to act so precipitously? And the many changes in sanitary regulations that had to be observed, such as wearing a mask (which was not mandatory at the beginning), represent for the analyst and his patient a series of disruptions, of actings, and of counter-actings.

While the notion of the *analytical frame* is very dear to my heart, I had not allowed myself or my patients a moment's thought to reflect upon and analyse this assault against the frame, just as I normally do when the frame is put to the test by a patient in session. How could it be that at no given moment did I say that in the face of such an unprecedented event, I might need a couple of days, if not an entire week, to think about this new state of affairs? Nor did I think of suspending sessions until the health situation stabilised. *A posteriori*, I realise now that my analytical capacities had completely failed me. I am able to accept that this might happen to me. But how can it be that the entire profession reacted in more or less the same way? And what could I have conveyed to my patients as to my anxieties and my psychic impropriety in acting in such a way—acting in complete contradiction to my usual approach, whereby I would take the time to think along with my analysands before reacting to any request? Had a maternal manner—of protecting, comforting, calming, appeasing my patients, like an animal protecting its young ones—awakened in me? Had my paternal function—external, reassuring, which would have allowed me to take some more time to think calmly—been completely swept away?

This pandemic has certainly reignited archaic anxieties that we all carry, buried within us, concerning the plagues that have decimated populations in the past. In proposing to my patients to continue our consultations, whether in the office or remotely, I was surely clinging to the life drive and to the idea that it was important to continue life and work as normally as possible. Was there not a hint of omnipotence in my brazen attitude, in continuing consultations, in exorcising my anxieties? (Naturally, I was convinced, and still am today, that the social distancing guidelines, as well as the masks and hydroalcoholic gels, offer us important protection.)

If continuing analytical work with most of my patients was at all possible, it is because they had been in analysis for years and had already been able to internalise the analytical frame and free association. I have no experience of preliminary meetings done remotely, nor *a fortiori* have I begun treatments that take place remotely from the outset.

Early lockdown

You may imagine my surprise when, during the first day of remote consultation, I realised that my patient had contacted me via Skype from bed. The next patient was in a nightgown at the breakfast table. I exchanged views on this subject with an American colleague, who told me that these were manifestations of a regressive attitude. Quite on the contrary, I felt that their entire verbal as well as non-verbal attitude conveyed seduction and seemed to me to be a *mise en scène* of infantile sexuality. Rather than justifying the patient's failing ego as my colleague had suggested, I thought that it was more important that the patient be able to evoke the fantasies that these situations—due to the virus, to lockdown, and to this new arrangement of sessions—conjured for them in the transferential relationship. I was mindful of the emotions that manifested themselves, and tried to perceive the unconscious representations that arose through the patient's narrative.

Some analysands had a somewhat paranoid reaction, since video conference sessions set off fears of intrusion and voyeurism in them: thanks to the camera, my eye penetrates into their homes, into "their interior". These patients, ordinarily very punctual for their sessions, often called me well after the session had begun.

Some analysands changed locations for each meeting: they would sit in their kitchen, in their bedroom, on a bench in the park, in their car, or at their partner's flat. For others, their children came to say hi to the camera. The most important thing for them was to maintain our connection no matter what, no matter how. And yet, as analysts, we take care to construct and frame that connection in a particular space within which a process of symbolisation may take place.

Some patients spoke more freely over the phone than in person, which points to the defensive aspects that some were experiencing within the analytical frame, despite the fact that it is conceived in order to facilitate free association. But we knew, the patient and I, that this supposedly freer speech over the phone was less consistent, was less "meaty", as one of them said to me.

We notice the same phenomenon more or less among analysts too. Some no longer sat in their offices for consultations, but chose instead any other location. Others remained in pyjamas all day long. Others still, since the end of lockdown, now allow for a floating frame: for some sessions the patient will come in person, and for others he will call or even Skype, depending on what suits him and on his whereabouts at that given moment.

After these initial experiences, I quickly understood that I had lost my bearings as regards too many aspects of the classical analytical frame, such as the place in which sessions took place (which would often change from one day to the next), or the presence of children and even of adults, or indeed the impression that some patients had of my presence invading their homes via the screen. For these reasons I decided to stop working with screens and only to propose over-the-phone remote sessions. I myself felt more at ease once the visual aspect was removed, a feeling Freud had already evoked and which led him to conceive of the idea of the couch. All of my patients, including those whom I had been seeing once a week in face-to-face sessions, clearly preferred the phone over Skype or Zoom.

The analytical frame is imposed on both patient and analyst, and it is up to the analyst to make sure that it is respected once established. Presently, this is not the case in many a situation—it is no longer the analyst who guarantees the frame, since it is the patient who decides where to make contact from; the patient has taken hold of the analyst's prerogative. This brings up interesting questions concerning analytical technique and interpretation that will have to await further time, experience, exploration, and discussion in order to develop further. Let us say simply that, for example, under the pretext of the crisis and the public health guidelines, some analysts have accepted these changes to the frame as if they somehow benefited from them, whereas before they took the utmost care, come hell or high water, to respect the analytical frame. For José Bleger (1966), the frame was the receptor of the patients' *symbiosis*—and surely of the analysts' as well—who used it as a depository for their mad parts. Changing the framework, or making it arbitrary, increases the risk for these mad parts, which had been immobilised in the frame, to erupt into the patient's life or into the session.

This is how I understood what had happened with two patients in analysis, as I watched the rapid, even spectacular, derailment of their family life, once territorial borders had closed and we decided to continue sessions over the phone. The effect was immediate: no longer able to contain their anxieties, they transferred their feelings of insecurity onto their preadolescent children, who in turn destroyed quite a bit of furniture at home and even struck their parents, to the point where the police had to intervene on several occasions. For these analysands, the fact that lockdown had been instituted was the proof that our social institutions, meant to organise life in society, were overwhelmed and could no longer protect us from the virus, which, invisible, was roaming freely all around. The change to the analytical frame confirms these fears, in that it contributes to the feeling of the collapse of normal life and the return of destructive psychotic anxieties. Some patients, having gone out for groceries, would undress upon entering home and immediately wash their clothes at high temperatures, and then leave their groceries untouched in the garage for several days. Were these necessary precautions, or rather paranoid fears that were not contained well enough through remote sessions? One patient chose total confinement away from her family, sure as she was that she would transmit to them this virus that in fact she was not carrying. Slowly but surely, she realised that the danger stemmed much more from her paranoid fears than from the actual threat that the virus presented.

These few clinical vignettes show the disorganising impact that the epidemic may have on the psyche of both patients and analysts. In hindsight, we are now coming to terms with the damage incurred to this analytical frame that we had so patiently constructed over the years and then abandoned from one day to the next. We are seeing a disintegration of the rules that analysts have pondered patiently over for decades, then implemented and transmitted to future generations of analysts in training. I sometimes found myself fantasising that this is how my colleagues have found a way to create their own little psychoanalytical societies, their own individual IPAs with their own little private rules.

The news that some colleagues will be continuing remote consultations for at least another year spread fast. I do not intend to doubt their personal and prudent decisions, but rather to reflect on the impact that these fears might have on our patients and our candidates. What do these fears say of us? While we work out of the very safe conditions that our private offices afford us, how shall we justify ourselves before the doctors and nurses who man the front lines at hospitals, or before the caregivers working at retirement homes?

Incidentally, a great many analysts in training were shocked and distraught by their analysts, supervisors, and other instructors, who, up until then, had insisted on respecting the frame, and who all of a sudden no longer took it into account. All of a sudden, they were taking extreme liberties under the superegoical aegis of government restrictions, without questioning the real-world as well as subjective implications of their actions. With regard to reality or the instructions issued by public health agencies, it took the psychoanalytical societies time to realise the disarray in which both analysts in training and members were left, as if the analytical institution had forgotten that besides its function in choosing candidates, it must also and most importantly accompany its members in the continual development of their analytical *being*.

The analytical frame

Many major francophone authors have recognised the importance of the analytical frame. René Roussillon (1995, p. 40) describes for example the complexity of the frame, which signifies a boundary but also back-drop, stage, screen, delimited as follows: "As part of its functions, the frame will at times suffice in simply calling attention to what it contains, and at times it will support it, bolster it, even cast it, molding its very form." The frame can take the form of its contents, or indeed constrain what it contains and impose its own form. Form and content exist in a relation of interdependence. Touching one modifies the other. The fundamental rule is part of the frame, which establishes free association for the patient and evenly suspended attention for the analyst. Leo Bleger (2021) mentions that André Green, in writing about Winnicott in 1974, refers to the facilitating and containing function of the frame, of its mothering function. He also highlights that, for Green, the frame allows for constructing symbolisation much more than any process of symbolisation does.

Évelyne Sechaud (2013), following Jean-Luc Donnet (2005), com-plexifies the notion in speaking of an analytical site which contains the frame. The site is first and foremost the site of language and "refers to the configuration of a site in which activity may take place. The constitu-tive elements of the analytical site precede its implementation; they are part of the *déjà-là.*" She then states that, at this site, the analyst must be able to rely upon the bisexual capacity of his self-assured identity. "This capacity for internal movement guarantees the freedom to think analyti-cally. For the analysand, these components of the site will function either as motivation or as resistance." We may say that in order for the analyst to enjoy the greatest psychic freedom within the site, the frame must be clear and firm. Altering the site has an effect on the analytical process.

It is the analyst who sets the frame in place; it is his role to watch over it and to maintain it. But once established, the frame applies to patient and to analyst alike. We cannot expect our patients to tend to the frame or to understand its importance and its meaning, at least not in the beginning of analytical work. On the contrary, we know perfectly well that the patient will attack it at some point and that this will represent a repetition in need of symbolisation. The analysand will gradually appre-hend the importance of the frame, through the analytical work the two of them perform. It is surely this internalisation of the analytical frame that allows for the possibility of real analytic work taking place.

This very specific apparatus characterises and defines psychoanalysis due to the fact that it is indispensable in the effort to investigate psychic processes that would otherwise remain inaccessible, according to Freud. Many analysts who up until now had worked with strict frames have suddenly discovered that remote work "will also do the trick", and all of a sudden they seem willing to accept a whole array of compromises. This begs the question of whether psychoanalysis, with all these somewhat erratic adaptations to the analytical frame, isn't running the risk of reducing itself to becoming only a limited form of psychotherapy, of becoming a space where anything is possible, where anything goes? How shall we attend to the frame if the analytical site has become arbitrary?

During this period, when so many things are being called into question, I think it is important to return to the basic reasons that incited Freud and Ferenczi to create the International Psychoanalytical Association (IPA), which serves as an exemplar for all other psychoanalytical societies in the world.

Freud and Ferenczi founded the IPA in order to counteract the lack of organisation among analysts, who until then were like scattered and unruly fanatics unlikely to be able to consistently apply themselves seriously. The lack of leadership, says Ferenczi, favoured an excessive proliferation of individual tendencies at the expense of the common aim to support and apply the central theses of psychoanalysis. He concluded that the creation of the IPA would guarantee "that its members effectively apply the psychoanalytical method according to Freud and not some method concocted for their personal use..." (Ferenczi, 1911). For Ferenczi, the ethics not only of our members but also of our institutions was at stake. He indicated the importance of federating analysts in the common effort of developing psychoanalysis. Founding the IPA, and by extension any other psychoanalytical society, is the analysts' effort to counter marginalisation and to create a space where they may meet, discuss, and develop together through the common lens of an analytical thought process.

Following Winnicott (1971), we may speak of institutions as a "potential space" that constitutes a safe environment in which the analyst is securely immersed and held in an atmosphere of institutional standards, practices, and agreed-upon terms of art. The "well-tempered" frame, in reference to the "well-tempered couch" of Jean-Luc Donnet (2002), usually exerts its protective function silently, as if it did not exist. With a public health crisis such as the one we have been living through, personal relations stretch thin, sometimes to the point of breaking, and the institutional frame no longer offers that space for the formal regression that allows analysts to think and to dream up their institution and psychoanalysis itself. This facilitating environment—thanks to which analysts may engage in calm, fruitful scientific exchange and carry out work of symbolisation on psychoanalysis, on their societies, on their place in relation to colleagues—is weakened. The group aspect, which is so indispensable to us, fritters away, and remote meetings are nothing but a poor substitute.

When the Covid-19 crisis broke out, the analytical institution no longer served either as a space for elaboration or as a container for its members' anxieties. At most, the institution gave out instructions as to how to adapt to the sanitary measures, but did not provide a space for thinking. In this sense, the analytical institution, as a space for elaboration and for thinking, was itself infected by the virus and contaminated in its essential functions.

Scientific seminars and international conferences were cancelled all over the world, thereby depriving analysts of the much-needed oxygen that results from meeting with their peers. Gradually, national and international analytical institutions such as the IPA began offering spaces for discussion over the internet, whose frank success only highlighted the analysts' need for communication, be it only remotely. The first IPA "webinars" were marked by the experiential narrativity of analysts, who spoke at length about their patients' anxieties. A lapse of time was required before analysts were able to speak also of their own fears, often masked by a compulsion to theorise everything and anything. This narrativity may have served as an abreaction to anxieties, but as Evelyne Sechaud writes (2013), it also has a defensive narcissistic advantage in that it "gives the impression of graciousness on the surface, if not of seduction, depending on the narrator's style".

Nevertheless, the consequences of this crisis for analytical institutions have barely been studied. Institutional life has been turned completely upside down; essential individual and group connections have disappeared. From one day to the next, our institutional spaces were emptied, with all the symbolic meaning that that entails. No more administrative meetings to organise the institutional and scientific life of its members, suspended seminars, and the fibre of analytical discussion unravelled.

Video conference meetings are useful: they assemble a large number of colleagues who do not have to travel and who can shut off the computer as soon as their interest wanes. But this kind of meeting will never replace physical meetings, where the bodily presence of analysts and their drives charge these exchanges with a different kind of energy. We have witnessed that institutional ties have become stretched to the point of breaking. By way of consequence, individualism is spreading.

I have noticed that the conflicts already present within the different psychoanalytical societies have been exacerbated in the absence of in-person discussions. Following José Bleger (1966), we may imagine that the members of a psychoanalytical society deposit their wildest analytical theories within the institutional frame, as well as the violence of any transferential, countertransferential, or inter-transferential residues that they may have accumulated, whether unanalysed or unanalysable. The symbolic institutional frame of fusion with the mother's body usually goes unspoken, except in situations of crisis where this fusional function is lost. Freud has shown that barbarism is related to the unconscious organisation of an individual, which is the reason why psychoanalytical institutions establish limits, derivations, sublimations, so as to allow their members to live and work together in spite of this barbarism. In this sense, institutions exorcise the "originary violence"[1] (Enriquez, 2006). With the outbreak of the crisis, our institutions have become virtual and much less capable of fulfilling the function of container and detoxifier of this violence. It is no surprise that conflicts have been exacerbated and that colleagues are now considering abandoning their posts in their respective analytical institutions, or retiring in isolation.

What possible future consequences?

The Covid-19 crisis may well persist for a long, indeterminate time. Realistically speaking, in-person meetings at our physical institutions will remain limited. No one knows what the future holds, but I shall try to propose some avenues for reflection.

---

[1] "*Violence originaire*" in French, which Enriquez describes as a type of violence that precedes institutions, that rebels against them, and that must be exorcised [translator's note].

This public health crisis is happening at a moment in time when the analytical institution has long been confronted with the effects of neoliberalism, which has profoundly changed the bonds between individuals and the connections that bond individuals to institutions. The modalities of social ties are changing, and we are witnessing a change in how the individual perceives himself, and how he perceives himself in society.

Psychoanalysis was born in a society or a set of institutions and traditions (such as family, village, group of affiliation, political party, religion, etc.), that linked people together through different forms of collective incorporation, which were indexed in turn on solidarity. The relation to others was governed by respect for traditions, customs, and ethical principles (Rosanvallon, 2018, pp. 357–358). As mentioned above, these ideas informed also Freud and Ferenczi's project to found the IPA.

As part of the change in our relationships with the other, Christophe Dejours (2014) notes a thinning of solidarity, of collective feeling, of coexistence, as well as the growing primacy of the notion of "It's every man for himself." He argues that mutual help and solidarity disappear, that we are left with the feeling of being alone among the multitude. Marcel Gauchet (2016, pp. 323–324) speaks of a "dissolution of the remains of religious structures" which would indicate the definitive disengagement from the religious framework that had fashioned relationships among individuals, as well as a disengagement from a pyramid-structure society.

Psychoanalytical societies provided a social structure for individuals and generated a collective consciousness in which the analyst saw himself channelled, framed by, and articulated through the collective sphere in his society. Under the influence of neoliberalism, we have seen demands of individual autonomy from the collective, with many analysts lacking belief in psychoanalytical societies and becoming members of institutional structures only after much resistance. The illusion of an analytical life without institutions, without common scientific policies, is on the ascendant. By eliminating oppositions that inevitably arise from one's confrontation with institutional structures, sexuality is eliminated. Our psychoanalytical societies are fragmenting, and individualism—societies of one—is replacing the desire or the need to live together. Put another way, the individual analyst is ever more becoming a consumer, rather than an active member, of his society.

If the link between the individual and his psychoanalytical society is threatened, so is his link with psychoanalysis. Our mode of coexistence, of each working together to construct the institution, its training, its ethics, is in danger of disintegrating.

Some analysts call for the levelling of the institutional structure, for the plain and simple suppression of any and all differences among members of a psychoanalytical society, and by way of consequence the suppression of full member training analysts. Psychoanalytical societies would then be reduced to a collective administration, a technical or regulatory body overseeing training and science programmes. This is the very essence of neoliberalism, where there are no ties to any form of collective and "which prescribes attitudes and characterizes a mode of interaction between people that lacks any vision of togetherness […], which is the mark and the effect of a void in social imagination" (Rosanvallon, 2018, p. 380). It is the negation of our psychoanalytical societies, which are steeped in transference and countertransference whether direct, lateral, or diffracted, that is to say, steeped in an instinctual depth and density.

In its desire to make everything the same, it is the idea of dissymmetry, a central notion of the Freudian project, that liberalism targets, under the pretence of the democratisation of the relations among members of a society and between patient and analyst. Laurence Kahn (2014, p. 8) says that the dissymmetry of the analytical relationship risks being jettisoned, and that the search for "truth [has been consigned to] subjective relativism, and practice to 'dialogue'". This is in direct opposition to the Freudian approach, where "each Freudian advance brings the very core of Freudian treatment to a point of crisis: the co-presence of radically heterogeneous orders whose mere consideration implies speculation" (Kahn, 2014, p. 13). Concepts revolving around interchange, interaction, the exchange between an analyst and patient "who understand each other" are attempts to do away with dissymmetry. This recalls the attempts made by some analysts to sweep away infantile sexuality and drive, or even transference, which are central and indispensable notions of the Freudian project.

Numerous colleagues affirm that, more than ever, nothing will be the same again after the Covid-19 crisis. If this tendency persists, of analysts accepting all alterations to and variations of the frame willy-nilly, it will lead to the mutual reinforcement of the coronavirus and of neoliberalism. The boundaries between psychoanalysis and psychotherapy will be blurred, becoming fuzzy, porous, soft, inconsistent. The symbolic and stabilising value of the institutional frame will fade, as will its capacity to set limits. Analytical identity as we know it would soon be lost.

We all know psychoanalysts who have taken a step back from institutional life, and whose psychoanalytical thinking we judge to have become all the poorer as a result of its removal from the vibrant space of institutional interaction. At the risk of sounding provocative, could we not even say that any analysis that distances itself too far away from a given orthodoxy runs the risk of working against psychoanalysis itself? Psychoanalytical societies are the safeguard against the risk that an isolated analyst runs of drifting, and it is imperative to preserve them.

It is advisable if not urgent that all societies initiate internal debates on their notions of the analytical frame and on the implications of its haphazard application. They should also reflect on the meaning that members accord to their own societies. During treatment, the way in which the analyst conceives of the frame is directly related to his notion of psychoanalysis. We may therefore deduce that the notion of the institutional frame relates to the way in which psychoanalysis is perceived within a given society. The way in which the institutional frame is understood affects the training of analysts as well as the notion of what an analyst represents for a given society. The institutional frame bears meaning. It is not neutral. If a society undergoes deep changes, so does its frame, and therefore its notion of training, its very notion of psychoanalysis.

The lack of overview that Rosanvallon describes leads to the levelling out of all differences, to their trivialisation. Everything is everything, everything is possible, no contradiction is to be found anywhere, everything is compatible. All analytical theories are of equal importance, there is no longer any reason to discuss and to debate in an effort to understand the source of our differences or their consequences on our practice. Discussions dry out as clinical narratives are dished out under the primacy of emotions. *Exit* any and all metapsychology.

The training of candidates would suffer if titular members applied the frame haphazardly. Would instructors suffer from these adaptations?

How would analysts in training take their instructors seriously if their teaching does not correspond to their practice?

We run the risk of finding ourselves in a similar situation to that of the IPA, which contains greatly diverging analytical notions, and by way of consequence, differing training for European, Latin American, and North American analysts. In order to avoid the fruitful and passionate debate that these conflicts require, a soft consensus has been reached that states that these are not essential differences, but rather simply different points of view. This is the spirit of the IPA slogan: one IPA for all.

Only time will allow us to analyse in depth the reorientations that this crisis has brought upon psychoanalysis and its institutions. Our priority should be to provide spaces for reflection on the essence of psychoanalysis, on the definition and preservation of psychoanalytic identity, on institutional structures, and on how our field integrates into culture and society. No psychoanalytical society can afford to forgo self-inspection. It is, as Rosanvallon says (2018), a "continuous history with no end […], a labor of exploration and experimentation, of understanding and of elaborating its very self".

Serge Frisch
September 2020

Translated from French by Shahar Fineberg

References

Bleger, J. (1966). Psychanalyse du cadre analytique. In: *Crise, rupture et dépassement* (1979). Paris: Dunod.

Bleger, L. (2021). What is the setting after all? In: C. Moguillansky & H. B. Levine (Eds.), *Psychoanalysis of the Psychoanalytic Frame Revisited: A New Look at Jose Bleger's Classic Work* (in preparation). Abingdon, UK: Routledge.

Dejours, C. (2014). La sublimation entre clinique du travail et psychanalyse. *Revue française de psychosomatique*, 46: 21–37.

Donnet, J.-L. (2002). *Le Divan bien tempéré*. La série, Le fil rouge. Paris: Presses Universitaires de France.

Donnet, J.-L. (2005). *La Situation analysante*. Paris: Presses Universitaires de France.

Enriquez, E. (2006). L'institution de la "vie mutilée". *Revue française de psychanalyse, 70*: 899–917.

Ferenczi, S. (1911). *De l'histoire du mouvement psychanalytique.* In: S. Ferenczi (Ed.), *Psychanalyse I, Œuvres complètes, 1908–1912* (pp. 162–171). Paris: Payot, 1990.

Gauchet, M. (2016). *Comprendre le malheur français.* Paris: Stock.

Green, A. (1974). L'analyste, la symbolisation et l'absence dans le cadre analytique. *Nouvelle Revue de psychanalyse, 10*: 63–102.

Haber, M. (1986). Mise en acte, acting-out et contre-transfert. *Revue belge de psychanalyse, 2*: 1–13.

Kahn, L. (2014). *Le Psychanalyste apathique et le patient postmoderne.* Paris: L'Olivier.

Rosanvallon, P. (2018). *Notre histoire intellectuelle et politique, 1968–2018.* Paris: Seuil.

Roussillon, R. (1995). *Logiques et archéologiques du cadre psychanalytique.* La série, Le fil rouge. Paris: Presses Universitaires de France.

Sechaud, É. (2013). Le féminin du site. *Annuel de l'APF*, pp. 145–162.

Winnicott, D. W. (1971). *Playing and Reality.* New York: Basic Books.

Part IV

Reconfigurations and changes
in practice

Body and soul in remote analysis: anguished countertransference, pandemic panic, and space–time limits*

Riccardo Lombardi
Rome, Italy

> *... and the plague, the fiery god of fever hurls down on the city, his lightning slashing through us—And black Death luxuriates in the raw, wailing miseries of Thebes.*
>
> —Sophocles, *Oedipus Rex*

The encounter with pestilence and death was among the fundamental sources that inspired Freud to create the clinical discipline known to us as psychoanalysis, and for which a broader reference can be found in the myth of Oedipus of that well-recognised triangular and parricidal conflict. On arriving in 1909 at the port of New York for the Clark University's conferences, Freud famously said to Jung, who had accompanied him, "We bring the plague and they don't know it yet." Apart from the belittling criticisms that he was subject to in Europe, which made him feel that he himself was plague-ridden, Freud was well aware of the relationship between his conception of the unconscious and the plague. Freud's view of confrontation with unconscious conflicts was

---

* A first, shorter version of this chapter was published as a paper in 2020, "Corona virus, social distancing, and the body in psychoanalysis", by the *Journal of the American Psychoanalytic Association* 68(3): 455–462. It is reproduced with the kind permission of SAGE.

that of tragedy, no different from a pestilence that necessitates learning to live with it.

The very same laceration of our internal reality is described by Bion (1970) as "terrifying evolving O", that is, the terrifying experience of contact with a mysterious and unknown internal dimension that evolves continuously within us in the course of an analysis: attempts to avoid this contact with O would lead to splitting that would destabilise and impoverish the personality (Klein, 1946). The precariousness and helplessness of facing the unknown is condensed in the myth of the Sphinx, which kills whoever does not resolve its enigmas. In this way Bion relocates psychoanalysis before Oedipus was hailed as king thanks to his success in solving the Sphinx's enigmas and underlines the importance for the analyst of tolerating uncertainty and ignorance, as essential elements in the search of one's personal identity.

All these risks are being overshadowed by a certain trend in contemporary psychoanalysis that identifies with its very own system of knowledge: the IPA statute defines psychoanalysis as its systems of theories, rather than a "probe" that explores the unknown, as Bion himself had wished. If the mental field of psychoanalytic theories tends towards saturation, our current patients' disturbances are more and more archaic, and increasingly insensitive to the common system of conventional psychoanalytic interpretations, including transference interpretations (Lombardi, 2019a, 2019b). In this situation the focus on the body, together with the transference of the analysand on to their own body (Lombardi, 2017, 2019b, 2021), becomes the essential point of reference in tracing the lost or disguised identities of our analysands and the point of departure for new and unexpected itineraries of thought.

The terror of our uncertainty and our bodily impotence seem to have become a concrete reality in the presence of the coronavirus, which appears to be infectious even up to a distance of several metres and persists on surfaces. The current state of the pandemic has had an extraordinary emotional impact on everyone, including ourselves and our analysands. The situation we are living in today presents a special opportunity in which the necessity of remote interactivity and resort to technological instruments can help us keep the psychoanalytic experience and research active. Reaching our analysands in atypical locations with respect to a normal analytic context—their homes, offices, vehicles—allows us to immerse ourselves "up to our necks" in their most intimate anxieties: an immersion that can occur only in the most fortunate and productive psychoanalytic moments. Hence, we are able more than ever to access the pulsating core of the unconscious by entering directly into the emotional density of life's situations. The body–mind dissociation that threatens the roots of mental life, today more than in the past (Lombardi, 2017), becomes more difficult in the current context, in which the body and its state of well-being are constantly called into question, and developing a *capacity for bodily concern* is required for our personal survival (Lombardi, 2018, 2019a). As one of my patients has remarked, had we suspended our sessions instead of continuing them remotely, we would have lost this unique occasion of taking analysis to a deeper level, and at the same time would have risked losing everything achieved up to this point, given the prospect of having to start analysis from the beginning once the pandemic has passed.

An essential theoretical framework on reality and the unconscious

Some analysts may have a concern working psychoanalytically in this period: how do we pursue something we would call "unconscious" (fantasy, belief, desire) when reality seems so immutably present and insistent? It's then perhaps useful to make explicit my theoretical view, which places external reality as a privileged counterpart of the unconscious.

Reflecting on the loss of contact with reality, Freud writes:

> The most extreme type of this turning away from reality is shown by certain cases of hallucinatory psychosis which seek to deny the particular event that occasioned the outbreak of their insanity.... But in fact, every neurotic does the same with some fragment of reality. And we are now confronted with *the task of investigating the development of the relation of neurotics and of mankind in general to reality*, and in this way of bringing the psychological significance of the real external world into the structure of our theories. (1911b, p. 218; emphasis added)

Thus, today more than ever we are faced with the task of *investigating the development of the relation of our patients to reality.*

The discovery of the primary process of oneiric logic allowed Freud (1900a) to elaborate the distortions of linear logic and of reality (Arieti, 1955; Matte Blanco, 1975) that characterise the domain of the unconscious. Highlighting the *form* of the unconscious and its spatio-temporal *violation of the normal parameters of consciousness*, I emphasise the *structurally catastrophic nature* of a psychoanalytic conception of the mind (Bion, 1970): a catastrophic nature that matches the catastrophe we are facing today.

Bion (1962) summarises the deformations imposed on the mind by the unconscious in his theory of the *defect of thinking* in which every patient is a reservoir of personal theories, that, influenced by the pleasure principle (Freud, 1911b), violate or alter in various ways the perception of reality itself: the working though of the unconscious consists of the emotive and cognitive restructuring of the patient's theories in order to draw them closer to reality. The choice of the patient "between modifying frustration and evading it" (Bion, 1962, p. 4) comes to the fore: tolerating frustration allows an emancipation from the pleasure principle, activating mental growth.

An aspect of reality that has a determining role in the functions of the ego is the relationship with the body, where "the ego is first and foremost a body ego" (Freud, 1923b, p. 26). This relationship is itself subject to distortions caused by anxieties, in particular death anxiety. Beyond the more renowned theory of the death instinct (Freud, 1920g), Freud (1914c) considered awareness of death the weak link in the narcissistic mental structure and thus a means of fostering progress towards mental growth (see Lombardi, 2013). The body, together with illness and death anxieties, becomes an elective arena in the confrontation between the unconscious and consciousness in the tragic context of a pandemic, placing the body–mind relationship at the centre of psychoanalytic attention.

The analyst's personal involvement

> *This is no longer the body that once was mine: I am a shadow now, a shadow of anxiety that breathes.*
>
> —Sophocles, *Oedipus at Colonus*

The analyst is neither a hologram nor a mental object, and not least an amalgam of psychoanalytic theories; he or she is a real person with a real body. If anything, the psychoanalytic hypotheses make sense if they are able to translate in an abstract manner the analyst's body–mind experience as the initial "concrete object", an ethological object limited in time and space (Ferrari, 2004), where the mental logic of the unconscious disregards these very elements of space and time (Freud, 1899a). And it is the body itself that makes its presence felt as the analyst grows old, as seen in Sophocles's second Oedipus play, stimulating the elaboration of the impact of time and the awareness of death as a human limit with which we need to learn to coexist. With respect to internal anxieties during the current pandemic I consider the analyst's *involvement* to not differ from that of the patient, even though the analyst possesses a greater degree of emotional containment. Let us examine a clinical sequence.

Giorgio begins the session calmly by telling me that he is becoming aware of his wrong conviction that he is *the only person with problems*: this is being challenged by the current situation, in which *nobody is exempt from problems and perils.*

At this point the patient stops and asks me: "How are you coping with the situation at the moment?"

Slightly disoriented, I realise that we are all in the shit and answer: "It's obviously a tragedy. I'm trying to cope with the severe difficulties and restrictions, just like anybody else."

Giorgio: Do you know that I always thought that you were perfect and immune from difficulties?

Lombardi: Now you can see that that is not true since I am battling with the same precariousness that is affecting everyone. You have constructed an image of my perfection in the same way that you have constructed an image of your own "perfection in the negative".

Giorgio: It's absolutely incredible that you are able to cope with the difficulties because you're able to maintain the nerve to face them. I always thought that these things came automatically.

Lombardi: If you wait for things to "happen automatically", you will never draw on your own resources and, more important, you won't gain the satisfaction of having been able to use them.

This aspect of my difficulties and restrictions, which in this case are disclosed to the patient to reduce his projections of omnipotence onto the analyst, are in this phase a part of the experience and of the so-called countertransference, as we will see more clearly further on. The analyst is expected to operate and monitor a continuous "transference on his or her own body" (Lombardi, 2017) in order to capture the most significant sensorial responses that accompany the relational experience with the patient. The transference onto the body is inevitably implied by the awareness of being exposed to the very same risks of illness and death that are elicited by a pandemic which has already taken the lives of more than a million people around the world.

The perception of the pandemic and of death

As soon as Elvira, fifty-five years old, lies down on the couch, she recounts a dream: "You paid a visit to me and my husband on your bike, and you were sitting in the living room near the window. At a certain point, a monster like Frankenstein comes down from upstairs and hurtles towards you. You manage to escape through the window even though Frankenstein has grabbed you by the ankle. You ride away on your bike." Elvira is frightened by this dream and associates it with the first news of the coronavirus that, after China, is spreading in Northern Italy. Currently both she and her husband suffer from immune system problems that would make a viral infection extremely dangerous for them. I tell her: "Death, from which I am escaping in your dream, seems to represent the risk of death in your own home, presumably due to this pandemic. And it is a threat against which it is possible to protect yourself, as seen by my own escape from Frankenstein." At this point Elvira asks me to continue the sessions remotely, to which I consent. Immediately afterwards, she takes further practical measures to protect herself and her family.

Elvira is the first of my patients to bring to a session a real alarm concerning the spread of the epidemic, in a period when the Italian government had still not taken any action. This episode provided me with the recognition that we were in danger and was the first incentive towards moving to teleanalysis with all my patients.

Lightening or burdening of anxieties

All my patients in analysis have registered an increase in anxiety during the pandemic and discussed how best to cope with their fears: for example, by creating a kind of protective filter with regard to the bombardment of tragic news in the media; this would include limiting one's access to the continuous newsfeed and being selective about one's reading, avoiding articles that might be experienced as too tragic or distressful.

One patient tells me: "I watched a terrifying TV show that searched for those responsible for the epidemic, the guilty ones who did not do enough to prevent it: a machine that only generates terror and hatred. I had to switch it off to protect myself from my own anxiety." Above all, in the patients most vulnerable to guilt and internal paranoia, exposure to the tragic news of the pandemic led to the necessity of an *unfolding* (Lombardi, 2009, 2015; Matte Blanco, 1988) of the distinction between body and mind, between external and internal reality, between objective tragedy and the imagined fear of an attack by an offender. There, where the "symmetry" (Matte Blanco, 1975) of the unconscious tends "like an acid" to cancel distinctions, the psychoanalytic task was to promote distinctions that stimulated discriminations, thought, and emotional containment.

The risk of "burdening" a reality that is already difficult emerged in the analysis of Anna, forty years old, who has suffered acute psychoses that in the past have required hospitalisation. Alongside her three-times-a-week analysis, she also receives pharmacological assistance from a psychiatrist. At the onset of the epidemic, Anna initially expressed doubt about whether she could continue her sessions remotely, fearing she might not be able to do it. Now, in a remote session, Anna describes how she had made some pancakes, adding an egg yolk more than the recipe called for because she thought the batter was too "light". The heaviness that resulted had been a disappointment. I suggest to Anna that she fears that she herself is "light" and inconsistent, lacking in resources, which makes her tend to overload with excessive anxieties. The result is that she becomes paralysed or even loses her mind, as has happened in the past. At this point she recalls having dreamt of her father, who has died, and who tells her in the dream that it is better for her to take into account her own mistakes. Anna comments that she is happy to have dreamt of her father, since he seemed to be encouraging in her dream. She adds that she could suggest to her psychiatrist that he replace her Haldol tablets with Serenase drops, giving greater flexibility in progressively reducing her medication. She adds that she is thinking of accepting a work proposal that would make her more optimistic about the future. I note that when she does not burden herself with anxieties, she is able to discover a "light" approach that implies more trust than she would normally allow herself.

Lockdown and hatred of limits

For the most problematic patients, lockdown with its limits and frustrations has been a particularly testing experience.

Ronaldo, twenty-five, is now in four-times-a-week analysis with me, after three psychotic breakdowns and several failed trials of psychotherapy. The requirement to stay in lockdown at home can lead to violence that explodes suddenly in the form of suicide attempts.

In a remote session Ronaldo's obstinate conviction emerges that there is life after death. The prospect of suicide would allow him access to a new life without the discomforts and limitations of his present life. In his mind he imagines a sequence from the film *Gladiator* (2000) in which the protagonist crosses a summer meadow representing the Elysian fields, the paradise Ronaldo believes he will enter after death. I tell him that in attempting to escape from frustrations, he creates a greater frustration by embracing death, since death is something from which no one can return.

In the following days, Ronaldo's hatred explodes against his parents; he threatens to kill them and then himself. This episode creates panic in the family, who rely on the psychiatrist and the consultant analyst for support.

Ronaldo skips the last session of the week, writing that he cannot make it, and does not respond to my attempts to contact him. The following Monday he declares intimidatingly that he wants to cancel Thursday sessions from now on. I discuss with him his tendency to attack the analysis and me, as he had done the previous Thursday; in the same manner he is driven to attack his parents and himself, rather than to think about and reflect on his hatred. He replies that he cannot tolerate the lockdown and will ask his psychiatrist for a government-required certificate authorising him to move to his beach house. I tell him that when there is a frustration, he acts out his hatred by cancelling limits: instead of remaining where he is, he goes against reality. Ronaldo seems to calm down and observes that now he can understand why he is unable to remain in the same place for any length of time. He can accept remaining in Rome and waiting until next month, when conditions might allow a trip to the beach. In the following session he shows me a book of poetry about the seaside town where he has a house; thinking about the beach through poetry, he says, has calmed him down.

The anguished countertransference and pandemic panic

The hatred of limits, particularly evident in Ronaldo's case, captures an element of experience to which not even the analyst is immune. The analyst is the bearer of a psychotic area of personality (Bion, 1962) with its disorganised and explosive implications, no less than that which may occur for all people. As is illustrated by the countertransference in the course of a treatment of the psychoses related to the risk of death, the analyst may experience an anguished countertransference characterised by a particularly intimate contact with psychotic anguish and the risk of actualisation of that anguish which at times may lead us to a near-death sensation. These feelings are accentuated in the context of a pandemic and implies the necessity of the analyst's specific engagement in continuously elaborating an intense emotional burden. The resulting "pandemic fatigue" (Zerbe, 2020) makes psychoanalysis much more demanding than it would be in normal times. For example, I have noted the increase in anxiety and hatred in all of my analysands, who have at times manifested uncontrolled explosions of hatred towards me over small incidents such as difficulties in telephone communications or a disturbed transmission. In those instances where I was unable to contact my analysands from my office, since I was at home or out of town, some of my patients found it most destabilising, resulting in an attack or denigration of my person, as if only the remote sessions from my office, as opposed to elsewhere, represented for them a factor of stability in the face of uncertainty and change.

Confronted with repeated expressions of hatred, I asked myself if this feeling could have a paradoxical *reparative* function with respect to their dehumanisation anxieties evoked by repetitive contact with the computer screen. This hatred, in other words, may have helped them to create a more real relationship with their analyst (Winnicott, 1969), even if in this case the continuity of the analytic relationship was paradoxically placed in peril by their tendency to act out.

In addition to the difficulties, I also sensed the risk of sudden panic, a "pandemic panic", which could emerge in a volcanic way when I least expected. For example, if the communication with the analysand became particularly obscure due to a slide into delirium or in a situation of negativity, the barrier of the screen contributed to amplifying a sense of "unreachableness" in the patient. Furthermore, personal factors also played a role: in the period in which my son had a high fever at home with no possibility of a diagnostic test, I noticed in myself severe hypochondriacal anxieties associated with the certainty of burning with a fever related to Covid-19, when the patient spoke of anxieties related to death. I experienced this correlation initially unconsciously and became aware of it only later on. On a side note, the risk of infection in my consulting room before starting remote analysis was very real since at least one of my patients had tested positive, even if being asymptomatic. This "anguished countertransference" implied the necessity of a greater investment on my part in those moments of "coming back into myself": moments of internal silence and self-analysis that enabled me to recalibrate my internal equilibrium in the face of a particularly demanding analytical situation.

Setting in teleanalysis

On this basis, I would say that the pandemic is not offering remote analysis as a "second level" instrument with respect to the "first class analysis" conducted in the habitual conditions of setting; instead it presents a particularly complex clinical challenge that demands all of our resources of psychoanalytic expertise in the elaboration of a very difficult field that is subject to several unexpected variables. It is important to realise that key conditions of the analytic setting don't simply disappear concurrently when the participants' real bodies cease to share the same room; that they continue to exist in teleanalysis. In particular, *time* (commitment to the schedule of the sessions and the continuity of the analytic work) and *money* (the payment of the analyst's fees) are particularly important to monitor and to protect against acting-out (Lombardi, 2005), because they offer a specific connection with reality, especially when the link to reality is weakened by the absence of sharing body proximity inside the analyst's office. The immobility of the time frame (temporal setting) is a determining condition for the patient's development, especially in a pandemic during which everything is unstable and unpredictable: "The most powerful, endurable, and at the same time least apparent, 'bulwark' is, then, the one that lies on the frame" (Bleger, 1967, p. 513).

If certain colleagues are of the opinion that psychoanalysis in the time of pandemic is the equivalent of setting up temporary tents outside the office while waiting for the return of our usual work with the normal parameters, to me this seems insufficient. This idea appears to me more a fantasy of temporal regression that contradicts the reality of linear time. On the contrary, I think this is an intense and productive moment for psychoanalysis, even if greatly impractical and tiring, which will probably have an important mutative impact on our identity as analysts and on the way we consider our science, leading to developments that are not yet foreseeable.

Controversies and conflicts among analysts

The necessity of introducing adjustments to the clinical work with respect to the common analytical practice has elicited diverse reactions among analysts, and the choice of resorting to remote analysis has not been shared by all. Some analysts have preferred to suspend treatments until the return of a normal external situation, or to give individual patients the choice of continuing their treatment or not. Other analysts have decided to continue to receive patients in their offices, despite the risk of infection and the limitations of lockdown, rejecting remote clinical work as not true psychoanalysis. Some of the latter have intimidatingly denounced remote clinical work as being against our ethical commitment to be analysts. From the harsh tones of this controversy, it can be easily deduced that the pandemic has incited hatred and intolerance among analysts, no less than that found in the rest of the population.

The advantageous side of these controversies is perhaps a partial fracture of the cohesion of the "power elite" in analytic institutions, an elite that generally shows criteria of absolute homogeneity that is the result of a tacit pact of belonging to a privileged class in a rigidly pyramidic hierarchical system in which membership is signalled by the empty performance of "sacred rituals". It is no mystery that whoever refuses to become the pet of some high representative of the class in power, who would lead them towards an institutional career, has no chance of placement in a corporate context and is excluded. The dispute of this system of monopoly and control caused by, for example, the public revelation of ethical violations, led to irremediable fractures and to the foundation of new institutions, as seen in Italy at the beginning of the 1990s when the IPA sent a site visit commission, which resulted in a scission and the foundation of a new IPA society. This event has been subsequently ignored in scientific debates over the thirty years that have followed.

"My body is in my soul" and the torment of distancing

In the face of the Covid crisis, I believe it has been important to guarantee continuity to the analytical experience through remote analysis, rather than undergo the serious risk of splitting (Klein, 1946) that may follow from the interruption of the continuity of the analysis. I consider the temporal parameter part of an important function of containment of the analysis especially in the context of the pandemic, since entire emotional sectors of the patient's life could risk disappearing together with a temporal interruption, putting the clinical work orientated to the integration of the personality in jeopardy.

Conversely, the absence of the physical body seemed to me more tolerable in remote working, both by telephone and by Zoom/Skype, and partially substituted by the containment of the setting's temporal parameter. As the medieval philosopher and mystic Meister Eckhart wrote, "My body is in my soul, more than my soul is in my body." A mental presence genuinely involved in emotions cannot be separated from a bodily reference, such that in remote psychoanalytical work we bring with us our bodies and our emotions. *Remote working is however not exempt from a significant torment of distancing and from the risk of a body–mind dissociation*, as was dramatically represented in the film *2001: A Space Odyssey* (Kubrick, 1968), where the mechanical mind of the computer on board, Hal 9000, refuses to allow the re-entry of the astronaut Dave Bowman when he enters into contact with the fear of death (see Lombardi, 2004).

A lengthy experience with patients dissociated from their own bodies has shown me that the physical presence of two bodies in the same room during the analysis certainly does not necessarily in and of itself lead to the realisation of the body–mind integration of the patient. Unfortunately, patients that are used to excluding their own bodies do it all the same, unless one directs the clinical work towards an examination of the conditions of their internal dissociations and specifically promotes the working through of a personal discovery of the body (Lombardi, 2017).

Between the two extremes of a body healthily integrated into their minds and a body–mind dissociation there are various intermediary levels, depending on the characteristics of mental or physical-sensorial dominance that identifies the single subject's body–mind disharmonies (Ferrari, 2004); and no personality is exempt from a certain level of disharmony. These aspects of the body–mind relationship could have conditioned the various types of personal reactions that have emerged during the pandemic, from a quite tolerable response to the torment of distancing, to the most extreme situations that have led to the sliding towards an evident psychotic state.

Hatred in a study group of analysts

I find it interesting to reflect on the reaction to the pandemic by two study groups I supervised on a monthly basis. In one of these groups it was possible to realise a continuity of work and to study together the analytic work during the pandemic, with an activation of the group's creative resources, such that every participant wrote and discussed in the group a clinical report on their own experience of clinical work with their patients. Instead in the second group unexpected complications arose that led to its interruption. I will briefly describe the experience of this second group.

Having advised participants three weeks prior that the next group meeting would be remote, on the day of the meeting I received notice that the group's participants (three people) had decided to cancel the meeting due to various difficulties arising from the pandemic, and because one of the participants was in mourning. The initial agreement of our group was that an honorary payment would be made even in the case of an absence, when there were difficulties of meeting, and I had agreed to their request to shift the date. This time, however, the pandemic had led to their univocal decision to cancel the meeting, which was imposed on me externally. When I pointed out the unilaterality of the decision and the agreement of the setting that had been defined from the beginning, my colleague A came forward saying, "Do you want some advice? Let it go!" I sensed a certain intimidation in this expression that seemed to attribute to the pandemic a higher order that was able to cancel all other established parameters. In reality, this occurred *not because of the pandemic, but because of a decision made by people.*

On the occasion of a group supervision "*in personam*", after two remote supervisions, I was able to enunciate at the end of the meeting our differences in evaluation, for which I was able to accept their non-payment for the missed session, as a choice of their own responsibility, although personally I maintained my difference of opinion with respect to the usefulness of respecting the setting's time parameters, which are as necessary working with groups as they are in analysis. I think that in the absence of *time* and *money*, which bind us to the concreteness of the shared world, the symbolic system of the analysis drifts towards an abstraction with no real foundation. It was sufficient to mention the missed session and our differences of opinion to activate my colleagues' intolerant objection, because the pandemic—according to them—modified the normal parameters. Colleague A commented that I was gratuitously rigid, where flexibility should be a characteristic of the analyst. On my part, however, the analyst's flexibility (Lombardi, 2010) cannot overlook time, as an essential parameter for thinking (Kant, 1781; Lombardi, 2003, 2005, 2013). Colleague B affirmed, however, that he does not make the patient pay in the case of absence due to mourning. Colleague A then confronted me in a clearly aggressive manner, raising his voice, and calling me arrogant, as was evident—according to him— by what he assumed was my preference to publish in foreign languages rather than in Italian, which "proved" my arrogant lack of attention to my countrymen.

Caught off guard by this direct manifestation of hatred, I briefly replied to A that he spoke of things irrelevant to the intentions of the study group. In the meantime, I asked myself if I was considered arrogant for not having accepted his "advice" to "let it go". Following his outburst, A suddenly approached me and, smiling, touched my hand: a rather confusing gesture that seemed to want to play down his attack. As such he violated the "social distancing" requirement that had been agreed upon in the context of personal meetings (as well as that established by the law). Immediately after, A headed for the door, hurriedly saying goodbye. This incident seems significant to me in observing the level of frustration, hatred, and the drive to action that has invested analysts during the pandemic. In consideration of social distancing, colleague A's precipitous touching my hand physically before leaving draws attention: a gesture that seems to suggest a difficulty in *tolerating physical distance imposed by the pandemic*. The emotional explosiveness had roughly shifted the main axis of the group's work plan towards a primitive axis dominated by basic assumptions (Bion, 1961): a shift that made it impossible to continue a scientific collaboration.

Lastly it must be noted that the work done by this group before its interruption did not involve topics specifically raised by the pandemic, in contrast to the other study group which made the specificities of dealing with the pandemic the object of its study.

Social distancing and individual space–time

Before concluding, let us now examine some new resources that the psychoanalysis during the pandemic facilitated in my analysands.

Elisa, forty-five, begins a session with: "Let me tell you a paradox: I'm afraid of ending the lockdown. In this period, I have discovered more than ever my need of my own personal space that is not spoiled by social situations." Like Elisa, other patients have used the lockdown as an *opportunity to treasure their personal space–time* in contrast to the fast pace of their pre-pandemic, normal lives. Three patients, having never cooked before, who had begun making their own fresh pasta at home, particularly struck me: tagliatelle, gnocchi, ravioli. In discussing these experiences, *a greater awareness of space–time limits* was recognised as something to be thought about more carefully and to treasure in the future.

Anchoring to personal space–time, correlated to the *discovery of internal silence*, has likewise been an important springboard for doctors and professionals in analysis with me, who were occupying positions of responsibility in the management of the national emergency: a focus on their own needs allowed them to enhance their relational and social engagement in their professions.

Creativity

The Italian government has required a mandatory self-declaration form, downloadable online, for those who leave the confines of their home: a permit that states their reason for going out. Its formulation has been updated several times, so that a series of out-of-date permits has accumulated.

Matteo, thirty-five, is an artist who is almost at the end of his analysis. He finds himself drawing pictures spontaneously on the out-of-date certificates. He then publishes these drawings on Instagram, encouraging others to upload their own illustrated self-declaration forms. The initiative grows. Within days 1,000, then 5,000 illustrated forms appear, hundreds of which are works with artistic and social value. This initiative has been featured in newspapers and on TV.

Struggling with body boundaries and acute anxieties has thus become a springboard for creativity.

"The contrast between man's ideological capacity to move at random through material and metaphysical spaces and his physical limitations, is the origin of all human tragedy....

Half-winged—half-imprisoned, this is man!" (Klee, 1925).[1]

Riccardo Lombardi
August 2020

References

Arieti, S. (1955). *Intepretation of Schizophrenia*. New York: Basic Books.
Bion, W. R. (1961). *Experiences in Groups*. New York: Basic Books.
Bion, W. R. (1962). *Learning from Experience*. London: Karnac, 1984.
Bion, W. R. (1970). *Attention and Interpretation*. London: Karnac, 1984.

---

[1] "Half-winged—half-imprisoned" (*Metà prigioniero Metà alato*) is also the title of the Italian edition of my book: *Body–Mind Dissociation in Psychoanalysis* (2017).

Bleger, J. (1967). Psycho-analysis of the psycho-analytic frame. *International Journal of Psychoanalysis*, 48: 511–519.

Ferrari A. B. (2004). *From the Eclipse of the Body to the Dawn of Thought*. London: Free Association.

Freud, S. (1899a). Screen memories. *S. E.*, 3: 301–322. London: Hogarth.

Freud, S. (1900a). *The Interpretation of Dreams. S. E.*, 4–5. London: Hogarth.

Freud, S. (1901b). *The Psychopathology of Everyday Life. S. E.*, 6. London: Hogarth.

Freud, S. (1911b). Formulations on the two principles of mental functioning. *S. E.*, 12: 218–226. London: Hogarth.

Freud, S. (1914c). On narcissism: an introduction. *S. E.*, 14: 73–102. London: Hogarth.

Freud, S. (1920g). *Beyond the Pleasure Principle. S. E.*, 18: 7–64. London: Hogarth.

Freud, S. (1923b). *The Ego and the Id. S. E.*, 19: 12–66. London: Hogarth.

Kant, E. (1781). *Critique of Pure Reason*. Basingstoke, UK: Palgrave Macmillan, 2003.

Klee, P. (1925). *Pedagogical Sketchbook*. S. Moholy-Nagy (Trans.). London: Faber & Faber, 1968.

Klein, M. (1946). Notes on some schizoid mechanisms. In: *Envy and Gratitude and Other Works 1946–1963*. London: Hogarth, 1975.

Lombardi, R. (2003). Knowledge and experience of time in primitive mental states. *International Journal of Psychoanalysis*, 84(6): 1531–1549.

Lombardi, R. (2004). Stanley Kubrick's swan song. *International Journal of Psychoanalysis*, 85(1): 209–218.

Lombardi, R. (2005). Setting e temporalità. In: G. Berti Cerone (Ed.), *Come cura la Psicoanalisi?* (pp. 302–331). Milan, Italy: Franco Angeli.

Lombardi, R. (2009). Through the eye of the needle: the unfolding of the unconscious body. *Journal of the American Psychoanalytic Association*, 57: 61–94.

Lombardi, R. (2010). The body emerging from the "neverland" of nothingness. *Psychoanalytic Quarterly*, 79: 879–909.

Lombardi, R. (2013). Death, time, and psychosis. *Journal of the American Psychoanalytic Association*, 61: 691–726.

Lombardi, R. (2015). *Formless Infinity. Clinical Explorations of Matte Blanco and Bion*. New York: Routledge.

Lombardi, R. (2017). *Body–Mind Dissociation in Psychoanalysis: Development after Bion*. New York: Routledge.

Lombardi, R. (2018). Entering one's own life as an aim of clinical psychoanalysis. *Journal of the American Psychoanalytic Association, 66*(5): 883–911.

Lombardi, R. (2019a). Developing a capacity for bodily concern: Antonio Damasio and the psychoanalysis of body–mind relationship. *Psychoanalytic Inquiry, 39*: 534–544.

Lombardi, R (2019b). Awakening the body. *Psychoanalysis in Europe, EPF Bulletin, 73*: 254–259.

Lombardi, R. (2021). *Le transfert sur le corps.* Larmor-Plage, France: Editions du Hublot.

Matte Blanco, I. (1975). *The Unconscious as Infinite Sets: An Essay in Bi-logic.* London: Karnac, 1998.

Matte Blanco, I. (1988). *Thinking, Feeling, and Being: Clinical Reflections on the Fundamental Antinomy of Human Beings and World.* New York: Routledge.

Winnicott, D. W. (1969). The use of an object. *International Journal of Psychoanalysis, 50*: 711–716.

Zerbe, K. (2020). Pandemic fatigue: facing the body's inexorable demands in the time of COVID-19. *Journal of the American Psychoanalytic Association, 68*: 475–478.

CHAPTER 10

A short circuit in the analytical process

François Lévy
Paris, France

> "We may be dealing with things which are so slight as to be virtually imperceptible, but which are so real that they could destroy us almost without our being aware of it."
>
> —Wilfred R. Bion (1976, p. 135)

The theme developed in this chapter stems from the experiences of patients which, during the uncanny global crisis brought about by the coronavirus lockdown beginning March 2020, shattered into pieces the analytical setting and its habitual aspects. This same setting had otherwise been established without difficulty and was in use for several years.

Some analysts have wondered whether this unprecedented event—which at the time of writing is far from over—would not compel analysts to reassess their sacrosanct analytical practice, and work towards establishing a "trauma setting" (Krzakowski, 2020) specific to the psychosocial aspects of the Covid event, as if a dictate against analytically informed use of one's subjectivity commanded them to submit their personal *analytic* practice to some extra-analytical fundamental rules.

But on a personal level, being the analyst that I am, I began by wondering whether the suspension of sessions wasn't perhaps equivalent to the ordinary stagnations encountered throughout the analytical process, apparent either at moments of so-called patient resistance, or indeed when it is the analyst who is responsible for his "retirement" from therapy. By way of example, I shall recount what happened to me fifteen years ago, when, for health reasons, I had to interrupt my activity for a not negligible period of time, and had informed my patients by post that our work would resume at a later date "where it had left off". One patient was quick to reply that for her, our work would resume not "where it had left off", but "where she herself would be in terms of this work at the moment of its resumption"!

Thus we have an important question, which consists of asking ourselves whether our position as analysts means that we are the guarantors of each patient's continued feeling of existence—in as much as they had previously identified this feeling within them (Lévy, 2014)!

In February–March 2020, before the public authorities instituted the "lockdown"—a term few people had been familiar with—I was receiving patients at my office and already asking them not only to submit to the official sanitary instructions, but also to a set of private precautions that seemed to me indispensable and which had to do mostly with my own personal frailties. I had suddenly become aware that "the great scythe" was swinging above our heads, and in particular above my own. For the grave illness that had caused me to interrupt my practice and which doctors had defeated fifteen years before had reappeared eighteen months earlier, deep within my organism, and a new treatment—very innovative in comparison to the first—had been prescribed to me. For fifteen years, an awareness of death had remained present in my mind. Following my remission, after such a close brush with death, I experienced what was virtually a "rebirth", and considered myself for a while to be an invincible and immortal being!

In my consultation room, some of my patients described with marvel what I have just evoked, or brought into sessions dreams in which certain oneiric figurations illustrated the dramatic consequences of this experience of immortality. Their faces as well as their haunted looks betrayed the hallucinatory world they just had travelled through. How indeed not to experience awe and anxiety when, in order to arrive at one's analyst, one must pass through streets, squares, avenues emptied of pedestrians, cars, motorcycles, bicycles, when silence now reigned majestically, having stifled the former daily commotion and noise of the city. Many pictures of deserted cities have been published since the advent of this extraordinary situation. Dream narratives have provided some of my patients with associations about their experiences of this irreality that had emerged from the disappearance of all forms of urban activity, and brought up painful childhood memories of solitude and isolation, as well as feelings of irreality concerning the places in which they had formerly lived. For others, they found themselves (once more) before a theatre scene or peering into a film set emptied of its extras and its actors, where the buildings, the shops, the pavements were made of cardboard or of wood and propped up on scaffolding.

Rigid and projective transformations

Psychoanalysis, in as much as it is meant to guide patients to transform profoundly their relations between the external and internal worlds, requires that childhood situations, which are replayed thanks to the transference in the analyst's office, take place in the presence of the analyst. The foundational moments of a realised life may not take place *in absentia*. In remote sessions, these essential movements can only be attempted via sound or virtual reality. However, in two treatments that continued remotely—one with an analysand who had left France and "chosen" Skype for future sessions, the other with an analysand who had opted for telephone sessions from abroad—I had already taken note of the isolation, the solitude, the distress that *I* was feeling, sat before my computer screen or holding a phone to my ear, when some sessions made me feel incapable of maintaining the psychic position of the "helper". My body was overwhelmed with a cold sensation; a moral pain rose within me the closer we got to the end of the session. I was convinced that these unusual manifestations in my practice reflected what Wilfred R. Bion had studied in depth when he adopted and remodelled the Kleinian notion of "projective identification".

Remote psychoanalysis thus appears as the negative of analytical practice, where the joint presence of analyst and patient in the office seems indispensable. I thus had negotiated with these patients their "repatriation" once a trimester, if not once a month, to Paris, so as to *restore presence*—the "skin-to-skin", as Esther Bick or Geneviève Haag would have said—or "co-presence", to use a term from Daniel Widlöcher (Widlöcher & Miller, 2003).[1]

When however, at the beginning of lockdown, I informed my patients—for lack of any better idea—of my proposition to continue sessions "remotely", over the phone or exceptionally via Skype, some of them accepted right away, while others said that they were not able to resign themselves to the idea of losing the normal conditions of their analytical work and that, as a result, they preferred suspending their sessions with me. For how long? No one could say. I detected in their rigid responses frank and non-negotiable opposition. As soon as I realised this, I uttered to myself a sentence that sounded like the bell tolling: "The analyst that I am is disavowed as if he exuded Death!" I will spare you the details of what effect this "verdict" had on me, who had only recently experienced the (mad) feelings of invincibility and immortality.

I then began to wonder whether I had not been mistaken from the start about some of these patients, and whether they were not indeed what is referred to in professional literature as "unanalysable": that is, patients who, from the beginning and sometimes in subtle ways, evade the establishment of the transferential link, who are subject to acting in and out so as to put themselves or their close ones in danger (not to mention their analyst), or who have lost all touch with reality and end up fleeing into delusion.

Those who had made me aware of this very *real* problem had until then accepted the analytical situation perfectly well. They did not seem to suffer from its more frustrating aspects, they never detached from reality, never acted out, be it in or outside sessions, nor did they manifest any somatisations. They seemed capable of taking into consideration the changes that had taken place in external reality (the silence, the empty streets that conjured oneiric and cinematic associations, an emptiness that was not devoid of beauty, which produced an uncanny— *unheimlich*—aesthetic effect, etc.). The most familiar places became foreign. The patients I am thinking of seemed more fragile in the face of the fake news that was circulating on social media before being picked up by official news outlets. This muddled information we were receiving seemed not so much to be issued by government sources as to be

---

[1] See below in the first clinical illustration.

stumbling out of them. Everyone quickly realised that the purpose of this information was not to prevent the spread of the disease throughout the population, nor to cure it. Its true purpose was to keep the hospitals from crumbling under the influx of patients. Everyone understood that the respiratory distress secondary or related to the virus was the principal risk at hand. Everyone knew that persons aged seventy and above were the most exposed, but the certainty of this information was undermined by the fact that 50% of patients in intensive care units were sixty years old and younger.

That being said, once the restrictive orders were issued relating to the exponential development of the pandemic, those same patients barricaded themselves in their defensive stance, resisting any adaptation to the frame, were opposed to the idea of continuing their analytic work under conditions that differed from what they were used to, and preferred "suspending" their sessions. Of course, their vigorous refusal could be attributed to something relating to the "fragility" of their psychic reality. It could also be understood from the point of view of disturbances that perturbed the symbolisation processes that foster an understanding of external reality. In other words, when the frame that the analyst provides the patient with is meant to allow the patient to (re)position their internal world as constituted during the infant stages of their history, it is often the difficulty to *symbolise* that emerges. This then requires the nurturing of this process during treatment, since, if it defaults, the conflict between a solidly established psychic reality and its modification, as imposed by the variability of external reality, intensifies. This, at any rate, is how I understood some patients who declined my offer of telephone sessions.

But if this difficult faculty of symbolisation expresses itself within the usual apparatus as established by any psychoanalyst who refers to the advice and instructions proffered by his predecessors since the frame was defined as such, it is that the value of this frame depends also on a general social and political situation that allows for psychoanalysis to be fully and freely exercised.[2] The frame is thus partially dependent

---

[2] On this subject, an anecdote comes to my mind that took place when, from 2005 to 2010, I hosted Dr Qin Wei, a brilliant doctor of traditional Chinese medicine, as well as professor of psychology at the University of Chengdu and psychoanalyst, invited by the

upon *group* conditions upon which it may be established and employed. Wilfred R. Bion was always attentive to this fact, considering that "classical" (in office) psychoanalysis takes place thanks to the constitution of a "group of two". For him, any analytical act, be it performed in group or in the office, is social and political, as well as an individual and group act. It is under these conditions that it may reveal itself to be therapeutic.

De visu

Among the patients whose behaviour made me reflect on the deeper causes of their refusal, let me mention the following case of a woman about forty years old, whom I had always received face to face. From our preliminary meeting, it seemed to me that asking her to lie down would risk completely disturbing the equilibrium she had found through what had been her first analysis, also carried out in face-to-face consultations, over five years and with a female analyst. This patient suffered for the past fifteen years from a case of multiple sclerosis whose development doctors had a hard time containing. If she was content with the work carried out during her first "piece" of analysis, she nevertheless never spoke of it or made reference to it. The vague idea that fluttered diffusely in my mind when I saw her made me think that for her, only the present existed, and only it could grab her attention.

She approached me due to professional concerns that required of her a kind of logical, organised, and structured thinking, of the sort found in international journals, which she felt to be totally lacking. She was the head of an important fundamental research laboratory and frequented many international conferences, where her scientific communications

---

Société de psychanalyse freudienne (SPF) to spend a year in Paris in order to increase his knowledge and engage with his peers. He had undergone analysis with a Lacanian psychoanalyst in China, had intensively learned French "in order to read Lacan in the original" and then spent a year at the University of Seattle (USA). As the aforementioned dates indicate, he ended up spending more than one year in France and began another "piece of analytical work" while discovering at the same time, thanks to various teachings, seminars, and supervisions, Sigmund Freud "in the original", Sandor Ferenczi, Melanie Klein, Donald W. Winnicott, Wilfred R. Bion, and Gisela Pankoff. It was towards the end of his third year that he declared to my wife and me: "I think I am only now beginning to understand the meaning of the Freudian expression of 'free association'."

were expected, all the more so due to the fact that her latest research was challenging—and apparently rightly so—the theses of certain Nobel prize laureates! During our work—over a long period of time—some *links* were established between very disparate and dispersed elements from her past, her memories, her knowledge, her associations, and between diverse domains—scientific, philosophical, mystical, religious, and, each time, she succeeded in finding coherencies that gave her a great deal of satisfaction.

Clearly, the "(re)discovery" in my presence of certain supposedly obvious connections filled her with a sense of relief. But, as I said above, since only the present seemed to be meaningful to her, as soon as the lockdown measures were imposed on us, it became unimaginable for her to continue her work with me if I were not to be *physically* present (unless the issue was that *she* would not be able to be physically present). Whether it was about me or her, or about the "analytical couple" that we formed in session, the *present* was *absent*, for if the presence—or the "co-presence", to use Daniel Widlöcher's expression again—was not present at the meeting, then no meeting had taken place at all. Clearly, this joint presence was meant to produce solutions to her problems of disorganised thinking, a sort of "analytical baby", provided, of course, that the analytical couple was able to *really* form, for otherwise the analytical baby could not be produced, not even through imagination.

I tried convincing her to stay in touch with me via telephone, especially when the initial lockdown was followed by a second, then a third, ever stricter and longer. My efforts were in vain. She did in fact re-emerge twice, via email, in order to "see how [I was] doing", to use her terms. But in reality, she was telling me how she was doing, in a formulaic, informative, indifferent tone. Clearly, the co-presence of two protagonists involved in this analytical apparatus had to be real, and any attempt on my part to shift this co-presence into an imaginary modality, indeed a symbolic one, was doomed to failure. I should state however that before the pandemic, this patient did experience a serious reorganisation in her modes of thinking, which afforded her a fresh reading of her history, of her early childhood links, and of her current familial and professional relationships. But in terms of the transferential link itself, she remained ignorant as to its essential role in the transformation she had undergone.

Since the end of lockdown, we have not yet been able to address the role of physical presence as an essential element in transference. I should add that the value of presence cannot be understood unless the (psychic) link between presence and absence is established. Freud's discussion of this matter, in the context of his grandson playing the "Fort-Da" game in the absence of his mother, is highly significant for our purposes (1920g, pp. 51–54). As I understand it, the importance of this case for Freud is in the value given to the game with the reel (= the mother) and to the movement of coming-and-going that the child engages in (presence/absence), and yet Freud neglects to accord as much attention to the link (= the thread) between the child and his mother. In his defence, Freud does approach this issue when he mentions in a footnote that the child will have sufficiently internalised this link when, a year later, his mother succumbs to the Spanish flu (1920) and he is able to endure a period of non-pathological mourning.

In contrast to this example, another patient, whom I have been receiving for a long while and who experiences intense hallucinations of a mostly visual character, has led me to ponder the etymology of the word "analysis", which Freud had adopted for his purposes and which, in Greek, signifies among other things the detailed examination of an object in an effort to discern its constituent parts. In psychoanalysis, this method of psychological investigation aids in making apparent to the mind (or the "soul" = *Seele*) its different components (memories, desires, figurations in images or in words, representations, fantasies, etc.). Like some others, this patient was opposed to my proposition to continue our work over the telephone, exclaiming: "I need to see you!" When sessions resumed approximately three months later, she arrived with a joyous air about her and declared that during our "separation" she had experienced a form of recentring upon the different components of her personality (a personality synthesis).

These two case histories make me think of the distinctions that Bernard Golse (2020) highlights in an online oral communication delivered during the lockdown period.[3] Golse's purpose was to maintain

---

[3] See: https://copes.fr/Presentation/Video/Resources/15802. The purpose of these communications was to maintain a link between analysts suddenly separated by bans

some sort of link between us analysts, who had suddenly found ourselves separated from our peers due to travel restrictions.

In this "chat" Golse highlighted the fact that we psychoanalysts tend to understand the consensual generalised expression of "object relations" in a somewhat academic way. For if we do not take care, we seem to understand it as follows. A meeting takes place between two objects that occupy the same space for the duration of a session. We call the elaboration we make of it the "metapsychology of the meeting" and forget about the complexities of the ruses that we employ in our attempt to reveal the linking mechanisms. This is why Bernard Golse goes to significant lengths in an effort to differentiate three levels of symbolisation, in what we call "object relations", that are indispensable for a correct understanding of this mechanism. In a way, he picks up Freud's discussion of the phenomenon's enigmatic nature, which occurs once two beings manage to "present(ify)" each other in an existential manner.

According to Golse, first—perhaps!—comes the "representation of the place of the object", which is not yet the object itself per se. Keeping a place within oneself for something that does not yet exist is in my opinion equivalent to replaying the creationary mechanism as described in Kabbalah: it is through the "reduction" (צמצום—*tsimtsum*) of divine energy that the existence of a reality exterior to Him comes into being. This then leads, Golse continues, to the *virtual* stage, contained in the Bionian term of "pre-conception", that serves to designate "the pre-representations with which the infant arrives into the world". Fidelity to Bion's innovative thought thereby requires of us to proclaim, somewhat scandalously, that every infant comes into this world equipped with "an inborn pre-conception that a breast that can satisfy its own incomplete nature exists" (Bion, 1962 p. 89).

At a second level, Golse insists on the establishment in the psyche of "the mental representation of linkings with the object". This is probably the most important of the three mechanisms, since the object, in as much as it does not exist as such[4]—a capital notion that indicates

---

on leaving their homes or offices, unless they had the title of medical doctors, which afforded them a much greater freedom of movement.

[4] Indeed, the remark is crucial in that it indicates that *the representation of the links* precedes, by far, the representation of the object (see below).

that the representation of linkings by far precedes the representation of the object itself (see below)—it is crucial to anchor it progressively using linkings ("cathexis", in Freudian terms) that orient it to its designated place.

As concerns the third "stage", that of the "representation of the object in and of itself", one must remember that, according to Freud, it is "what is most variable" (1915c, p. 122), since it persists so long as it provides us with the satisfaction we expect from it, and that the withdrawal of cathexis from it only occurs once it no longer supplies us with that for which it had been chosen.

It is easy to understand that hyper-cathexis in an object, as may occur in transference, can become a source of suffering when the object itself "modifies the rule" unilaterally, as was the case with the SARS-CoV-2 pandemic of spring 2020. An analyst who announces to his patients that he is "retiring" and requests that they accept a purely vocal link from now on must necessarily require of them that they mourn a non-dead object—and not just any object, if we recall that Lacan added the voice (and the gaze) to Freud's list of "partial objects"! This may cause a particular form of traumatism, remarkably described by Louis-René des Forêts in the conclusion to one of his most touching short stories: "… Anna to whom a beautiful voice was so dear that she appeared to mourn it" (1960, p. 62).

Lack of psychic pain?

I shall now discuss the case of a man, about seventy years old, in analysis with me for eight or nine years, who comes from a sociocultural background open to the world of ideas—including those of psychoanalysis, seeing as one of his parents had undergone analysis. This man disappeared after I had left him a vocal message at the beginning of lockdown, explaining my proposition to continue sessions "remotely". I knew this patient well (or thought I did!), which is why I did not contact him again with a second message after he had failed to respond to the first. It was at this point that I came to understand fully the extent to which his relationships had always been precarious—including ours? I wondered about this man, who had never missed a session.

Once lockdown had ended, I received from him a letter by post, reproduced here (with his consent):

Hello,

I am writing to you after a long silence (for you) and an extremely loud commotion (for me), and I ask of you first of all to excuse the fact that I had not got in touch with you since mid-March, seeing as I was incapable of it.

As I told you over the phone the day that lockdown began, my wife and I had spent the weekend in the countryside and, upon hearing the news, decided against returning to Paris.

When I called you on Tuesday morning to tell you that I would not be coming to my session, I felt assaulted when you retorted—and I am aware of the fact that it is a strong word—that if I wanted to find a way to (come) talk with you, I would certainly find one.

It was that "come" (which I have placed in parentheses, since to this day I am not sure that you actually said it) that I felt to be violent. Your sentence, I took it to be an incitement to desire my session with you to the point of disregarding the lockdown, and I began fearing—in particular, fearing speaking to you, fearing you!

The violence was contained in the words with which you had formulated your reply. Thereupon my health began worsening. I had left Paris with a troublesome rhinitis and cough. In the countryside, my fatigue and cough worsened, followed by a secondary infection of the bronchi.

One weekend in April, I slept for thirty hours straight and, upon waking, had the impression of having left something behind. My primary care physician prescribed me an antibiotic against bronchial or pulmonary infections.

Slowly, very slowly, I retrieved a capacity for thought that had completely deserted me.

I then thought of you, without however being able to bring myself to call you. For me, calling you would have meant letting you into my house, letting you "break and enter" into my home, my intimacy, and this I deemed impossible. Analysis with you, in my eyes, cannot take place anywhere but in your office, and of course, in your presence.

I will probably be returning to Paris on June 8 to resume my professional activity. I will then be able to resume my work with you and relate what I have described in the present letter in person and in detail, should you accept to continue seeing me, after the silence I have imposed on you!

Best,

X

To say that these patients are unable to establish *linking* (to use the term employed essentially by Wilfred R. Bion (1959, pp. 105–123)) would be wrong. Indeed I can positively attest to the seriousness and dedication of their efforts during the years of analytical work they had carried out with me. Bion's choice of using the gerundive grammatical form of *–ing* (in *linking*) indicated that this is ever an *active* process—the process of linking, the establishment of a link, the function of linkage—which attests to the active involvement of a patient in the analytical process. But whereas linking is possible, these patients seem to suffer from a deficient identity, from a void that translates into a veritable disturbance in terms of thought.

As mentioned above, these patients found themselves in environments marked by a certain irreality (deserted streets, cardboard buildings, absent extras, lack of activity, a "deathly" silence that causes birdsong to stand out all the more when it ceases with sundown, etc.) that, during such moments, relate back to childhood situations comparable with hallucinatory experiences. In accordance with Bion's conceptualisation, these subjects lack an "alpha function" that would furnish them with the elements necessary to contemplate otherness, and in particular psychic otherness. Since childhood, they have not been able to construct fantasies capable of being repressed and thereby capable of serving them as "psychic capital" (cf. McDougall, 1978) that exists in a safe place and that can be mobilised in situations of catastrophe. Didn't one of these patients ask me, upon declining my invitation: "If something happened to *you*, what would become of *me*?" They also lack the elements that provide the means to contemplate suffering. Consequently, they cannot speak of it.

Consultation in the absence of physicality?

Each one of the aforementioned analyses affords us a glimpse into the fact that a long learning process may lead the analyst–analysand pair to go through a shared mutative experience. At first, this made me wonder whether I had not taken a wrong turn at the beginning of my work with each of these difficult patients, or whether I had been inattentive to the point of overlooking certain essential transferential elements. My long analytic training has, however, led me to take into account these elements that an analyst observes, precisely because they manifest *in their absence*, and imprint the course of analysis with a static and negative force that produces no effect on that which, since the beginning, appeared to be split—and which remains so.

To put it bluntly, these patients speak of things and of people, but they never speak of the *relationship* between those things or the *relationships* between people, no more than they speak of relationships *with* things or *with* people. Similarly, we never hear them speak of the fact that one may find "proximities" between the dream world and the world of consciousness, that is to say, between primary and secondary processes. When they exist, the sensory links (linking), the links between past and present, the links qualified as affective, preclude one from speaking confidently of "object linking". One may then conclude that in transference, no reviviscence takes place. And if it does, it does not manifest itself through affective expressions. "Transference", Freud already wrote, "is the one thing the presence of which has to be detected" (1905e, p. 116. See also Muller, 2004). Object relations, as evoked by such patients, seem to be preserved only in order to maintain a more or less stable life, or not to have to separate from the object of their resentment. Even in this last case, no trace of such relations remains vis-à-vis the analyst. The foundational otherness of subjectivity resembles an object lost within oneself. One may say that subjectivity is disavowed in this case (this is the second time I have used this term, to which I shall return below). We must not therefore be surprised when we find ourselves wondering *who* and *what* we are observing.

Whenever this question arises, it is only answered—if at all—by *one* mechanism, *one* process, *one* line of questioning, *one* analytical mode, that is difficult, painful, complex: the analysis of countertransference! For these "refusals" can at first be understood as (massive) failures in terms of our analytical function, and can cause us an intense countertransferential suffering that leads to a narcissistic wound that we "treat" through the cathectic withdrawal from the patient. We must thereupon question the resistance that had prevented us from anticipating this refusal with which we are faced. There is no use in sharing with such patients the hypotheses that point to the fact that we surely comported ourselves like deprived analysts, firstly because such assessments may have persecutory effects on ourselves, and secondly since such interpretations may also be persecutory for the patients, leading them to wonder what kind of the problems their analysts may be suffering from.

Refusal, denial, or disavowal?

Everyone is obviously subject to *his own* individual psychic functioning, whether they be analyst or patient, and Bion insisted on the importance of our own ignorance in this domain. He speaks in terms of "limits", as if to say that vocabulary itself does not possess the words that might describe the content of thought (conscious, and even more so unconscious), which the analyst observes in practice.[5]

In *Attention and Interpretation* (1970), Bion compares each analytical experience to an adventure during which we "introduce" a probe (successfully or otherwise) into the psyche, at an exact spot and at varying depths, and that the glimpse we get during this exploration is not always decipherable:

> It [the mental domain] cannot be *contained* within the framework of psycho-analytic theory. [...] Psycho-analysis cannot be *contained* permanently within the definitions they use. [...] Psycho-analysis cannot "*contain*" the mental domain because it is not a "*container*" but a "*probe*". (p. 283; my italics)

In other terms, each analytical experience allows for the exploration of a different "territory" of the container/contained relationship. Bion never claims that exhaustive knowledge is possible, and insists on other aspects

---

[5] As to the denial of trauma employed by patients, it is a denial that analysts are prone to credit and susceptible to maintain, especially when they espouse loyalty towards the "orthodoxy" of the IPA. It is imperative to take into account the "brave" comments of Louise de Urtubey concerning a patient who, "in good faith", related an anecdote a priori without interest in an analytical narrative. I have taken the liberty of reproducing this episode at the end of the chapter.

of the encounter. The permanent acknowledgement of the immensity of our ignorance conflicts with the "subject supposed to know" which, according to Lacan, is the distinctive mark of the analyst. In this Wilfred R. Bion joins Blaise Pascal, who asserts that *"le silence éternel de ces espaces infinis m'effraie"*[6] (1670, p. 230).

For her part, Joyce McDougall, in the French edition of her *Plea for a Measure of Abnormality* (1978, p. 111) adds:

> We all have blind spots where certain opinions, certain traits of character that elude symbolisation, are constructed based on stereotype, or on preconceptions in Bionian terms, constructed on rules of thinking, that is, on inauthentic thinking. What matters is perhaps the extent of our collective blindness.

Cheek to cheek?

When the analyst adheres to governmental health instructions and decides to impose on his patients the profound upheaval of the analytical apparatus, one can understand Samuel, a patient whose interview with Elise Karlin appeared in the *Le Monde* supplement of August 28, 2020.[7] Samuel rebelled before his analyst who until then had perfectly respected the precepts acquired during his training.[8] Samuel was shocked at first:

> Analysis over the phone! With my psychologist, usually so strict about the frame, so respectful of the classical norms of treatment! I suddenly got angry, thinking that she fears me, that I represent a potential threat, capable of introducing the virus into her office. Then I became disappointed by the fact that she feared for herself, just like anyone else, whereas for me she had been like my own

---

[6] "The eternal silence of these infinite spaces frightens me," always quoted in French by Bion.

[7] "Avec le Covid-19, la psychanalyse fait sa révolution," by Elise Karlin.

[8] One may mock so-called "traditional" or "orthodox" training, which is not dissimilar to the punishment that the poor Condemned Man receives in Franz Kafka's *In the Penal Colony* (1914), which consists of having inscribed "on his bare hide a speech whose subject knows neither its meaning nor its text, nor in which language it is written, nor even that it has been tattooed to him" (Lacan, 1960, p. 290).

commandatore's statute.[9] Then I thought about it. In the end,
I was reassured by the fact that she was able to adapt, that she was
not giving up on me, wasn't telling me: "Come back when this
will all be done with."

He adds that he discovered that he was also able to evoke over the phone
a highly problematic situation that he had been living through and
which until then he had been incapable of recounting: "*This could never
have taken place if not via telephone*," he later declared. It appears that, in
these devices modified by the analyst, it is the unreality of the object that
facilitates the attacks against it.

It is true that on March 17, after French president Emmanuel
Macron's address to the nation, psychiatrists, psychologists, and other
mental health practitioners had to urgently rethink everything, imagine consultations with no physical presence, language reduced to
words, the disintegration of the ritual, while knowing full well that the
telephone asepticises the non-verbal elements indispensable to transference. They persevered in these changes, however, claiming that they
would not abandon anyone to suffering—not to mention the fact that
this enabled them to continue making a living. "We had to answer the
request," as some maintained, who otherwise used to proclaim loud
and clear that analysts did not deal with requests but with desires. Others went so far as to send an SMS to their patients to propose to them
this new "service" that would allow them to stay in touch without having to speak!

Once the communication link was re-established (through wireless
devices), some discovered an ever more accentuated proximity thanks to
the use of headphones, and "appreciated" the fact that the phone allowed
for an exchange that they described as "equal to equal".[10]

The idea of "responding to our analysands' new constraints" sounds
strange to my ears, since, when I read this (or hear it), I recall the

---

[9] From Mozart's opera *Don Giovanni*, which cautions Don Giovanni and offers him one
last chance to repent before being condemned to Hell (translator's note).
[10] What did they do with what they had experienced in their own analyses, and which
analysts call proximity thanks to "subjective disparity"?

paragraphs that Freud had consecrated to genes and to the hardship he himself had experienced when faced with patients, and which altered his mode of listening (let us recall the man who was telling him how everything was going perfectly well in his marriage while ceaselessly sliding his wedding band on and off).

In conclusion, just as I gave an account of the feelings of solitude and, most importantly, of impotence, that I had felt when listening to some of my patients over the phone during lockdown, I am in agreement with Christophe Dejours (*Le Monde* supplement of August 28, 2020), who recognises honestly that: "I need presence, smells, fears—in the absence of physical bodies, there is no affect."

We hear from all over the world a call to "reinvent psychoanalysis", but let us not forget to specify that if it is to retain its effectiveness, it must be invented … "just the same"!

Appendix

The following is a narrative describing a patient's denial, which the analyst interprets while taking into account the political context of the totalitarian country in which the analysis takes place (cf. de Urtubey, 1982):

> The patient told her that someone had come to his house and left a cabbage in the refrigerator. If de Urtubey had only taken into account the associations that her patient was able to produce due to psychic reality—fantasies, infantile sexual theories (that babies are made in cabbages, etc.), Oedipal dynamics, etc.—her patient would have surely lost his life. Instead, she understood that she was dealing with a denial related to external political reality, an active denial in the case of this patient. Upon serious reflection as to her role as an analyst in providing direct interpretations of a patient's denial, an act typically contrary to the classical recommendation of not intervening in the patient's daily reality, she made up her mind: she told her patient that one does not keep cabbages in the fridge. The patient then leaped up from the couch, ran home and tossed the cabbage out the window.

Ten minutes later, the police arrived at his home and immediately checked the fridge. There was something in that cabbage that would have led to the imprisonment and condemnation of that patient. More so than in the cabbage, the Devil was in the patient's denial.

François Lévy
September 2020

Translated from French by Shahar Fineberg

References

Bion, W. R. (1959). Attacks on linking. In: *Second Thoughts. The Complete Works of Wilfred R. Bion, Vol. IV*. London: Karnac, 2014.

Bion, W. R. (1962). *Learning from Experience*. In: *Second Thoughts. The Complete Works of Wilfred R. Bion, Vol. IV*. London: Karnac, 2014.

Bion, W. R. (1970). *Attention and Interpretation*. In: *The Complete Works of Wilfred R. Bion, Vol. IV*. London: Karnac, 2014.

De Urtubey, L. (1982). Quand une inquiétante réalité envahit le travail du psychanalyste. *Revue française de psychanalyse, 46*(2, special issue): 389–396.

Des Forêts, L.-R. (1960). Les grands moments d'un chanteur. In: *La Chambre des enfants*. Paris: Gallimard.

Freud, S. (1905e). Fragment of an analysis of a case of hysteria. *S. E., 7*. London: Hogarth.

Freud, S. (1915c). Instincts and their vicissitudes. *S. E., 14*. London: Hogarth.

Freud, S. (1920g). *Beyond the Pleasure Principle. S. E., 18*. London: Hogarth.

Golse, B. (2020). Pour une métapsychologie du lien et de la rencontre. Unpublished. Available at: https://copes.fr/Presentation/Video/Resources/15802 (last accessed December 21, 2020).

Kafka, F. (1914). *In the Penal Colony*. Available at: https://kafka-online.info/in-the-penal-colony.html (last accessed December 21, 2020).

Krzakowski, P. (2020). Psychanalyste par temps de Covid, un métier inessentiel?. Unpublished.

Lacan, J. (1960). The subversion of the subject and the dialectic of desire. In: *Écrits* (1966). Paris: Éditions du Seuil.

Lévy, F. (2014). *Psychoanalysis with Wilfred R. Bion*. London: Routledge, 2020.

McDougall, J. (1978). *Plaidoyer pour une certaine anormalité*. Paris, Gallimard.

Muller, C. (2004). *L'Énigme du transfert*. Ramonville Saint-Agne, France: Érès.

Pascal, B. (1670). *Pensées*. Paris: Georges Bridel Éditeur, 1857.

Widlöcher, D., & Miller, J.-A. (2003). L'Avenir de la psychanalyse. Discussion with Bernard Granger, June 1, 2002. *Psychiatrie, Sciences humaines, Neurosciences*, 1(1). Available at: https://materiologiques.com/fr/20-psychiatrie-sciences-humaines-neurosciences (last accessed December 21, 2020).

CHAPTER 11

Beyond the all-traumatic: narrative imagination and new temporalities in the analytic session

Jean-Jacques Tyszler
(with Dr Corinne Tyszler, paedopsychiatrist)
Paris, France

The global health crisis that we have been living through since March 2020 has brought our collective feeling of uncertainty to new heights. Will the pandemic subside or will it surge? Is such and such medication helpful or harmful? Does the mask protect us sufficiently? Will vaccines be developed soon, and will they be readily available for all? Uncertainty reigns supreme over questions of employment, social welfare, freedom of movement, human contact, etc.

What if the Freudian axiom of *Wo Es war, soll Ich werden*, "Where id was, shall ego be", is currently being pushed to unprecedented limits, both in the sense of an obstructing limit and of a limit that will serve as a crutch for when the tide finally turns? To anticipate the future, we must look to the past—that is what the analytical treatment is all about. But with such an unforeseeable future, where each passing day may be the one where I may get infected or indeed infect another, every memory seems like a loss, if not a renunciation. We are experiencing a sort of melancholia linked to the loss of meaning.[1] For many people, nothing seems today like it will return to be "like before": *la bise* (the customary

---

[1] A loss of meaning close perhaps to that evoked by Christopher Bollas (2018).

French cheek kiss used to greet another), shaking hands, all of our most simple and most human pleasures are now barricaded behind masks and preventive measures. These times of uncertainty have profoundly upset the way adults behave with children (not to mention the elderly and precarious populations such as asylum seekers). It is in this unprecedented context that I propose three points of investigation:

- Alterations to professional practice, both private and institutional, and more specifically, that which this pandemic has allowed us, me and my colleagues, to better understand about the function of the frame, notably the *temporality of sessions and of treatment.*
- The pandemic has reaffirmed our need to revisit the notion of that which we call traumatic, but also of the fantasmatic. We should focus on the pragmatics concerning the changes in our way of conducting treatment, whether in our offices or in our institutions.
- Finally, I would like to plead for breaking down the barriers surrounding some of our psychoanalytical perspectives. The present crisis, and its subsequent practical and conceptual reshuffling, have made this possible. We will thus catch a rare glimpse of the surprising proximities between the Freudian and Lacanian principles that inspire me and many others, and their links to some of the remarkable advances made by the British schools (of Bion, for example).

Material changes to the analytical frame: inventions and extensions

I work as a psychoanalyst in Paris at two different locations, in a private office and in the psychopaediatric service of a medical-psycho-pedagogical centre. If private practice is similar in many regards all over the world, this is not the case with the very particular French institutions that are called medical-psycho-pedagogical centres (CMPP). In contrast with the medical-psychological centres (CMP) in France, which are affiliated to university psychiatric services that receive adults, adolescents, and children, CMPPs deal mostly with children. They usually operate as part of large non-governmental associations (such as the Red Cross), but also enjoy considerable public funding. In addition, they have strong ties to social and judicial child protection services and to schools.

The centre that I direct operates through a very big insurance company that provides insurance and medical treatment to education workers in France. The system as a whole, CMP and CMPP together, aims at providing free psychological care to the entire population, an extremely important social benefit politically speaking, and one of the hallmarks of the French health system. I shall return to this need for universality below. But over time, the CMPP and CMP have slowly diverged: CMPs, which depend on university centres and therefore on *world psychiatry* (DSM, psychopharmacology, etc.), have in some cases become less receptive to psychoanalysis. On the other hand, the relative institutional autonomy of CMPPs has often allowed them to maintain a strong psychoanalysis component in child and adolescent care. This is one of the factors that explains the French exception: a strong and vibrant presence of psychoanalytical paedopsychiatry within public institutions.

Such a framework allows for very sick children to be taken care of on a very long-term basis, in coordination not only with their parents but also with their schools and sometimes with the judicial system. Individual and group psychotherapy is the norm, as we are relatively free of financial constraints (such as limitations to the number of sessions or to the duration of treatments), with deeply engaged caregivers. The institution as such does not create an obstacle for the establishment of transference.

The pandemic has turned all of this upside down: we had never practised over-the-phone sessions until now and, for the younger children, we feared that we might have to cease treatment completely. Some of the points of reference established during psychoanalytical sessions were jeopardised. Schedules, for example, quickly lost their meaning. Patients sometimes called late at night, over the weekend, even during the summer holidays. It was no longer possible to interpret a patient arriving late or missing a session. Our practice is going through a crisis concerning temporality as we usually understand it.

At the CMPP, the psychologists' inventiveness simply astonished me.[2] The changes in the clinical situation required by the pandemic meant

---

[2] Cf. online, Jean-Jacques Tyszler and Ilaria Pirone, "Tenir le fil de la vie par la voix", available on the Association générale des enseignants de maternelle (AGEEM) website: https://delecolealamaison.ageem.org/tenir-le-fil-de-la-voix-par-la-voie/

that therapists worked via voice only, over the phone, and things were going relatively smoothly. However, the autistic or psychotic children could not keep still under the sole yoke of the voice, and required Skype to help create a space for different types of presence. Whereas psychologists may have feared penetrating the intimacy of their patients' homes, this system required parental participation that also allowed parents to feel more involved. And this cooperative dimension, often sidelined in ordinary paedopsychiatric services due to time constraints, has once again shown its value: the parents' anxiety must be addressed, since otherwise the child will manifest in his symptoms the suffering of his close family circle. At the behest of a kindergarten instructors' association, and for the same reasons, we have also produced texts meant to support the efforts of teachers in maintaining an educational link with children confined to their homes.[3]

To be sure, finding a substitute for group therapy was a more difficult task, and this reinforced the isolation felt by many of our little patients. The experience, however, turned out to be beneficial elsewhere: almost every family was able to enjoy not only more regular monitoring, but more frequent follow-up than usual. Finally, thanks to video linking, some Winnicottian aspects of the child's drawing were still able to be solicited. They sometimes replaced for a while the objects available to the children within the usual therapeutic game area, with very pleasurable results. And yet, new problems arose. For the slightly older children, around ten years old, we noticed an increase in nightmares, and even night terrors, as well as very widespread phobias as we neared the end of lockdown.[4]

Some new elements appeared, which we have integrated into our practice in our private office, whereas they had first developed in institutions. A first adjustment appeared of its own with our classically treated analysands. We spoke openly *with no appreciable dissymmetry* of the shared experience we had been going through. In terms of our usual practice and theory, this change was not trivial. Here in France, such an

---

[3] Ibid.

[4] We share the benefits of this experience in a recently published book: *Vocabulaire de la psychanalyse avec l'enfant et adolescent*, Paris, Érès, 2021, under the direction of C. Rey, D. Janin, and C. Tyszler.

attitude is more common among analysts when dealing with psychotics. With a psychotic patient, we discuss literature, poetry, art, and we sometimes respond to the questions he asks us about our personal life, our family, our profession ... This is a *savoir-faire* that, in France, comes from the tradition of institutional psychotherapy as it was practised in certain psychiatric wards.

Freud (1950a) used the expression of *Nebenmensch*, our "fellow human", whereas Lacan (1986; 2006, pp. 224–225) spoke of the otherness of our "fellow" man, insisting on the real problem that this poses, seeing as other humans are unassimilable for the subject. What we have discovered seems more like the *Mitmensch*, "the man beside whom we stand", side by side, shoulder to shoulder. Analysands will nevertheless invariably express the wish to return to dream stories and free association. This moment of common experience, albeit real and assuredly necessary, could nevertheless only take place for a determined and limited period of time. From it I have retained that dimension of *sharing the period of uncertainty*, which I allow to seep into the frame of our sessions. This is a notable inflection to our Freudo-Lacanian practice and in no way a regression to idle talk, but rather an ethical necessity. The veritable parameters of the place from which an analyst acts are determined, so it seems, by the psychic wound that no one can escape, seeing as it is collective.

Of all these material changes, it seems that temporality is the parameter most affected. It has become commonplace to critique the generalised acceleration of contemporary life (cf. Rosa, 2015), whose harmful impact on psychic care we can see in France. But is it possible that the analytical frame, and in particular the duration of a session, might remain unperturbed by this question? The question is a formidable one. In opposition to the classical Freudian analysts, Lacan launched a movement to shorten sessions, called "short sessions". He justified this by the use of an interpretive practice that was based on a literal game of signifiers, which sought to elicit the effects of signification as induced by scansion acts, or by interruptions to analysands' utterances. If the underlying metapsychological hypothesis is that psychoanalysis deals with the subject of the signifier structure, and if the subject appears in this structure in an essentially *synchronic* manner, then one may deduce that it is hardly necessary to wait long for it to manifest itself, and interpretive scansion can indeed occur very quickly. This strategy is clearly in opposition to any idea of the subject in analysis who must take his time before achieving narcissistic withdrawal.[5] Taking into account the literalness within signifying associations, or in other words going straight towards the dry-cut symbolic quotient that dreams inversely dilate during psychological image-time, this is Jacques Lacan's innovative contribution, his "return to Freud". And yet, in so doing, he authorised the use of techniques and methods of treatment which, essentially, espouse the spirit of our times: ever going faster. The waiting room is full, we must act fast, ever faster. And this does not concern only the duration of sessions.

Our experience working with psychotic patients, and then with children and adolescents, had already modified our methods, and we took the time we needed, which was not codified as imperatively short, but rather as variable. The pandemic corroborated this idea. It does not perhaps seem to be a radical opposition to the so-called "logical" comprehension that Lacan promoted, and his way of reconstructing the signifying genesis of the ego's typical "certainty" (meaning its fundamental unknowing of the unconscious (Lacan, 1945)), but rather this led me to notice two things: first, that this logical certainty presupposes a social order, or an order that structures discourse, which was articulated in a specific way, in which there was no doubt that every subject was deeply "subjected" to a whole system of common signifiers, of explicit collective ideals, etc. I shall return to this matter shortly. But, second, I observed quite simply that this logical temporality can be embodied concretely only at the very moment when the subject is going through a period of crisis and of collective uncertainty, such as we are presently. Thus understood, Lacan's "time for seeing" is already that in which the collective effects (of the current configuration of daily life, work, health) are seen. This is followed by a "time for understanding" the singularity of each case, since we obviously listen to each patient on a case-by-case basis. As for the "time for concluding" an interpretation, a reminder, a question—this presupposes the two other "times" to occur during the time of a session. A way of reading Lacan in a more logical and abstract way than what he meant would neglect this substrate—especially noticeable during the

---

[5] Which makes of Lacan's critique of narcissism and of withdrawal a central thesis in his position. Cf. the recent essay by Renato Mezan (2020).

current period—since it does not take into account only the ego isolated within its "certainties" and its unknowing of the unconscious, but also solidarity and fraternity during hardship.

But we also believe that the emphasis placed on the symbolic, or on the signifier, is now reaching its limit in praxis. For often in clinical work we are faced with a lack of imagination, or with difficulties in creating a story. At these moments we require tools that, if not unknown, are at the very least unusual in our field of Lacanian analysis.

All is not traumatic: the defection[6] of fantasy as a theoretical and clinical proposition

The health crisis that we are living through is inevitably a traumatic moment for us all: we live with the daily fear for our loved ones and are permanently alarmed by the news. Freud warns us that fear—*Schrek* in German—is the point of "undialectalisability" and irrepresentability, for it is beyond the typical neurotic horizon (cf. Freud, 1920g, 1926d. See also Tyszler, 2010). We must not forget this, since Freudian traumatism is not measured by the psychic experience of pain or by any specific kind of pain. That is the psychological and pain-based popular opinion. As far as psychoanalysis is concerned, trauma is first and foremost a true breach of one's psychic armour, of the very functional mechanisms of the subjective structure. This may certainly manifest itself through a total incapacity to feel psychic pain. Freudian fear attacks the *form* that an experience may take, and one must not allow oneself to become fascinated by its ultimately rich and manifold *contents*.

At the CMPP that I run, we are all the more attentive to the fact of having assumed the delicate responsibility of intervening among a population that no one else wanted to address: the children of migrants, and especially of the masses of Syrians, Iraqis, and Afghans who ended up a few years ago on the pavements of northern Paris, hoping in part to

---

[6] Editors' note: The word "defection" is a neologism that we have retained for its evocative possibilities. It contains the dual meanings of a deficiency or incapacity (a "defect") and designates one who deserts his or her post (a "defector"). In this context, it will refer to patients who have lost or never acquired the capacity to elaborate the "facts" of their existence through imagination, fantasy, or dreams.

make it to the UK. We cooperated with the institutions that receive these refugee families, so that their children may have access to psychoanalytic psychic care. Well before the health crisis, our paedopsychiatric ward in Paris volunteered to help in addressing the migrant crisis. And we were able to see for ourselves to what extent the fear encountered during their journeys of exile had a particular traumatic aspect, linked to the impossibility to mourn. We treated young people, often very young, accompanied by their families or what was left of them, and who had managed to make it all the way to Paris.

We quickly encountered a clinical fact that I would only be able to qualify as a "freezing of temporality". Children would tell or draw the same scenes at each session, the same traumatic scenes of abuse, of murder, of rape which they might have seen or suffered from. Transferentially speaking, it is difficult to bear this freezing of temporality, since we were not dealing with ordinary Freudian repetitions. The same monstrous drawing comes back week after week, identical, with the same identical darkness. Each child was under the care of an individual therapist from our service, who were all very personally invested, but the normal procedures would not suffice. Not to mention the therapists themselves and the great difficulties they had in the face of the breadth of these traumas.

Armed with the experience we had gained, we slowly began realising how counterproductive it was to treat clinical questions when a young subject showed himself to be so devasted in light of what we might call the "all-traumatic". And to my great surprise, the global health crisis, rich as it is in traumatising occurrences, rather reinforced this hypothesis. It is as if our encounter with the children of these abused exiles had prepared us for the new traumatisms of the pandemic, providing us with some tools to deal with it. This is the point I now wish to develop.

It is therefore through the perspective of fantasy and its defection, and not through that of traumatism, that we prefer addressing the matter. Indeed, fantasy is like a window onto a world that suffers from having lost its horizon, whose vanishing point has been destroyed: without a fantasisable future, there is no erotisation of our linking mechanisms. A type of hypochondria may well appear in this context, not as a psychotic reaction but as a defence mechanism against the invisible enemy carried by our neighbours, our friends, our colleagues … our spouse. It is as if hypochondria suddenly became generalised: everyone is infected, everyone can infect everyone else. Suddenly we ascribe a pathogenic and pathological quality to social ties in general.

The question becomes: how do we restore the colours of the fantasmatic scenario?

The problem lies in the fact that we cannot directly shape fantasmatic narratives (i.e. the signifiers of fantasmatic expressions, with their links and permutations, understood herein as based on the logico-verbal pattern of "A child is being beaten"). Any slightly contrived interpretation, which we are apt sometimes to propose (as Freud did) for the hysteric cases, would seem too raw, if not obscene, in the context of trauma. When dealing with children, we nevertheless tend to suggest to parents that they *re-poeticise* their personal and spousal life, so that the child may understand that desire is quite simply still a possibility. If the parental other does not act, the child will remain in this regard immobile and frozen. Re-poeticising takes place through the simplest of acts: offering flowers, holding hands during a walk, performing affectionate gestures. Clinical work has shown to what extent the child's drawing will then take on fresh colours and stop repeating nightmarish scenes filled with monsters of the night.

It is nevertheless through another general proposition that we may characterise what is meant by "restoring the colours" of fantasmatic life. We base ourselves on what we call *imaginations*, in the plural. Following Lacanian imagination (Lacan, 1962a, 1962b), we distinguish between a) the imagination that refers to the "mirror stage" (which Lacan (1949), and then Winnicott (1967) add, following Freud), b) the fantasmatic imagination (that Lacan received from Freud), and c) a third imagination that we call "narrative". In the enterprise that consists in "restoring the colours" of fantasy, it is this third type of imagination that we must call upon.

Let us use an image to give an idea of what we mean: the stained-glass windows of a cathedral. The stained-glass window is a *visual story* whose elements reveal their colours through daylight. This story always recounts the mysteries of life, the great dogmas of faith, the conception we may have of death, but also of love. Just as we must make an effort in order to produce a literal reading of the unconscious, so must we work to decipher the stained-glass window. In Lacanian terms, this story is woven of words, as per the symbolic dimension, but is also laced with "colours", which then produce images and even the stuff of dreams and daydreams. This is the imaginary, which always borders on the real. In other terms, it is beyond any symbolic order that manifests itself as an impossible essential (as is the case with the "mysteries" of religion, first and foremost those of evil and redemption through the death of Christ).

But where shall we find this imagination that I call "narrative"? Where does its specific, revitalising power come from? I'd posit that the power of this narrative imagination is to be found in myths, legends, and fairy-tales. One might say the children but also adults have been cruelly cut off from it. Much ink has been spilt over the decline of our grand narratives (such as that of communist emancipation), which indeed served as the cornerstone for postmodernism (Lyotard, 1979). Will ecology pick up the slack? When confronted with the difficulties of children and ado-lescents, the psychoanalyst might not have to express himself on these ideological and cultural generalities. He cannot but take note of the dry, arid articulations of this universe of rigid signifiers, or of literal and dis-incarnated symbols, more real than symbolic, that offer the sad choice between automated, calculating thinking and cracked, split thinking (schizo-paranoid?).

The defection of fantasy—as if the elements that make up the stained-glass window could no longer vibrate and diffract their rich colours in the sun, and thus animate the elements of the symbolic—confront us with the little-known factor of the *inability to imagine a story, to weave a narrative*. This inability manifests itself overwhelmingly in the psychic life of the children of migrants; it is the anxious reflection not only of a familial and personal disaster, but of a political, social, cultural one, which landed them on the streets of Paris.

This impossibility to create a story has intensified due to the health crisis that we are facing. The scientific data are impossibly difficult to represent (beyond their simple depiction as curves, which mean nothing to children). The generalised uncertainty that we evoked above inhibits *both* symbolisation *and* imaginative elaboration. The coronavirus has propagated all over the world precisely what we have been dealing with for several years with the children of migrants and their precarious par-ents: not exactly traumatic after-effects, but a deficit in the capacity to fantasmatically imagine the world.

That being so, I shall limit myself here to description. These three strands of the imagination (Lacan's mirror, Freudian dream and fantasy, and that which I call "narrative") are tied together, and we must work towards their separation and articulation in the effort to restore the consistency both of the individual strands and of the braid they make together.

To return to the metaphor of the stained-glass window, we may recall that the optical mixing of pure, separate hues according to rational methods was a technique that appeared rather late in history. The history of painting had to await the arrival of impressionism and neo-impressionism. It was Georges Seurat who instigated it with *Un dimanche après-midi à la Grande-Jatte,* but so did Camille Pissaro, his son Lucien, and Paul Signac. The last of these recounts it best:

> The neo-impressionists, just like the impressionists, only keep pure colours on their palette, but they repudiate any mixture on the palette itself, with the exception of contiguous colours on the chromatic circle. [...] But, through the proportional optic mixing of these few pure colours, they obtain an infinite spectrum of hues, from the most intense to the greyest. (Signac, 1899, p. 63)

Restoring light, contrast, and colour to the imagination is just the same for psychoanalysis, where all the strands must exist separately before they can be juxtaposed and finally braided together.

Let us first examine the mirror stage. It is described as part of early childhood, but as a matter of fact it actualises itself all throughout life, a point which is not often highlighted: during adolescence, when the body changes and sexualisation makes its mark, during pregnancy, during various accidents that affect the body and its image, and finally at the dawn of old age, of course. The image in the mirror is solicited by specialised therapists in the treatment of autistic children and of psychotics. But working on the image in the mirror may also be of interest in treating anorexia and bulimia, not to mention the different chronic psychoses where all forms of *mise en scène* and theatricalisation of presence are solicited (notably via art therapy). Let us not forget how we require the simplest of things from a patient, that he or she accept to dress themselves, to mind their appearance before heading to a session, whether private or at an institution. All of this restores colours to the image in the mirror.

Whereas we do not at this stage intervene abruptly in how fantasy is imagined, we must recall that it is in construction since the very first scene, but is also reactualised throughout the erotic life of the senses.

In this regard, it is necessary to recognise that one's intimate and spousal life were deeply affected during lockdown. All over the world, we watched as women suffered from domestic tyranny, but we also saw something less frequently commented, namely a desexualisation in the form of renunciation of any activity with one's partner. The pandemic has, in our opinion, accelerated a tendency that we have reported in our book entitled *Actualité du fantasme de la psychanalyse* (Tyszler, 2019), namely the cessation of all sexuality, the choice of being "asexual".

This is a strange, poorly explained phenomenon, which statistics (concerning mostly Americans) indicate is widespread among an entire class of youth, affecting men more than women, but equally present among homosexuals and heterosexuals. Generalised hypochondria, the fear of anything that stems from the body, is not trivial in this unprecedented "freezing" of fantasy. Practically speaking, in each session of psychoanalysis, when confronted with this hypochondria, we had to address each of the cliches commonly heard about the transmission of the virus. But it was clear that there were more obscure processes taking place in the undercurrents, unconscious processes that were impermeable to explanation, which were clearly not directly related to traumatism, but more precisely due to some alteration in the capacity to fantasise—an alteration that has a relatively independent logic to itself, occasionally intertwining with the traumatic.[7]

---

[7] To give a lateral but important example of our work on image, erotisation, and narration, let us cite a recent experience from the CMPP: the extremely important encounters with exiled women who had come to seek refuge in France due to the ritual sexual mutilations they had undergone in their countries of origin. They left not so much to protect themselves as to shield their daughters. Thanks to the complicit and attentive presence of some of our female psychologist clinicians and of our social workers, these women were able to evoke their sexuality, the types of mutilations they had suffered, the repercussions on their feelings of self-worth, on their capacity to receive and to give in the act of love-making. While trying to remain tactful, we were able to indicate to these mostly young women that they did not have to give up on feminine desire or on the prospect of living with dignity as wives, mothers, lovers, daughters ... We referred some of them to restorative surgery departments, which were beginning to emerge at the time. This kind of intervention is meant to restore one's confidence in both one's image and one's anatomy, not only for the subject but also for her fantasmatic partner. It is also meant to authorise the pleasure and the enjoyments previously forbidden or refused (and we know that feminine sexuality is richer in nuance than what Freud had allowed for back in his day).

Once these two first strands of the imagination have been recalled and specified, what kind of tools have we developed to help in reactivating this "narrative" imagination? How have we adapted what we had elaborated in the context of extreme trauma, with children and migrants, to the moral and psychological crisis provoked by Covid-19?

At the behest of our colleague Ilaria Pirone (who teaches also education science), we set up a workshop called "Mythos". This is a therapeutic group for children on the subject of myths. Some might be surprised by the fact that we read Greek mythology with children who come from such a different culture. This was partly because we did not wish to single out these little exiled subjects in a special workshop meant only for them, but to include them in the programmes set up for the other children and adolescents that they would soon be meeting. Furthermore, Greek myths carry in them stories of a *universality* that children can grasp regardless of their place of origin. In saying this we do not wish to oppose either transcultural psychiatry or ethno-psychiatry, but we nevertheless chose to remain in the tradition of universalism that Freud himself had called upon when he generalised Oedipus for all of humanity (and which the French cherish all the more so, seeing as universalism is a "republican" principle).

How do things work? A child begins reading, since it is always a child who reads or who is assisted in reading. The hero enters the Minotaur's cave, for example. From a certain point of view, time is already frozen, as we already know that no one comes back alive from his encounter with the monster. Nevertheless, the hero continues, just like the child continues reading one word after the next, letter after letter, and there, all of a sudden, a spectacular moment, an *unheimlich* irruption from the mirror: the beast's gaze emerges. We then ask for a moment of silence in the reading, since the following scene is of capital importance: when they lock eyes, Theseus discovers to his astonishment the *childlike* gaze of the Minotaur, seeing as this monster was himself an unsightly child who was cast aside and, as a consequence, became monstrous. Another child picks up the reading and will rush headlong into the threshold of

---

Still, the therapist and the plastic surgeon must know how to *create a story* of the possible changes, which until then had been unthinkable, that is, *beyond fantasmatisation*. In our service, these treatments were extremely moving and educational.

the *real*, that is, the impossible absolute: that Death is going to smite one of our two protagonists.

Following this scene of recognition of their shared humanity, of their shared childhood, the shared exile and shared abandonment, the fight to the death begins. And, in order to win, the hero must strictly imitate the gestures of the monster he is faced with. It is at this moment that the entire fantasmatic imagination of the child is "coloured", as I like to call it, through the spectacular unfolding of the Freudian theme, which must be understood in terms of its structural truth: "A child is being beaten" (or even *killed*). A small child, barely seven years old, once made this incredible remark: "So, when you enter the labyrinth, you become a monster." He was able to interpret better than any us this identification, which only psychoanalysis is quite capable of accepting.

Myth, let it be said once more, has an uncanny ability to link between the distinct registers of temporality and of the coloration of fantasmatic life. Death, love often unrequited or rejected, all the grand themes of psychic life are present in it. Most wonderful of all is that children distinguish very well, and very young, between a myth, a legend, and a fairy tale: "A fairy tale generally ends well"; "A legend, that's in honour of a great figure"; "A myth, that's maybe true"—that's what the child says. Just like the child, psychoanalysis is capable of assigning truth (and not accuracy) to some kinds of discourses. The only slight objection that sometimes arises has to do with the plurality of the gods: "Oh really, there are many gods?" some wonder. We must then put monotheism and polytheism into perspective.

Our "Mythos" workshop thus served us as a laboratory. It was the responses and the reactions of these children to myths, legends, and fairy tales that allowed us to better perceive why it is necessary to distinguish between the ravages of trauma and those related to the defection of fantasy, even though, in many cases, both are bound together. The same therapeutic inventiveness which had been first implemented with the traumatised children of migrants revealed itself to be particularly precious during lockdown, in treating the effects that the Covid-19 crisis had on children. As we may see, it is not about repairing the wounds of the ego, nor is it about reassurance as regards a future of normality. We must rather be able to rearm the capacity to fantasise, while respecting the potentialities of very young subjects for desire. And indeed, in order to be able to conceptualise this slight displacement, imposed on us by circumstance, we had to revise our theoretical positions on two issues: a) the time required to "restore the colours" of imagination through the use of "narrative" imagination (a relatively different time framework than is typically considered from within Lacanian theory); and b) a certain rehabilitation of imagination, whose dimension does not at all appear—in contrast to common Lacanian theory—as the negative site of the illusion of ego and of the sedimentation of symptoms. On the contrary, it having a strong consistency becomes essential for the psychic life of the subject.

Returning to Freud and decompartmentalising psychoanalytical theory

In the global health crisis that we are living through, there is probably a fertile dimension of unknowing that is at work, hiding behind the words that we normally employ, such as "traumatism". I have made use in this chapter of several hitherto unfamiliar expressions: "generalised hypochondria", "freezing of the story". We have yet to systematise their usage in new clinical work, but the Freudian compass guides us. We are fully engaged in the process of elaboration.[8]

This theoretical uncertainty reaffirms, in our opinion, the utility of a certain decompartmentalisation—which is already underway—of the dogmatic traditions of psychoanalysis. In a French paedopsychiatric service, practitioners are quite far removed from any exclusive use of either Freud or Lacan, in contrast to their practice in treating adults. They refer also to the great names of the Anglo-Saxon tradition, such as Winnicott and Melanie Klein, but also to Bion and to many other American and British authors. Even clinicians trained on Lacanian couches seek to remove themselves from the formalistic excesses that stem from a taste for mathematisation present in some Lacanian schools.

---

[8] I have proposed (Tyszler, 2019), in view of the preceding considerations on fantasy, to revisit contemporary clinical work based on the idea of "post-Freudian neurosis" or "neurosis *a*", in reference to Lacan's object (a). But I am well aware of the fact that this all remains to be seen.

We ourselves have learned from Bion's crucial teachings on groups, which is in no way reducible to what Freud had said about group psychology. On the other hand, we have been pleasantly surprised by the references that Freudian or Anglo-American authors have been making to Lacan (cf. *inter al.*, Feher-Gurewich, Tort, & Fairfield, 1999). In Latin America, such a blend is quite common, and does not for all intents and purposes seem to give rise to a mishmash of unrelated ideas. It seems to us that the crisis as we know it will only accelerate the process of schools opening up to one another, and will perhaps allow for a re-enchantment of doctrine.

At any rate, it seems worthwhile to explore the idea of knowing whether the displacement proposed in this chapter, which complexifies the question of traumatism in adding the element of the defection of fantasy, may not share an affinity with some of Bion's famous suggestions. Indeed, one might compare, at least in some respects, the idea of "narrative" imagination with that of *reverie* that the British master suggests. In the same spirit, is it not possible that the displacement that I am suggesting, as regards the formal primacy of the Lacanian signifier and of the symbolic order, might allow us to make use of Bion's notion of the "container"? Finally, it seems worthwhile to me to note that these displacements and these reorderings stem from a *practical* origin, and that this origin is the "therapy group" with children. It is the way in which they grasped the myths we proposed that gives clinical credence to my proposition, in particular because what seemed valid for children who had been extremely traumatised by the violence of exile was also pertinent in negotiating the difficult consequences of the current health crisis, which affects so many more lives. At the current state of our reflection, all of this clearly remains hypothetical. Let us simply say that this opening towards Bion does not really stem from a confrontation between theories. It results from practical changes imposed on us by extraordinary circumstances.

Speaking more generally, psychoanalysis might find it useful to revisit some of its concepts not for the sake of difficult exegetic or conceptual joustings, but rather because reality beckons. In order for this pressure coming from reality to be truly fertile, we should not, in my opinion, sweep everything under the rug as "traumatisms", and we should take into consideration the notions of fantasy and of narrative imagination in and of themselves. In doing so, hitherto theoretically exclusive approaches would reinvigorate each other under a new light. In the best-case scenario, crisis kindles jolts of inventiveness and renewal.

The health crisis, at any rate, leads us to ponder a collection of elements situated halfway between traditional nosography and true innovations. Some of the elements we were expecting include of course widespread phobic reactions due to lockdown, whereby some subjects remain terrified by public space, whether in public transport or even in the street. Some youth have taken the virus as a pretext to isolate themselves even further, limiting their social exchanges to social media. Obsessive washing rituals have intensified, seeing as it is now commonly agreed that they are part of the "preventive measures" required and demanded by all. Manifestations of collective hysteria have also made a comeback, sometimes in the form of protests or provocations in the face of governmental instructions. This is taking place all over the world, sometimes paradoxically, at the behest of certain world leaders themselves ... There is an overarching climate of paranoia, in particular as regards anything to do with medical advice and instruction, ranging from "social distancing" to eventual treatments and vaccines.

Many overtly think that we are living through some sort of vast conspiracy. This form, of what may be called "ordinary paranoia", is not strictly speaking psychosis but has much more serious collective effects, since it lumps together individuals as if they made up some "one" thing. Let us note in passing that complex psychic troubles accompany the convalescence of coronavirus victims. Somatically speaking, the after-effects are many, affecting various organs including the central nervous system. There is a whole slew of neuropathic and somato-psychiatric disorders that researchers are only beginning to explore (this recalls what happened in the 1920s, with von Economo and encephalitis). A specific form of hypochondria tends to emerge, since some patients who seem to be in good health, having recovered from the virus, complain of diffuse pains that are impossible to identify (for the time being). Not to mention depression. Some cases are very understandable, due to effects on the life, work, and future of many. There are other, more complex cases, which feed into the semiology of "bipolarity". In these specific cases, we are not yet able to decide what is truly new and what is less so. But it is precisely this time of uncertainty that dominates us all, and forces us to adjust all the more so, on a case-by-case basis, without jumping to conclusions. Should we coin names for new syndromes? No one can tell.

But that's not all. There is also the unpredictable, unprecedented movements of subjectivity which we cannot classify as easily as in the aforementioned examples. And psychoanalysis remains an excellent method, if not the only method, to pay them the attention they deserve. We thus spoke of the notion of fantasy. But there is also drive, and especially the death drive, whose historical importance is undeniable. One need only turn on the radio or leaf through the morning papers to encounter it: even in a period as traumatised by the virus as our own, acts of war and of barbarity persist. Man is never quite done with his destructivity. It's not finished, it keeps growing, just like the Freudian *Drang*, just like the (death) drive. Primo Levi said that each of us was perhaps the unwitting Cain of some Abel whom he will strike down in the middle of a field. Freud (1915b, p. 292) takes up this theme in his own terms, in "Thoughts for the Times on War and Death", and tells us that "hence the primaeval history of man is filled with murder. Even to-day, the history of the world which our children learn at school is essentially a series of murders of peoples."

We would then need to "redialectalise" this axiom, and rejoin Freud's effort to offer an answer to the discontents present in our civilisation. The current health crisis, and whatever is brewing for the years to come, should most certainly be envisaged under the light of what it tells us of the death drive. The ambivalence that entire swathes of the population are expressing in regard to what should or should not be done is shared the world over. Some are unfazed by the death of the elderly and the weak; it's natural selection, they claim. Others, more learned, argue that it is the economy that dictates everything, and that the most important thing we can do is consume. The most contradictory arguments come from movements with strong mechanisms of splitting, of denial, of the quasi-loss of any notion of reality. While writing this essay at this time, we notice that most of the clinical words used are hereby subject to some future reshuffling that will clarify itself with time. Sticking to our *terra firma* of certitudes, it seems to us all the more so necessary to return, through fantasy or identification, to the cornerstones of the Freudian edifice.

Let us conclude provisionally with the words of a wonderful and great philosopher, Rachel Bespaloff (Bespaloff & Weil, 1943, p. 90), exiled to the United States during WWII, who killed herself in 1949:

> The crises which disrupt the individual do not alter the constants of human Becoming. History remains a tangled succession of catastrophes and breathing spaces, of problems provisionally set, resolved or conjured away. But the man who has felt the terrible pressure of total impotence and survived that experience does not resign himself to living as if it had never happened to him. He tries to keep hold of the supreme resources revealed to him by despair.

Jean-Jacques Tyszler
with Dr Corinne Tyszler, paedopsychiatrist
Summer 2020

Translated from French by Shahar Fineberg

References

Bespaloff, R., & Weil, S. (1943). *War and The Iliad.* New York: NYRB Classics, 2005.

Bollas, C. (2018). *Meaning and Melancholia, Life in the Age of Bewilderment.* London: Routledge.

Feher-Gurewich, J., & Tort, M. (Eds.) (1999). *Lacan and the New Wave in American Psychoanalysis.* New York: The Other Press.

Freud, S. (1915b). Thoughts for the times on war and death. *S. E., 14*: 275–300. London: Hogarth.

Freud, S. (1920g). *Beyond the Pleasure Principle. S. E., 18*: 3–66. London: Hogarth.

Freud, S. (1926d). Inhibitions, symptoms and anxiety. *Psychoanalytic Quarterly, 5*: 415–443.

Freud, S. (1950a). A project for a scientific psychology. *S. E., 1*: 330–332. London: Hogarth.

Lacan, J. (1945). Logical time and the assertion of anticipated certainty. In: *Écrits* (pp. 161–175). New York: W. W. Norton, 1966.

Lacan, J. (1949). The mirror stage as formative of the *I* function as revealed in psychoanalytic experience. In: *Écrits* (pp. 75–81). New York: W. W. Norton, 1966.

Lacan, J. (1962a). *L'Identification, séminaire IX*. Paris: Le Seuil.

Lacan, J. (1962b). *Anxiety: The Seminar of Jacques Lacan Book X*. Cambridge: Polity, 2014.

Lacan, J. (1986). *The Seminar of Jacques Lacan: The Ethics of Psychoanalysis. Book VII*. New York: W. W. Norton, 1997.

Lacan, J. (2006). *D'un Autre à l'autre*. Paris: Le Seuil, pp. 224–225.

Lyotard, J.-F. (1979). *The Postmodern Condition*. Minneapolis, MN: University of Minnesota Press, 1984.

Mezan, R. (2020). *Lacan, Stein et le narcissisme primaire*. Paris: Ithaque.

RFP (2018). Lacan aujourd'hui. *Revue française de psychanalyse, 82*(4).

Rosa, H. (2015). *Social Acceleration: A New Theory of Modernity*. New York: Columbia University Press.

Signac, P. (1899). *D'Eugène Delacroix au néo-impressionnisme*. Paris: H. Fleury Libraire-Éditeur, 1911.

Tyszler, J.-J. (2010). Freud et le traumatisme. *Journal français de psychiatrie, 1*(36) : 3–4.

Tyszler, J.-J. (2019). *Actualité du fantasme de la psychanalyse*. Paris: Stilus.

Winnicott, D. W. (1967). Mirror-role of mother and family in child development. In: *Playing and Reality* (pp. 111–118). New York: Basic Books, 1971.

Part V

Clinical journals

CHAPTER 12

Katabasis, anabasis: working in a post-ICU Covid-19 unit in a public hospital

Steven Jaron
Paris, France

adame B lies on her bed in the hospital room, rolled up into a ball and pressing her knees tightly into her abdomen. Her face writhes in pain and she's gasping for breath. She tries to calm the pain and slow the breathing down by hyperventilating herself. She loosens her knees and unfolds her legs. In what seems like nothing more than a split second, she looks up and notices me, although my feeling is that she's already sensed my presence in the room. It's as if she knows she's being observed but does not wish to let the observer know that she's aware of him. I introduce myself and tell her that my medical doctor colleague has asked me to see her.

She doesn't understand what's happened to her. Between grimaces and controlled breathing she explains that she'd been out with friends having a drink and telling them about her work with an NGO in sub-Saharan Africa. She then collapsed on the café terrace. Her friends thought she was choking on something she'd eaten but she managed to tell them that she was having trouble breathing. She lost consciousness. An ambulance was called and she was brought to the hospital. Her evening out took place only two days before the lockdown measures were put into place in France, on March 17. She was among the first to be hospitalised in the newly organised Covid-19 units throughout the country.

She was seemingly well prepared for working in perilous conditions. Ever since she was a young girl, she'd wanted to help others. When she was old enough, she trained in first aid and became involved in non-profit organisations. She left for a conflict zone as soon as she could. She felt in her element there. The problem, which she did not at first realise as such, was that leaving France meant leaving her boyfriend, too. She felt that she could handle the temporary separation but he wasn't so sure. He became involved with another woman. She was devastated by the betrayal. After all, she was sacrificing so much of herself in order to go and try to help the destitute.

While she's recounting her story, she's still trying to slow down her breathing. She's also fumbling with an oximeter, clumsily placing it on her index finger. She calms down when she reads the measurement. "It's all OK," she informs me. "I'm getting enough oxygen." I'm surprised to see her manipulating the instrument, which isn't part of the hospital equipment but counts among her own belongings. Her face screws up and she grasps at her stomach again. I'm struck by the auto-eroticism of the gesture of quantifying her blood-oxygen value on her own and I suggest to her that she's trying to care for herself, whereas those who are important to her had let her down. She looks at me like I'm half crazy.

I ask Mme B how long she'd stayed in the other hospital. It was only two days. They'd run all the tests possible to see if she had contracted the virus. Everything came back negative. Patients were streaming in. They had to free up a bed and she was transferred to our hospital.

I meet my colleague who'd first spoken to me about Mme B. She confesses that she was uncomfortable with her. "This is the kind of patient I have a lot of trouble handling. Nothing explains her symptoms. To all appearances the patient is experiencing intense abdominal pain and intermittent respiratory distress but the clinical examinations haven't revealed any organic disorder. She can't be discharged, if only out of precaution." She asks me how it's gone with her. It appears to me that she's a hysteric. "Conversion disorder?" she asks, taken aback but, at the same time, intrigued. Her symptoms mimic those which individuals suffering from a severe respiratory infection have. Her self, in Christopher Bollas's words, has *"transformed into an event"* (Bollas, 2000, p. 108;

his emphasis). The outward event enacts her unconscious conflict. My colleague finds this explanation compelling and we agree that the coronavirus has not only taken hold of individuals physically but also mentally.

Given the limitations of Madame B's hospitalisation, it won't be possible to go too far into a psychotherapy but it might be helpful to start to connect her symptoms with her history. This is what I do during my following meetings with her when we elaborate together, in an almost playful way, her florid gestures. Behind the troubled breathing and abdominal pain, we imagine a woman in labour but wholly on her own, as if she were giving birth without a midwife. The symptoms largely recede. Once she is discharged, Mme B might begin further psychotherapy with an analyst colleague closer to her home.

Another patient I see repeatedly during the peak period for only brief interviews—all he can bear—has had a tooth removed in order to facilitate intubation. He is thin and tall and wears a yarmulke, while sitting in an armchair. When Monsieur P awoke from the medically induced coma, he noticed the tooth was missing. This occurred in another hospital, since ours does not have an intensive care unit. At this point, he only speaks about how much he's vexed because this particular tooth was used to anchor his denture. He doesn't express any affect and appears indifferent to the month he was unconscious while on a ventilator, and even to my presence. An exercise pedaller is at his feet, which he uses to strengthen his legs. He's physically weak and undergoing physical therapy. I observe him looking down at the floor and moving his arms and hands around himself as if he were searching for the lost object. It is a matter of a repetition compulsion in the face of unspoken and perhaps unspeakable actual traumatic experience—that of losing his breath and fearing it could not be found again; that of dying—that cannot yet be recalled and worked through. His movements suggest to me that he feels the primitive anxiety of falling to pieces. The repetition compulsion appears to fill in what is missing, the tooth. But not only the tooth. More importantly, what's missing is an implicated and conscious understanding of the trauma or, as Thomas Ogden writes in reference to Winnicott, "the fear of breakdown is a fear of a breakdown that has *already happened*, but has *not yet been experienced*" (Ogden, 2014, p. 55; his emphasis).

Still another patient, Monsieur D, a sixty-year-old man, is recovering satisfactorily with the help of non-invasive oxygen therapy and he's physically well enough to return home. During the morning staff meeting, however, my colleagues describe him as "depressed and withdrawn". I go to see him in his room. He's sitting on his made-up bed, his belongings packed in a small suitcase beside him. He's expecting to see me and invites me to sit in an armchair a few feet away from the bed. I ask how he's feeling. He tries to smile as he tells me that he doesn't really know. I see that he's confused. When he explains that he'll be discharged that afternoon, I feel that his departure might be premature. His friend will come to pick him up. The friend won't be allowed to enter the hospital—no visitors are permitted—but an orderly will bring him down to meet him and the friend will drive him back to his apartment. Given his look of confusion, I want to know something about his cognitive state and ask if he understands why his friend is not allowed to enter the hospital and come up to his room. He says that he does.

I remark to myself that till then Monsieur D hasn't told me anything about how he's feeling. I ask him how long he's been in our hospital. "Just over a week." He'd previously been in another hospital for three weeks, two on ventilation while in an induced coma. He doesn't recall anything of that time. I ask him how he came to the other hospital. "In an ambulance." Again, a perfunctory answer. He then develops his reply a little. He'd been alone in the apartment. His wife was already hospitalised in still another hospital. She'd fallen ill a few days before he did. He's silent. I ask myself what lies below the silence as I look at him from behind my mask and see his frail body. Monsieur D's face seems thin and his neck and shoulders hardly seem able to support his head. He tells me that the staff have been wonderful, that they've even contacted his building's concierge who will go out and do some grocery shopping for him since he'll be confined to his apartment. I sense that he's trying to reassure himself about the conditions of his departure from the hospital.

I begin to think about what he's been telling me. Again, nothing about how he's feeling or how he experienced—is experiencing—his ordeal. His speech is descriptive and he emphasises procedures. I have no representation of his inner world other than what seems to be its emptiness. We sit quietly facing each other. I let the silence do the work of opening up a space in which Monsieur D might begin to express himself.

He begins to speak about his apartment, telling me that he's not sure what he's going to find there when he returns home. He becomes quiet again as his gaze turns towards the window. I follow it intentionally, telling myself that this might be a way of offering a counter-cathexis to his psychic withdrawal. Let's share the reverie and see what happens. The Covid-19 unit is up on the fifth floor of the hospital, its top floor, and together we look out on to the Parisian skyline consisting mainly of grey rooftops under a cloudy sky. I'm comforted in my technical wager when I hear him freely associate with the bleak cityscape outside.

"The apartment is essentially empty, save a few pieces of furniture. There's nothing on the walls."

I ask why there's nothing.

He explains that shortly before he and his wife became ill, just before the virus spread wildly, the apartment had been repainted. The couple had been excited about doing it over but repainting required a great deal of preparation, which had tired them as they removed everything from the walls and put most of the furniture into storage. They then moved back a week or so before his wife had to be hospitalised, followed by his own hospitalisation.

"There's really nothing there, it's all quite empty."

Again he's silent.

He goes on to speak. "My case was relatively light. Not so for my wife. I learned that she wasn't going to make it even as I was being taken to the hospital. I was feeling very weak before then, I was feverish and coughing. My daughter told me I had to call the ambulance right away. We knew that my wife was dying. She's been cremated, her ashes are in an urn." It occurs to him that he doesn't know where the urn is. "Everything has happened so quickly," he says, placing each word carefully as if he were laying the foundations on which an edifice will be built. He then tries to reassure himself again by recalling that the concierge will take care of the grocery shopping, that everything has been looked after.

The crisis that Monsieur D had undergone—seeing his wife become ill followed by his own illness and then her death—had little if any meaning for him at the time I saw him. The experience of psychic pain went unexpressed. In the brief time of our encounter (but a single meeting) it was nevertheless possible to help him initiate a mental process in which a representation of his fear, confusion, and loss could take shape along the lines, to quote Howard Levine, "of weaving a path to repair the unity of a torn fabric" (2013, p. 53).

* * *

From the middle of March through the remainder of spring, I held sessions over a remote setting from my office very early in the morning and then later in the afternoon and into the evening (Jaron, 2020). Most of the day, however, was spent at the Quinze-Vingts Hospital, which specialises in the treatment of patients presenting ophthalmological disorders and conditions. When the health crisis arose, a post-intensive care unit was set up. We took on patients recovering from the coronavirus and who had been hospitalised in other Parisian hospitals which needed to free up beds in their ICUs for patients requiring ventilation and heavy sedation over weeks of time. In other words, the patients we saw in this unit had been through the worst of it elsewhere; we monitored them further until they'd regained sufficient strength before moving on to a centre for specialised physical therapy or returning home.

When we first reorganised the Quinze-Vingts in the second half of March in order to receive the Covid-19 patients (while still seeing the regular patients), my department head approached me for a discussion. We sat in my office and there he told me that he wanted me on staff for as long as possible in order to work with patients and their families. (Contact with family members would occur only by telephone.) I was struck by the expression, *as long as possible.* It was still early in the epidemic and many questions were asked about contagion and protecting oneself from infection. Our hospital was fortunate not to suffer from the material penury others did (though at times we were only a few days from exhausting our stock) but some of the personnel had already become infected. It goes without saying how conscious I was of the potential danger to my mental and physical health while working in this setting. Death anxiety was an essential part of my countertransference in doubtless all the clinical encounters I engaged in.

Public transport was discouraged as the virus spread and so I took to my bicycle to go to and from the hospital. One morning in the beginning of April, just after I passed by the Pitié-Salpêtrière Hospital and neared the Austerlitz railway station, the little traffic was redirected by cones positioned on the boulevard. As I approached the train station there were lines of armed military police in black uniforms motioning authoritatively. What on earth were they doing so early in the otherwise peaceful, quiet morning with no one, other than a few delivery vehicle drivers and the occasional cyclist like me, to police? I then recalled a news report I'd read the previous evening. As Parisian hospitals had reached their capacity, a high-speed train was being equipped with ventilators and staffed by medical personnel to evacuate Covid-19 patients to hospitals in Brittany. The train would be leaving from the Austerlitz station. Clearly, the government didn't want anyone interfering with the operation. Riding my bicycle with the military police guarding the Covid-19 patients only a few feet away, I was in the throes of disbelief at what I would be facing in only a matter of minutes with my own patients at the Quinze-Vingts.

From a psycho-geographical perspective, the journey to the hospital aroused in my mind an image of a descent. My private office is located on the outer edge of the left bank of the city and the Quinze-Vingts Hospital is on the right bank, not far from the Seine and near the Bastille. The bicycle ride thus took me downwards to near the centre of the city where over millions of years the river has cut a depression into the earth. All hospital entrances and exits had been sealed in order to restrict movement in and out of the building, save the main entrance. Normally patients, visitors, and personnel come and go as they wish. Now they were obliged to pass through a *zone de tri*, or processing centre, in which anyone entering the hospital would have their temperature checked and be given hand sanitiser and a surgical mask by nurses in full protective clothing, a kind of second skin. Arriving at the hospital after my twenty-minute long bicycle ride in the very early spring, my body temperature was always frightfully low. In a temporary state of hypothermia, I might have been dying. As the nurses' faces were fully covered, I could not recognise them as they greeted me. Shivering, I felt embarrassed as one of them would aim the thermometer at my forehead and read the temperature. It averaged a very chilly 32 or 33 degrees Celsius (89.6 or 91.4 degrees Fahrenheit). In order to ease my awkwardness at not recognising my colleagues, I would joke, in a moment of gallows humour expressing my ambient death anxiety, that I was undead in a zombie apocalypse. I would then go to my office, warm myself up, and prepare for work. Hours later, after my shift had ended, I was so relieved that I imagined myself returning to the earth's surface.

Every day was a cyclical *katabasis, anabasis* which began with a descent into the cold and was followed by a warm resurfacing, relatively speaking, at least. This cycle brought to mind those terrible lines addressed to Aeneas by the Cumaean Sibyl as he passes into the Underworld:

> [...] facilis descensus Averno:
> noctes atque dies patet atri ianua Ditis;
> sed revocare gradum superasque evadere ad auras,
> hoc opus, hic labor est. [...] (Virgil, *Aeneid, VI*: lines 126–129,
> quoted in Heaney, 2016)

which Seamus Heaney translates as:

> It is easy to descend into Avernus
> Death's dark door stands open day and night.
> But to retrace your steps and get back to upper air
> That is the task, that is the undertaking. (Heaney, 2016, *Aeneid,*
> *VI*: lines 174–177)

Heaney, I should note, is alluding in his translation to at least two of his works: his second collection of poetry, *Door into the Dark* (1969), in which he describes the entrance to a forge as "a dark door" (a poem is forged, as is the conscience, individual or national), and *Human Chain*, his final collection (2010), in which he writes about his recovery from a stroke (returning "to upper air") but also the birth of a first grandchild, all the while using *Aeneid, VI* as an archetypal template. Throughout his writing life, Seamus Heaney saw Virgil as a contemporary.

Ideally I would like to set the weeks spent in the hospital's Covid-19 unit as "in parenthesis", to use David Jones's formula, an expression which gave the title to his poem-testimony of soldiering in the Great War. "This writing is called 'In Parenthesis,'" Jones states in the preface,

> because I have written it in a kind of space in between—I don't
> know quite what—but as you turn aside to do something; and
> because for us amateur soldiers [...] the war itself was a paren-
> thesis—how glad we thought we were to step outside its brackets

at the end of '18—and also because our curious type of existence here is altogether in parenthesis. (Jones, 1937, p. xv)

This way of putting it, "in parenthesis", fits how I feel about those weeks when the pandemic first threatened France with havoc. They have settled, however superficially, "in a kind of space in between": it is a liminal space between the time before the coronavirus spread, and now that it has been mostly contained, at least in this country and at least for the time being. This is but fantasy. In reality, the parenthesis did not close for David Jones at the end of 1918—he suffered breakdowns throughout his life, and, further, the onset of another war was only a few years off. Nor is our own parenthesis definitively closed. We are conscious (the degree of awareness varies from individual to individual) that the coronavirus has been neither wholly eradicated nor entirely subdued; it may well flare up again, taking with it its victims and once more stoking the flames of fear among the general population (a good portion will remain in denial).

Laying out the setting of his work for the reader, David Jones shifts between the first person singular—writing about himself as an infantry soldier—and the first person plural—"*our* curious type of existence" (my emphasis). His experience is his own, it bears the indelible imprint of a particular subjectivity. But he believes that it reflects the experience of others. This articulation of shared experience brings to mind another poem-testimony of hell experienced "in between". I am thinking of *The Inferno*, whose first line reads:

> *Nel mezzo del cammin di nostra vita*
> Midway in the journey of our life (Dante Alighieri, 1320, pp. 2–3)

The poet is in the middle not only of *his* life but *our* life. This first verse is followed by "*mi ritrovai*" ("I found myself"), which indicates that the poet is nevertheless speaking about himself in the first person. And he is speaking about a time that is occurring again, as the prefix *ri-* indicates: in telling, *there* he finds himself once more: a period that is past but is relived in its recounting. Further, when he uses the plural *nostra*, he is suggesting that the experiences his poem conveys are emblematic for others; that is, for others who might relate to what he is describing. In the instance of Dante, it is a matter of time: the events that he recounts, like those in David Jones's poem, take place "in a kind of space in between". But Dante is not merely telling a story; he is, more pertinently, describing *a state of mind* characterised by disarray or mental confusion. Charles Singleton's otherwise very helpful translation only partially captures the *shape* of the mental states that the Italian expresses: *Nel mezzo del* may also be rendered as "In the middle of the". I wish to emphasise the pictographic dimension of the words because their pattern is something of a mirror. If one breaks apart the key word, the pivotal sign, *mezzo*, we obtain: *nel mez / zo del*.

The rest of the opening tercet reads:

> [...] *per una selva oscura,*
> *che la diritta via era smarrita.*
> [...] in a dark wood,
> for the straight way was lost (Dante Alighieri, 1320, pp. 2–3)

The mere thought of recollecting the memory of being lost in "a dark wood" fills the poet with "fear" ("*la paura*"), and I imagine him trembling with fright. Those who become disoriented while in the obscurity of the forest have two options: they may back up or forge ahead. Another option is to wait and see, to think before acting. I pause and then return to the opening of the poem, *Nel mezzo del*. In light of the lines that complete the tercet, in consideration of their *après-coup*, the repetition of two letters, *l* and *z*, previously unremarked, becomes significant. The letter *l* is straight and has the solidity of a column while the letter *z* is a wandering zigzag. The shape of the thought informing Dante's poem is depicted in its very first words as if he were saying, "If only were the path straight; it is not and I am deeply confused and fearful."

The frightening state of being *Nel mezzo*, in between, is developed throughout *The Inferno*. One particular moment stands out, however, if only because we come across *mezzo* once again. Well into his testimony of his descent into hell, Dante recounts how he mounts the dragon, Geryon, with his "master" and "author", his "guide" and "leader" Virgil seated behind as they prepare to reach deeper circles still. This occurs in the seventeenth canto, that is, in the very middle of *The Inferno* (comprised of thirty-four cantos). Dante offers what seems to me a highly significant detail of the mounting of Geryon. Virgil is already astride the "*fiero animale*" ("fierce beast") (Dante Alighieri, 1320, pp. 178–179) and he advises the poet, encouraging him when he's fearful:

> *Or sie forte et ardito.*
> *Omai si scende per sì fatte scale;*
> *Monta dinanzi, ch'i' voglio esser mezzo,*
> *Sì che la coda non possa far male.*
> > Now be strong and bold:
> henceforward the descent is by such stairs as these.
> Mount in front, for I wish to be in between,
> > so that the tail may not harm you. (Dante Alighieri, 1320, pp. 178–179)

Geryon's "*coda aguzza*", his "pointed tail" (Dante Alighieri, 1320, pp. 172–173) will swing wildly and stealthily (the sin of fraud is the subject of the canto), and Virgil, not only acting as guide, likewise seeks to protect Dante from its thrashing. He therefore "wishes to be *mezzo*", "middle", or positioned between the tail and the poet. *Mezzo* recalls not only the opening line of the poem, in which Dante is "in the middle", but also the place this particular canto is situated. The quality of being in between, of dwelling on the threshold of dark horror, terror, and fear, defines the mental atmosphere of *The Inferno* as Virgil and Dante fuse into one another—each is *mezzo*—while on Geryon's back.

A contemporary commentary with David Jones (for whom Dante was not, in his own estimation, a contemporary as such because, he surmised, he was unable to read him in the original) brings out another significant quality of Geryon as a poetic figure. Ossip Mandelstam draws our attention not to the poem's contents but to a specific aspect of Dante's work, the "link" "as a continuous metamorphosis of the substrate which is for him poetic matter" (1933, pp. 42–43). He suggests that this operation is possible because the phonetic, material, and semantic components of poetic matter possess a transformative potential, whose precedent is Ovid's *Metamorphoses*, which he terms "convertibility" or "mutability" (1933, p. 88). Clarence Brown describes this process as "the subtle chain of association and implication which causes one image to give birth to another and that to a third, imparting to the whole a sense, however unconscious, of inevitable rightness and logic" (1965, p. 61; see also Brown, 1973, p. 285). Mandelstam adds that the poem itself, consisting of poetic matter, is the result of a "creative explosion" which, he argues, is more important than the poem's syntax, which "muddles" or "obfuscates" (1933, p. 87). True poetic matter is subject not only to "convertibility" but also to "reversibility" (Mandelstam, 1933, p. 88): a nominative may and *should* be reversed into a dative if there is to be an interdependency between the poem and its interpretation. These principles of substitution and reversibility are likewise an essential part of Freud's thought. They are observed most frequently in the dream work. Manifest content could express the contrary of latent material (Freud, 1916–17, p. 178). Or the beginning of a dream might foretell its end (Freud, 1909a, pp. 230–231). This is akin to how a psychoanalyst listens to a patient's speech, attuned to possibilities of what Christopher Bollas calls "trains of thought" "linked by some hidden logic that connects seemingly disconnected ideas" (2009, p. 6) expressed in moments of free association. The obscurity of the unconscious, then, may be thought of as a subterranean river (Acheron, Styx, Lethe) of thought, a stream of unconsciousness, which we seek to bring to light through interpretation in the course of a psychoanalysis. *Katabasis* radically transforms into *anabasis*.

If Virgil's *"ombra"*, his "shade" (Dante Alighieri, 1320, pp. 6–7) is a contemporary to Dante, and if Dante is a contemporary to Mandelstam just as Virgil is to Seamus Heaney, both antique poets are contemporaries to Freud. But Freud does more than undertake an imagined dialogue with these figures; in a sense, he merges with them. It is more than a matter of stating his affinity or kinship; it is nothing less than the introjection of the object. We observe this in his letter of August 6, 1899 to Fliess, in which he writes (almost light-heartedly) concerning how he'd conceived the structure of *The Interpretation of Dreams*:

> The whole thing is planned on the model of an imaginary walk. At the beginning, the dark forest of authors (who do not see the trees), hopelessly lost on wrong tracks. Then a concealed pass through which I lead the reader—my specimen dream with its particularities, details, indiscretions, bad jokes—and then suddenly the high ground and the view and the question: which way do you wish to go now? (Freud, 1899, p. 365)

The allusions to *Aeneid* and *The Inferno* are not even thinly dissimulated; they belong rather to the unconscious fabric of Freud's thought. This also occurs early in chapter seven, the final chapter of the dream book:

> For it must be clearly understood that the easy and agreeable portion of our journey lies behind us. Hitherto, unless I am greatly mistaken, all the paths along which we have travelled have led us towards the light—towards elucidation and fuller understanding. But as soon as we endeavor to penetrate more deeply into the mental processes involved in dreaming, every path will end in darkness. (Freud, 1900a, p. 511)

Freud further quotes, consciously, here, *Aeneid* as the epigraph to the dream book—*Flectere si nequeo superos, Acheronta movebo*: "If I cannot bend the Higher Powers, I will move the Infernal Regions" (Freud, 1900a, p. ix and 608 note 1)—and in chapter seven, in the course of his discussion of primary and secondary process in which he emphasises that the "*interpretation of dreams is the Via regia which leads to the knowledge of the unconscious in psychic life*" (p. 608; translation modified and as quoted in Starobinski, 1987, p. 396). Jean Starobinski suggests that Freud's quotation not once but twice of this line from Virgil, referring to the dream as vehicle for lifting what is repressed in the unconscious, makes it a framing motif of the book's argument (1987, p. 396f.).

Freud, then, will both enlighten and seek enlightenment, he will guide and be guided while having strayed from the "straight path" in the "dark wood" of the unconscious's "Infernal Regions". In this foundational work of psychoanalysis, he has done nothing if not fuse himself into the reasoning and purpose of Virgil and Dante.

* * *

By bicycle (Geryon, in a manner of speaking) I return to my office after a morning shift which lasts well into the afternoon and begin my therapies and analyses over the telephone or video platform, finishing just before 8pm. I cannot count the number of patients I've seen at the hospital and each of those I see privately are facing the complexities of lockdown, set against their respective psychic organisations. I have alluded only to

Madame B, a hysteric; Monsieur P, flooded with primitive anxiety and struggling against actual traumatic neurosis; and Monsieur D, as he begins to emerge from a psychic retreat while sketching out a representation of his emptiness and perhaps face his psychic pain. I feel exhausted and over-whelmed, and I'm relieved to close my office for the evening and begin the short walk back home where I "reach the surface".

I leave the building and I'm out on the avenue d'Italie. Night is falling and not a single car passes on the deserted avenue, there are no passers-by and all the restaurants and cafés are closed. There's what seems to be a perfect silence which I relish for a moment before it's broken by the sound of a window opening and then another. An air horn blasts, as if there were a sports stadium nearby. Whistles blow and pots are banged with wooden spoons. I look upwards and see apartment dwellers leaning out of their windows, whistling and cheering. I truly don't know what's happening. I'm alone in the street. But I quickly realise what the din is all about. It will become a regular evening occurrence for the weeks to come. A lump forms in my throat. No one applauding above knows how I've spent the day and I can hardly admit that what they're doing is intended for people like me. I tell myself that I don't want any of this but it's something, I suppose, that I have to accept. Their intentions, after all, are sincere and it's surely good for the collective morale. It's not that I don't want their expressions of gratitude; rather, I don't want *any* of this for I am deeply conscious of how our world has changed and the great and long-lasting turmoil this change has plunged us into. More still, I'm troubled by another expression of this radical change arising in the social body: there have been incidents of attacks against hospital person-nel through physical violence, psychological intimidation, and property destruction (the actors, certainly far fewer than the 8pm applauders, presume us to be vectors for contagion and thus subject to stigmatisa-tion), and the director of human resources has circulated a police memo detailing how, when off duty, we should keep the fact that we work in a hospital discreet lest we ourselves become targets. There are thus two opposing features to the viral group's unconscious, what Freud calls the "polarity of love and hatred with a hypothetical opposition between the life and death drives" (1921c, p. 102, note 1 [translation modified]), and I find myself, along with my fellow health practitioners, impossibly on both sides of it.

"Or sie forte et ardito."

The next morning, I'm back at my office to hold sessions over the telephone or a video platform. A school playground lies just a few feet from the window of my waiting room. Patients who have their sessions during the daytime come into the consulting room and regularly remark on the joyful chatter and cries they hear coming from the outside. Birdsong also sounds from a group of trees nearby. The children's revelry and the birds' twerps and tweets may go unnoticed for some while for others they resonate with something intimate. It is unexceptional to state that associations differ from patient to patient.

During the deeply unsettling height of the Covid-19 time, I did not receive any of my patients in the office itself. While speaking to each other over one device or another, none mentioned what they'd at times spoken of while on the couch, namely, the sounds entering the waiting room window. As I pondered this detail in the change in the setting, Virgil and *Aeneid* came back to mind and in particular the horrifying thought that, as its etymology suggests, in Avernus there are no birds. I felt a moment of nauseating silence opening within myself as I imagined that there are no groups of children playing happily, or viciously, for that matter, in the Underworld, neither in Virgil's nor in Dante's.

Steven Jaron
March–May 2020

References

Bollas, C. (2000). *Hysteria*. London: Routledge.

Bollas, C. (2009). Free association. In: *The Evocative Object World* (pp. 5–45). London: Routledge.

Brown, C. (1965). The prose of Mandelstam. In: *The Prose of Osip Mandelstam: The Noise of Time, Theodosia, The Egyptian Stamp* (pp. 3–65). Translated from the Russian by C. Brown. Princeton, NJ: Princeton University Press.

Brown, C. (1973). *Mandelstam*. Cambridge: Cambridge University Press.

Dante Alighieri (1320). *The Divine Comedy: Inferno*. Italian text with English translation by C. S. Singleton. Princeton, NJ: Princeton University Press, 1970.

Freud, S. (1899). Letter of August 6th, 1899. *The Complete Letters of Sigmund Freud to Wilhelm Fliess, 1887–1904* (pp. 365–366). J. Moussaieff Masson (Ed. & Trans.). Cambridge, MA: The Belknap Press of Harvard University Press, 1985.

Freud, S. (1900a). *The Interpretation of Dreams. S. E.,* 4–5. London: Hogarth.

Freud, S. (1909a). Some general remarks on hysterical attacks. *S. E.,* 9: 229–234. London: Hogarth.

Freud, S. (1916–17). *Introductory Lectures on Psycho-Analysis. S. E.,* 15–16. London: Hogarth.

Freud, S. (1921c). *Group Psychology and the Analysis of the Ego. S. E.,* 18: 69–143. London: Hogarth.

Heaney, S. (1969). *Door into the Dark.* New York: Faber & Faber.

Heaney, S. (2010). *Human Chain.* London: Faber & Faber.

Heaney, S. (2016). *Aeneid Book VI: A New Verse Translation,* bilingual edition. New York: Farrar, Straus and Giroux.

Jaron, S. (2020). Psychoanalysis in the time of Covid-19. *Psychoanalysis Today.* http://psychoanalysis.today/en-GB/PT-Covid-19/Psychoanalysis-in-the-Time-of-Covid-19.aspx (retrieved July 3, 2020).

Jones, D. (1937). *In Parenthesis: seinnyessit e gledyf ym penn mameu.* Introductory note by T. S. Eliot. New York: Chilmark, 1961.

Levine, H. B. (2013). The colourless canvas: representation, therapeutic action, and the creation of mind. In: H. B. Levine, G. S. Reed, & D. Scarfone (Eds.), *Unrepresented States and the Construction of Meaning: Clinical and Theoretical Contributions* (pp. 42–71). London: Karnac.

Mandelstam, O. (1933). Entretien sur Dante. *Entretien sur Dante* précédé de *La Pelisse* (pp. 15–88). Translated from Russian into French by J.-C. Schneider in collaboration with V. Linhartová. F. Rodari (preface). Geneva: La Dogana, 2012.

Ogden, T. (2014). Fear of breakdown and the unlived life. In: *Reclaiming Unlived Life: Experiences in Psychoanalysis* (pp. 47–67). London: Routledge, 2016.

Starobinski, J. (1987). Acheronta Movebo. F. Meltzer (Trans.). *Critical Inquiry,* 13(2): 394–407.

CHAPTER 13

Where does the psychoanalyst live? The online setting in the psychoanalysis of a three-year-old girl on the autistic spectrum

Patricia Cardoso de Mello
São Paulo, Brazil

Where does the psychoanalyst live? The answer to this enigmatic question would be given emphatically by many of our young patients: in the office. In fact, it is not uncommon for them to express the fantasy that the office is the analyst's home.

This seemingly simple response reveals itself to be very deep. After all, it is in the office that the analyst becomes an analyst. He entertains a very peculiar relationship with his place of work. Apparently, there is something of his identity living there: something dense and essential that is transferred. Indeed, we also exist in our things.

With the arrival of the pandemic, however, psychoanalysts have been prevented from receiving patients in their office. Remote sessions have become practically inevitable and practised by the majority of analysts, in what seems to me to be a significant step in the direction of the movement of renewal that André Green (2006) called the end of the reign of the divan. In any case, there is no doubt that contemporary analysts have been strongly invited by the necessities of the Covid pandemic to leave behind the classic in search of new ways to psychoanalyse.

At the same time, we know that the psychoanalytic work needs certain conditions in order to unfold. For there to be a process, for regressive movements to be possible, for conflicts to be heard and the inner world to be transformed, the analyst and patient must be supported by a set number of the setting's constitutive elements.

Within a theory that revisits and complements the points made by Bleger (1967) about the setting, Green (2002) proposes we separate the variables (made up of material and formal aspects, such as the frequency of the sessions, the fees, the use of the divan, etc.) from the permanent (defined by the dialogic nucleus of the analytic process regarding the verbal and non-verbal communication between analyst and analysand). In this context, changes to material and formal aspects are aimed at maintaining the dialogic nucleus's ability to function—the symbolising matrix that embodies the Freudian method and provides the foundation for the analytic process.

Developing his ideas on clinical thinking, Green (1997) introduces the notion of the "analyst's inner frame". The function of the inner frame is to ensure the symbolising dimension of the analyst's clinical thinking and guarantee the analytic role of the process, placing it beyond the circumstantial variations of the external setting and the impasses inherent to the psychoanalytic journey (Urribarri, 2005). Thanks to it, we are able to carry out aspects of psychoanalysis within the most varied of places—in psychiatric hospitals, public clinics, on the street, online. If the analyst lives in the office, we could say that the analytic process lives in the internal setting.

While barring us from face-to-face sessions, social isolation has given us the opportunity to experiment. To construct new settings. To root around our internal settings. In short, to transform ourselves as psychoanalysts.

This text will take a brief look at this experimentation and the technical knowledge it has given rise to. It contemplates sessions through a smartphone for a three-year-old girl with autism, showing the impact of the confinement imposed by the pandemic on her life and our relationship. Over the course of five months of work, we see that the brutal rupture of the analytic setting led to the construction of a new, online setting that is able to produce therapeutic effects as interesting as they are unexpected. In particular, I will describe the surprising role of the smartphone and its dual condition: as a device that organises the analytic situation and as a toy/tool for subjectivation.

What now?

At our last face-to-face session, when I said goodbye to Lélia (three years and nine months) and her parents, all four of us were disoriented. Lélia did not fully understand what made this farewell so different from the others. The parents did not understand how they would cope without the support of our sessions, while I did not understand how I would work remotely with such a young girl, whose symbolic resources were still so precarious.

Lélia's parents had sought me out based on a recommendation from a paediatrician, due to a typical condition of autistic withdrawal: an absence of relations with others, avoiding eye contact, stereotypical manifestations, and a lack of language. After a year and a half of work, she had evolved considerably: she was opening up progressively and had created live bonds with her parents. Words and then simple sentences began to appear. The words came fully formed, ready, while the sentences were almost complete, although both were still very infrequent.

The parents had built up a relationship of trust with me and were strongly supported by our work. With the arrival of the pandemic and the subsequent need to interrupt face-to-face sessions, intense feelings of abandonment arose. I was also very apprehensive, given that situations of this kind—unexpected ruptures, long separations, uncertain futures—represent a gigantic risk of intensifying the diffidence of children with autism.

Before the pandemic

On the foundations of the analytic process and the setting's symbolising function

When they first arrived at my office, Lélia's parents quickly accepted my suggestion to come, talk, and think together. They both made a point of being present at every session (twice weekly with their daughter, once a week without), showing real availability to help the child. However, in the sessions with Lélia, I faced issues that acted as barriers to the implementation of the analytic work. First, the parents stimulated her with too much intensity, creating a situation of invasive excess for Lélia.[1] Then, they maintained an intense phallic-narcissistic struggle for the child. They each wanted to take her for themselves, establishing a dual, devouring relationship with her with no space for a third or for thought. This experience was profoundly disorganising for Lélia. She was stranded in the middle, split between two antagonistic movements—"like a dog with two masters", in the words of the father—and was falling apart. Her extremely fragile ego was permanently overloaded by excessive and chaotic investment. By trying to approach her, even seeking to regulate the parents' overinvestment, I ended up functioning as yet another source of potential overstimulation, contributing to increase the excess, instead of moderating it.

The bond between Lélia and her mother was extremely fragile. Lélia swung between indifference and avoidance. These behaviours were milder in the relationship with the father.[2] However, in trying to support his daughter, the father would end up taking possession of her, leaving the mother on the outside, suffering. Fathers and mothers tend to alternate with greater or lesser balance when it comes to care and functions, but here there was an impoverishment of the maternal place.

Third, the parents found it difficult to not join in on my interventions, to take a more passive position, and to give me space. In the relationship with the daughter, they were unable to make the regressive movements that would allow them to reach her. They had a kind of desire to be the protagonist and a need for narcissistic affirmation that steamrollered the child.

In the sessions with the parents, we discussed this dynamic. I spoke of the importance of entering into a partnership to look after the daughter, and we were able to put into words the rivalry between them. The father brought the idea that both of them—successful engineers who were used to leading teams—"had too much leadership and did not accept being led". He proposed an interesting formulation that they needed to learn to play "Follow the leader", the children's game where the objective is just to copy

---

[1] We know that the lack of response in autistic children to requests from parents generates a desperate behaviour of hyperstimulation, which, in turn, ends up reinforcing the withdrawal. This phenomenon is called up-regulation.

[2] In my experience with autistic children, avoidance regarding the mother is primary and then progressively generalises to other relationships.

the movements of whoever is leading the game. They needed to learn to follow each other's bodies, to follow their daughter, to follow the analyst.

However, despite our conversations, the situation would not change. In the sessions with Lélia, identifying with her left me feeling anguished and invaded. I was stuck, no matter how fast I ran. I was building on swampland and it was impossible to carry on in that way.

So, I decided to propose something unexpected to the parents. Instead of both being present during Lélia's sessions, they should attend one each, separately. I was, however, hesitant about the proposal, because, in my experience, sessions with both parents and the child comprise a special place for the construction of primary bonds. As it happened, this intervention yielded decisive results. It allowed something fundamental relating to the child's narcissistic bases to begin organising itself. The fact of each parent having a guaranteed place, under no threat from the other—in an acknowledgment of their narcissism as parents—generated the conditions for the emergence of otherness. With the parents' places guaranteed, the child's place could now "be", too.

This transformed, to an extent, the two "devouring mothers" into a father and a mother with separate places, allowing for the integrity of the child. To avoid splitting Lélia in half, we split the time in two. The setting was perfectly suited to these arrangements.

Thus, it was possible to support the parents so that they could be capable of favouring the construction of the child's narcissism, converting it gradually into "The leader" or "Her Majesty the Little Girl" (Freud, 1914). In this context, the weekly session with the couple took on an extra function: integrating the experiences each had acquired in their individual sessions with Lélia, favouring the formation of a common child.

Over the years, seeing children and teens, I have carried out this kind of therapeutic action that I call a "framing intervention". It is the changing of a precise and concrete aspect of the setting. It works by exercising the tertiary function that supports the transitional, favouring the creation/transformation of the patient's limits of the ego. This action on the intersubjective plane installs a certain practice and materialises in a change in the functioning of the variable part of the setting.[3] The concrete aspect of

---

[3] Often, instead of modifying a temporal element, the intervention happens in relation to space.

this solution seems fundamental to me, even if its symbolic character is the real reason for its efficacy.

This kind of intervention is based on a patient and painstaking comprehension of the analytic field (Baranger & Baranger, 1969). It is built up through a process; that is, through a number of small transference-countertransference movements that are gradually adjusted until a crisis and an impasse are produced, which press the analyst in the direction of change. In his thinking about the "analyst's framing function", Urribarri (2010) emphasises the "framing/deframing/reframing" tripod as an essential tool for working with non-neurotic patients.

Here, reconfiguring the devices and dynamics of the relationships, the intervention produced the conditions needed for the analytic process to, literally, have a space. My work of creating bonds and attributing meaning now had a place in which to happen and this is how we were progressing when the pandemic hit.

Knock! Knock!: the first video session

The first video session necessitated by the pandemic took place with Lélia and her mother at their home, on the latter's smartphone. A few seconds into the call, the three of us "entered" Lelia's toy room, a place where our meetings could potentially happen. On entering, I felt completely out of place in that new and strange space. The room seemed vast, arid, impersonal. Countertransferentially, it was as if all the delicate progress we had made over the many months of work had been lost, left behind.

During the session, the mother told me what the first days of isolation had been like, as Lélia walked around the room, seemingly oblivious to our conversation. The mother tried to engage her a few times, but without success. At a certain moment, however, Lélia went to her bookshelf and, to my surprise, picked up the book, *Knock! Knock!*. She walked a few steps in our direction, sat down on the floor and started "reading", by flicking through the pages. I began talking about the book and the mother drew closer to her daughter, to better frame her with the smartphone camera, creating a moment of intimacy among us. *Knock! Knock!* is a book I have at the office and that I read to Lélia occasionally at the beginning of the session. Her parents bought a copy to have at home, something I was unaware of until that moment.

Knock! Knock! shows the story of a young boy coming home, alone, during the day. He opens colourful doors, one after the other. The doors are the size of the pages, so that turning a page corresponds to opening a door. Before opening each door, the boy names its colour and knocks. After opening each door, the boy asks if anybody is home, then describes the curious scene before him: for example, four monkeys having a pillow fight. This goes on until the boy opens the final door and finds himself outside. He says, "Nobody's home ... The moon is shining, let's go ..."[4]

Young children love this book. Apparently simple, it condenses a series of organisers of symbolisation expressed in pairs of opposites: open/close, full/empty, day/night, inside/outside, near/far, together/apart, present/absent. It is a kind of hide-and-seek, trying to find the other in a very particular rhythm. And, furthermore, it has beautiful pastel colours that are in sync with the experience of separation.

The narrative's powerful moment is the interruption of the rhythm, arriving at the emptiness outside the house, at night: "Nobody's home ..." It is set up by the repetition of the question, "Anybody home?", asked when each new door appears. The rising intonation of the question juxtaposes against the falling intonation of the answer, modulating feelings of expectation and disappointment. Outside, night-time, nobody home: the last page in the book shows feelings of emptiness and abandonment. We have left the house, we are alone, the book has ended.

When I now read the book to Lélia and her mother, during this first session in a new place, she looks at me with great intensity, precisely in the moment I say, sadly: "Nobody's home ... The moon is shining, let's go ..." This brief glance of extreme depth appears every time I tell Lélia something very precise that makes sense to her. In these moments, there is a real meeting of gazes between us, where she is.

I am able to put into words, in line with the feelings present in the book, how sad we are to not be able to meet, to not be at the office, together. I say, "No more office. Poor Lélia, poor Patricia, poor mummy," referencing the game we played for months on end, where she would

---

[4] Freely translated from the Portuguese edition of the book, originally published in Sweden.

leave me with no grape juice and say, seriously, "No more grape," the first sentence she spoke in her life, followed by, a few sessions later, "Poor Patricia." These sentences symbolise the experience of losing the mother, with the birth of Clara, her sister, who is two years younger. Linked in the game, they transform her passive experience into an active one, placing in me all her suffering.

In this context, *Knock!, Knock!* is doubtlessly an allusion to the interrupted sessions, to my office, and to the desire to meet me again. The house where she lives is, actually, amusingly similar to the house in the book. It seems very significant to me that Lélia chose from the toy room an element identical to one in my office. Probably the only identical one in that whole room. The relationship of identity established through this choice tries to restore the continuity lost through the massive rupture of the setting that represents having the sessions in a different place, without my physical presence. Creating a bridge between the past and the present, Lélia brings back our office. Fort and Da! (Freud, 1920).

At the same time, the book unexpectedly shows my entry into Lélia's house for the first time, into the toy room, our new space. All these aspects are condensed in the choice of the book. When Lélia chose it to read together, I knew that she was still connected to me through the smartphone—where my image and voice now lived—and that the remote treatment would be possible.

The haunted hut

The social isolation required by the pandemic implied multiple losses for Lélia. In addition to losing people, relationships, and spaces, she lost her routine—which represents a kind of earthquake for the mind of a child with autism.

During the first two weeks, feelings of a depressive nature arose. She spent a lot of time lying down, sucking a dummy (pacifier), and clinging to her cushion. She became highly sensitive to frustrations and fits of crying would ensue. She said, once, "Leli is very sad."

Almost always, the trigger for the fits would be in connection with Clara, for whom Lélia nurtured devastating feelings of jealousy. During the confinement, being locked in, at home, with her sister has been challenging for her. Invaded by hate, she desperately tries to control the little one's movements. She says, repetitively, "Clara will not play downstairs," "Clara is going to nap," and "That's mine!", uttered in regard to objects, always in the feminine and probably referring to the mother.[5]

At the end of these two weeks, the depressive feelings vanished and Lélia began to be overcome by a growing agitation. There was an expressive increase in autistic behaviours. She would spend long moments alone, lying on the floor, pushing toy cars and making engine noises, unreachable to others. The stereotypical actions became more frequent: she nodded forward, bending over with her arms behind her, twisting her closed fists. She would run back and forth repeatedly, grunting gutturally.

A regressive period then followed, lasting about ten days and causing great anguish in the parents. On the one hand, Lélia lost control of her bowels and bladder, which had not happened in months. On the other, for the first time, she began to act like her sister, asking for milk in a bottle, in the mother's lap. "Leli wants the bottle," she would say.

After this first, turbulent month of quarantine, we had what seems to have been a watershed session. When the mother turned on the camera, Clara was inside a small indigenous hut, which Lélia was shaking, agitatedly and with all her might. Trying to start a game, I said, "Wow, it looks like the wind is shaking that hut! Help! The wind is so strong! Is the hut going to blow apart? How frightening!" However, she ends up pushing her sister, who is removed by the nanny.

Lélia then picks up a car, lies down on the floor, and starts pushing it back and forth, making motor sounds. The mother tries to interact, but she seems impenetrable. The mother tells me that Lélia has been even more "focused" the past two days, after coming back from the beach, where the family has been isolating half the time. She tells me Lélia woke up screaming last night, terrified. They were unable to get her back to sleep again.

I speak at length about the fear of being left alone, again, at night, without mummy and daddy in her room, because at the beach house she normally sleeps in their bed. And about her having had such a frightening nightmare. I ask aloud, playfully, what the nightmare could have been about. Could Lélia be frightened of Clara becoming a ghost

---

[5] Portuguese is a language with grammatical gender.

and coming to haunt her in the middle of the night, when she is asleep? Something like she was doing, shaking the hut with Clara inside?

She becomes very interested in what I am saying, getting up and walking towards me. She looks closely, taking her time, smiling broadly. It is the first time she has been able to hold my gaze since we started the remote sessions. She begins making a "mmmm" sound, pressing both lips between her teeth, as if trying to speak while gagged, which is a new gesture. I copy her and she bursts out laughing, reminding me of the "no more grape" game, when I would make a similar sound while pretending to cry, much to her delight. We stayed like that for a few minutes, in eye contact, then she covered her mouth with her hands, but continued making the sound. I say that it is so difficult to be locked up in the flat, in the city, without being able to go outside. That it looks like she feels imprisoned inside the house, like her voice and her crying, which are imprisoned inside her mouth, trying but failing to escape. I also say that in the flat, it looks like Clara is everywhere, that she owns the place, even owns mummy. That Clara does not stop moving, that it is impossible to control her movements and that this causes a lot of fear and anger.

Having finished, Lélia organises herself and calms down significantly. The mother proposes that she sits at the table, to paint. She asks for red paint—the first sentence of the session—and I talk about the family's red boat, which she is obsessed about. It was moored at the beach house and she showed me it during our last session. Thus, we recover the representation of that object in which she has invested narcissistically, favouring a reorganising movement of the disorganising experience of returning from the beach. Saying our goodbyes, the mother notes that Lélia "seems like a completely different girl".

In this session, we see how the new rupture that represents the return to the city, as well as the fact of being locked up in the flat with the sister, added to the difficulty of bearing the parents sleeping together, without her, seem to make Lélia more fragile. Her ego is invaded by uncontrollable feelings of hate and jealousy and she becomes disorganised. The storm of drives threatens to destroy the fragile indigenous hut. Aggressive fantasies haunt her. It is unbearable to be outside and unbearable to be inside.

The theme of invasion is a central one in autism. The gaps in the constitution of the boundaries of the primary narcissistic structure force the ego to install a defensive system of highly rigid withdrawal. To avoid the driving invasion triggered by the movements of the object, the ego drastically blocks its borders, making them completely impenetrable. At the same time, there is a disinvestment in the process of representation, which aims to suppress the presence of the other in the internal world (disobjectalisation).[6] In clinical practice, we see children who actively close their orifices and their senses, blocking every and any entry by others. Children who do not open their eyes, who seem to not see and hear well, who develop strabismus, etc.—these are desperate attempts to keep others outside their perceptual field.

It seems to me that the autistic child seeks to negativise others to avoid the storm of drives that they are capable of provoking. The other is not the primary object of the avoidance. They are rejected as the object-trauma trigger of the drive, the pain, the feelings of abandonment. In this sense, the baby is thrown out with the bathwater. That is, to combat the effects of the other, the other is suppressed—through the radical implementation of a negative narcissistic functioning (Green, 1983).

Part of the transforming effect of the session's interventions seems to arise from having established the figurability that creates the symbolic nexus between the various interiors: the buccal cavity, the hut, the dark room. The following day, Lélia tells the nanny that, "Leli had a dream with the red boat. Leli was startled by the red boat." For the first time, she organises a narrative about this other mental state of mind that is dreaming. She verbalises, with relief, that she had a nightmare, suggesting an acknowledgement of the dream dreamt as an experience of the internal world—the expression of a new step of subjectification in the construction of the double limit of the self (with the object and the id).

---

[6] Editors' note: For those readers not familiar with the formulations of André Green (e.g., 2002), he draws a distinction between the notation of a perception of an object and the transformation of that perception into a psychically alive presence that we would then qualify as an internal object. He calls this transformational process *objectalisation* and assigns its functioning under the aegis of Eros, which creates and binds. By the same token, there is an opposite function, *disobjectalisation*, that operates under the aegis of Thanatos (death instinct) that dismantles, fragments, and destroys internal objects. Disobjectalisation in Green's theory is an operation at the maladaptive pole of the work of the negative.

Making little houses

The following week, an interesting passage inaugurates a long series of games in which Lélia comes to explore, with pleasure, the interior of objects and spaces.

Lélia and her mother are seated on the floor, playing at filling up a truck bed. To let me see the scene, the mother places the smartphone with my image on the couch. The truck is filling up with small musical instruments. "Load the truck." Then, "The truck is full of construction." The piled-up objects begin to slide and fall out. Anxiously, she asks the mother to help and spends a long moment holding up the precarious set to avoid the overflow/collapse.

After a while, she places the truck on the couch, right next to the smartphone, which is left between a cushion and the back of the vehicle. The sight amuses her, but I do not immediately understand. She then slowly starts pulling the xylophone from the truck, so that it hangs over the smartphone, like a roof. This puts the smartphone perfectly framed by the "roof", the two "walls", and the "floor". The mother notes that it is as if the device—and, therefore, the image of my face—were inside a little house. That is what made her smile. The anticipation that she makes what could come to be a house seems important.

Then, she tries to stick her head inside the little house, bringing her face very close to mine, giving me the sensation of us being in an enclosed space. She moves back and forth a few times, slowly, looking me right in the eyes. It feels like the "little hut" game that young children play: nose to nose, hands cupped between faces, providing "walls" and a "roof", creating a sensation of an intimate, dark environment for two.

These games that young children adore, of being with others in a restricted, very limited interior space—little houses, hiding places, under the blanket—place on the stage fantasies regarding the consolidation of the primary narcissism. Against a backdrop of a primary subject–object separation, the meeting is pleasantly explored in the construction of the experience of intimacy. Making a little house is enjoying the pleasure of being inside and together.

In the passage above, there are feelings of well-being that arise from the pleasure of affectionate sharing, with the mother and with me. However, the continence is still under threat, revealing that the bond with others has not been stably internalised: it depends on the mother to physically hold the objects inside/on top of the truck, and probably on my presence inside the little house to make it habitable. Green (in Urribarri, 2005) states that the subject is what is left when the object leaves. In this sense, we still do not have a fully formed subject.

The new setting

The new setting gradually came together within the context of the remote sessions, against a backdrop of my own malleability (Milner, 1952). As described, the first session took place using a smartphone. In the following sessions, the father made a few attempts to use the computer or television, to increase the size of the screen, but after experimenting, I chose to remain with the smartphone. First, because eye contact, which is a vital part of working with Lélia, is easier on it than the larger devices. Second, because, being mobile, the device allows me to follow the child's movements closely. In fact, the father and mother have spent much of the sessions holding the device in order to show me their daughter, which they do precisely and naturally.

In the first weeks of work, the sessions took place in the toy room. However, spontaneously and gradually, Lélia and her parents began to move around the house and, before I realised it, there was no longer one set place for our sessions.

Given the child's age and functioning, I thought it would not be productive to restrain her movements. In my office, which contains several rooms and a small garden, when seeing young children I tend to use different spaces according to what we are working on. From this point of view, we recreated a similar dynamic, establishing a relationship of continuity with the face-to-face sessions.

In the absence of a constant physical space, without realising it, the smartphone transformed into the only stable, concrete object present in every session. It became the permanent and principal element of the material dimension of the setting. This contributed to it being invested in and objectalised, such that it acquired a decisive function in Lélia's process of symbolisation.

The smartphone

Before the pandemic, Lélia rarely used a smartphone, but, since then, she has developed a real passion for this object. I see two reasons for this. One, working from home, the parents have held many meetings through their smartphones-objects-of-desire. Two, the smartphone is the instrument through which she relates with me.[7]

Since the start of the remote sessions, I was very surprised by her ability to maintain a connection with me through the screen. During the first month, she would give me furtive glances and, sometimes, repeat something I had said. Even at a considerable distance and without looking at me, she remained connected to my voice and words. Eventually, she addressed me, directly. After a few weeks, with the support of the parents, she came to say "Hello!" and "Goodbye!" with pleasure at the start and end of the sessions. Gradually, over the five months of work described here, the moments of interaction with me became more extended and increasingly rich, and less repetitive games were created.

As we will see, in this process, there was a surprising transformation in the role of the smartphone. At the beginning, the smartphone and analyst are identified, maintaining between them a relationship of concreteness. The smartphone is the analyst. Or the analyst lives in the smartphone. However, Lélia progressively playfully explored and discovered the smartphone's representative and communicative functions, which provoke the differentiation between the representation of the analyst and her image on the screen. Lélia appropriates the smartphone and uses it as a device for symbolisation. It gains a transitional

---

[7] We know that electronic devices carry a significant risk of alienation for any child, given their addictive and de-subjectifying potential. In the case of children with autism, their use can easily increase withdrawal, contributing to leaving the other outside the drive circuit. However, in certain circumstances, they can be used in the service of creativity and relating to others. In this sense, over the past few years, I have often worked with electronics in the office.

function. Finally, Lélia begins to lean on the functioning of the device to develop her own representative abilities. This culminated, at the end of the fifth month of quarantine, in a notable evolution of language. The smartphone is then conceived as a means of representing and the analyst gains her own existence, being clearly separate. The development of the function of representation is correlated with the passage from the predominance of negative narcissism to the predominance of positive narcissism.

At the beginning of the second month of remote sessions, a situation arose that illustrates how the smartphone and person of the analyst are still undifferentiated—at the same time, it shows how the device is over-invested, because it supports the entire weight of the material setting. In a session, the father's smartphone, with my image on it, slipped on the table where it had been placed. Lélia was startled and said "Ah, ah, ah" repeatedly, in great agitation. I then said, "Goodness, what a fright! It looked like Patricia fell, but it was only the phone." She stood up the device and knocked it flat several times, actively revisiting the anxiety-generating situation to elaborate on it. This movement opens the work of symbolisation that distinguishes between the analyst's image (on the screen) and the analyst's person, giving rise internally to the dimension of representation of the object.

That same week, Lélia discovered she could enlarge or shrink my image on the smartphone, while also making her image simultaneously and inversely smaller or bigger. She was very intrigued by this possibility. During various sessions, she experimented with this alternation, showing pleasure at being able to make me bigger or smaller, farther or nearer. As if she could on some level control the distance and separation. A digital and elementary Fort-Da game (Freud, 1920): at the touch of a finger, as if by magic, the analyst is sent far away and then brought back close.

Unlike people, machines rapidly and precisely follow commands with a reassuring predictability. While the human world is chaotic and hypercomplex, the mechanical world of machines does not leave you guessing. The issue of unpredictability is critical for those with autism, directly touching the problem of the object's reliability. The construction of a reliable object is one of the essential conditions for overcoming autistic functioning.

Since a very young age, Lélia has been fascinated by machines: blenders, coffee makers, printers, lawnmowers, vehicles, etc. This fascination seems related to the power of machines and the fact they have no emotions. They are objects that are idealised and, at the same time, feared.[8] The peculiarity of the machine in question—the smartphone—is that it circumscribes my living image, live. Thus, it can be handled, managed, and dominated, counting on the dimension of reliability. Yet it also brings a connection with the human presence of the analyst and the entire analytic universe, full of meanings and emotions. It is a complex, compound object with this dual nature.

Another important change began to happen upon Lélia's discovery of the ability to change the sizes of our images on the screen. She would make her image larger and mine smaller for several minutes at a time, gazing longingly at the screen, as if into a mirror. When she did something new, such as playing an instrument, she would come closer to repeat the action while looking at herself, clearly enjoying the narcissistic pleasure. Her interest in mirrors had already appeared at the office, giving us indications about the formation of a unified body image (Lacan, 1949). However, the peculiarity, here, is that by looking at herself in the smartphone/mirror, she would see me too. I was in the reduced image, looking at her. The smartphone was like a mirror with eyes. A less dangerous mirror than the gaze of the other, but a more human one than that of a glass mirror. A mirror where it is pleasurable to see yourself being seen and that can, in this way, perform an auxiliary function in the organisation of the narcissism. We could imagine that this is the kind of experience of looking at oneself in the presence of the other, akin to that described by Winnicott (1958).

The mother's gaze, which commonly has a primordial role in the construction of the ego (Winnicott, 1967), does not perform that role in children with autism. The gaze of the other is experienced as intrusive and disorganises the narcissism, instead of organising it. This is why it is so drastically avoided, in turn drastically blocking the process of construction of specularity and identity.

---

[8] I often find, in children with autism, the fear and desire to transform into inanimate objects.

The sensitivity of children with autism to the gaze of the other is immense. A few times, Lélia would come closer to the smartphone, looking into my eyes, and I would react spontaneously, moving slightly closer, too, causing her to move back. Even through the screen, my slight approximation was too abrupt. For there to be a pleasurable interpenetration of looks, a great deal of delicacy is required (Haag, 2008). In the office, we would spend many minutes face-to-face, her inside and me outside, in the garden, staring at each other through the window, in a repetitive game of jumping and gesturing where I would imitate her. She would stand on a low table to bring our eyes level. In this way—mediated by the window and the imitation—she was able to sustain prolonged eye contact with pleasure.

Midway through the second month of remote sessions, something else new appeared. Lélia began to ask the parents to film her carrying out some action, such as a forward roll. "Want the video!" she would say. She would then watch the clip over and over, proud of her accomplishment. Here, too, the smartphone has a narcissistic function, yet, beyond that, it seems to play an important role in constructing the representation of oneself, which then leads to the ability to self-invest libidinously.

Soon, Lélia began to film and photograph without the parents' help. She would just take one of the smartphones and use it. Later, the parents would find hundreds of photos and short clips she had taken. In this period, she wanted to do everything on her own. She rapidly gained autonomy over a number of everyday tasks.

An unprecedented movement of opposition and confrontation by the parents arose over the course of the third month of confinement. It was triggered by the mother's decision to no longer allow Lélia to use a nappy when defecating—despite having full control of her sphincter, she still needed this subterfuge in order to separate herself from the faeces. However, she flat-out refused to evacuate without them and, a few weeks later, the mother gave up on her project. Here, Lélia is able to say no to the object in order to say yes to herself (Green, 1993)—a crucial moment in the constitution of the ego.

In this context, the mother's precious work smartphone becomes an element of a passionate struggle between them. In a tug-of-war with the mother, Lélia grabs the smartphone against the rules, throwing it on the floor in provocation, etc. As a sign of protest against the fact of the parents having spent a weekend without their daughters, she shattered the object into a million pieces, throwing it against a wall. This rageful movement is highly significant, marking Lélia's ability to express hate and exercise aggression in relation to the mother.

In the beginning of the fourth month of quarantine, Lélia began to ask the parents to recreate scenes that surprised her, to film them and watch them again. For example, one day the mother tripped and Lélia asked her to trip again, to film her tripping and be able to watch it repeatedly, making it predictable.

Another example in the same vein came when Lélia fell and hit her head, requiring a trip to the hospital for some stitches. A few days later, in a session with the mother, she began to play doctor, inverting the roles in terms of passivity/activity. First, she examines and looks after the mother. Then, she asks her to cry and begins to film her crying face. With her other hand, she slowly hits her, to make her cry more, still as part of the game. However, at a given moment, she hits her with all her might and the mother yells in surprise. She says, "Doctor Lélia hit mummy's leg." The clip shows the mother's face precisely when she yells out in surprise and pain. She watches it over and over.

In these two scenes, we see how the smartphone transforms into a tool for subjective appropriation of potentially traumatic events. It allows for an unpleasant scene to be recorded, so it can then be repeated, represented, and elaborated. These essential functions of the mind become as if extended to the smartphone, which becomes a tool of the process of symbolisation.

The function of representation that finds support in the smartphone is a derivation of the analytic process. I am the one who puts into words the difficult situations Lélia undergoes, helping her to metabolise the impactful events, seeing as the parents have little resources to do so.

In this period, Lélia is given an old smartphone. She then begins to record and photograph her own body, as well as record her own voice. She records the engine noises she makes with her mouth, her yells and singing, then listens to them. The smartphone is like a tool for self-knowledge. Through the transference of the symbolising function of the analyst on the smartphone, it is transformed into a subjectifying device.

At the same time, the handset converts itself into an instrument for investigating the world. Lélia seems to record video and audio, and to photograph to research and comprehend the nature of things. In one session, in the arms of the mother, who is moving around the house, she takes photographs of the surroundings and then looks at the photos repeatedly, reconstructing the route taken. In other moments, she has fun throwing the smartphone in the air while recording, so that she can watch the trajectory from its point of view (of the observer). Curiosity about the world, others, and herself are signs that the process of objectifying is running its course.

In autistic withdrawal, there is a most severe state of disobjectalising. The complete victory of this process gives rise to "classic" autism, such as described by Kanner (1943), where the effects and consequences, including neurological ones, caused by the lack of relations with others, are devastating. From my point of view, autism is an extreme form of negative narcissism, where withdrawal is actively implemented to neutralise the pain of helplessness coming from a radical inability to connect with the primary objects.[9]

In every activity where Lélia uses the smartphone as a recording object, there is an aspect that seems fundamental to me. The audio and video recordings can be played back ad infinitum, unlike real life, which unfolds without the ability to return. Thus, there is the expression of the desire to control time. To capture the present, preventing experiences from passing and being lost.[10] The smartphone as a magical object that supports omnipotence—an essential experience to overcome the negative logic originating from abandonment.

The use of the smartphone in the sessions seems to have operated like a support for communication, encouraging Lélia to use other means to establish the relationship with the distant other. Thus, she began to use the device to make calls and send messages. During the sessions, she would sometimes send me emojis and type out a jumble of letters, as if they were words. She would call the parents using the inter-phone system, the father's smartwatch, or the baby monitor, calling them when

---

[9] Which, evidently, does not discount the possible existence of constitutional factors in the child when determining this process.

[10] The fear of losing them reminds one of the fragility of memories and, at the same time, the hyperamnesia of many children with autism.

she needed. This intense desire to communicate is obviously significant in the context of Lélia's autistic functioning.

This objectifying process, of investing into the world and the other, allows for a slow passage from negative narcissism (predominance of withdrawal, disobjectalising, and de-investment) to positive narcissism (libidinous self-investment, the emergence of otherness, and the representational process). Lélia is opening up, creating more consistent bonds with others and leaving behind withdrawal for increasingly longer moments.

Thought is a house built of words

At the end of the fifth month of remote sessions, after a period of ten days of separation from the mother, Lélia began to say many sentences, each more complex and less repetitive than the last, even if they were disconnected and not organised in a dialogue with the other. From one or two sentences spoken per session, at the beginning of the pandemic, to a dozen before the mother's trip, they then numbered fifty or so, many of them directed at me.

This unexpected flourishing of language witnesses the important work of elaborating absence that Lélia has been able to do in analysis. Currently, the analyst and smartphone are clearly differentiated. The former is represented, imagined, as being present in a different place—a space that Lélia is able to conceive and name. She says, "Patricia will play house in her room," or "Patricia will arrive at daddy's house." The development of the use of language in sessions is inscribed on the work dynamic begun with the "No more grape" game, which Lélia transforms and makes more sophisticated, always ensuring I explicitly state, playfully, her frustrations and feelings of abandonment and hate: "Patricia won't get any sweets," "Patricia doesn't get to see Leli's bed," "Patricia, you get nothing," "No more Leli, Patricia," "Patricia, mummy is going to punish you," and so on.

With my support, Lélia learned how to play at making me live the hardships that she experiences and put into words what she is feeling, so that her emotions become thinkable and bearable. She says, "Patricia will be scared of the dog," "Patricia is scared of the red boat," "Patricia, are you scared of mummy?", so that I can verbalise, in the form of a game, without dread. She needs me to enact her feelings, transforming them, so that, later, they can be internalised by her. It is about wearing down the feelings so that they become less psychically harmful, in transformative work that makes us think of the theories of Bion's (1962) on the function of maternal reverie, alpha function, and container/contained. All this metabolisation of the negative—absence, pain, frustration—is fundamental, because it liberates the ego from the death drive, allowing for positive investment into oneself and the object. In certain moments, it feels like I am a kind of double for Lélia: another Lélia, one who lives and expresses what she feels, allowing for an elaborative circuit instead of expulsion. A double, able to live with raw emotions. And able to sustain certain positions: for example, recently, when the father was playing at nibbling her stomach in a way that bothered her, she said, "Patricia doesn't allow that." Later, the sentence became, "I don't allow that," and is used with vehemence when she does not want something to happen.

In moments of fragility, instead of becoming disorganised or needing the concrete presence of the other to recover, Lélia has started to be able to express herself using words—sometimes with an unexpected clarity. In a session by the beach, when the mother called, Lélia said, "Patricia is not going to see Lélia," and "Patricia is not going to see anything," in an effort to keep me away and the mother just for her, before adding "Mummy is going to leave Patricia here," referring to the sea. Then, "Bye Patricia, enjoy your work!" This sequence of spontaneous, connected sentences shows how Lélia is acquiring the ability to say no and how her thinking is being structured (Freud, 1925).

Lélia shows us how thoughts expressed in words exercise the function of establishing limits with the other, slowly substituting what was once a very strict system of autistic withdrawal. In a recent session at the beach house, we came up with a game where she hides in the hammock-house, leaving me outside, unhappy and cold. She says, "It is Leli's house and Patricia is not coming in," an exquisite phrase that shows signs of the advances in the process of appropriating herself and constructing her own limits.

Lélia's analysis shows us the mind's extraordinary potential for change. Despite the extremely adverse environmental and relational conditions brought about by the pandemic—confinement, the change in routines, the breaking of the analytic setting—we see this three-year-old girl with autism managing to support herself in a new and unlikely setting, using it as a path to a surprising advance in the process of subjectification.

Patricia Cardoso de Mello
October 2020

Translated from Portuguese by Henrik Carbonnier

References

Baranger, W., & Baranger, M. (1969). La situación analítica como cámpo dinámico. *Problemas del campo psicoanalítico* (pp. 129–164). Buenos Aires: Kargieman.

Bleger, J. (1967). Psicoanálisis del encuadre psicoanalítico. *Simbiosis y ambigüedad: estudio psicoanalítico* (pp. 237–250). Buenos Aires: Paidós.

Bion, W. R. (1962). *Learning from Experience*. London: Karnac, 1984.

Freud, S. (1914). Introdução ao Narcisismo. *Obras Completas, Volume 12 (1914–1916)* (pp. 13–50). São Paulo, Brazil: Companhia das Letras.

Freud, S. (1920). Além do Princípio do Prazer. *Obras Completas, Volume 14 (1917–1920)* (pp. 120–178). São Paulo, Brazil: Companhia das Letras.

Freud, S. (1925). A Negação. *Obras Completas, Volume 16 (1923–1925)* (pp. 249–255). São Paulo, Brazil: Companhia das Letras.

Green, A. (1983). *Narcisisme de vie, narcissisme de mort*. Paris: Minuit.

Green, A. (1993). *Le travail du négatif*. Paris: Minuit.

Green, A. (1997). Le cadre psychanalytique. Son intériorisation chez l'analyste et son application dans la pratique. In: *La clinique psychanalytique contemporaine* (pp. 5–29). Paris: Ithaque, 2012.

Green, A. (2002). *La pensée clinique*. Paris: Odile Jacob.

Green, A. (2006). *Unité et diversité des pratiques du psychanalyste: colloque de la Société psychanalytique de Paris*. Paris: Presses Universitaires de France.

Haag, G. (2008). De quelques fonctions précoces du regard à travers l'observation directe et la clinique des états archaïques du psychisme. *Enfances & Psy*, *41*(4): 14–22.

Kanner, L. (1943). Autistic disturbances of affective contact. *Nervous Child*, 2: 217–250.

Lacan, J. (1949). Le stade du miroir. *Écrits* (pp. 93–100). Paris: Seuil.

Milner, M. (1952). The role of illusion in symbol formation. In: *The Suppressed Madness of Sane Men. Forty-four Years of Exploring Psychoanalysis* (pp. 83–113). London: Tavistock, 1987.

Urribarri, F. (2005). *Le cadre de la représentation dans la psychanalyse contemporaine*. In: F. Richard & F. Urribarri (Eds.), *Autour de l'oeuvre d'André Green: Enjeux pour une psychanalyse contemporaine* (pp. 201–216). Paris: Presses Universitaires de France.

Urribarri, F. (2010). Passion clinique, pensée complexe [postface]. In: Green, A., *Illusions et désillusions du travail psychanalytique* (pp. 243–271). Paris: Odile Jacob.

Winnicott, D. W. (1958). The capacity to be alone. *International Journal of Psychoanalysis, 39*: 416–420.

Winnicott, D. W. (1967). Mirror-role of mother and family in child development. In: *Playing and Reality* (pp. 111–118). London: Tavistock, 1971.

CHAPTER 14

Where does the Covid live?
Osmotic/diffuse anxieties, isolation, and containment in times of the plague

Joshua Durban
Tel Aviv, Israel

> Exile is more than a geographical concept. You can be an exile in your homeland, in your own house, in a room.
>
> —Mahmoud Darwish

I have completed the construction of my burrow and it seems to be successful. All that can be seen from outside is a big hole; that, however, really leads nowhere; if you take a few steps you strike against natural firm rock. I can make no boast of having contrived this ruse intentionally; it is simply the remains of one of my many abortive building attempts, but finally it seemed to me advisable to leave this one hole without filling it in. True, some ruses are so subtle that they defeat themselves, I know that better than anyone, and it is certainly a risk to draw attention by this hole to the fact that there may be something in the vicinity worth inquiring into. But you do not know me if you think I am afraid, or that I built my burrow simply out of fear. At a distance of some thousand paces from this hole lies, covered by a movable layer of moss, the real entrance to the burrow; it is secured as safely as anything in this world can be secured; yet someone could step on the moss or break through it, and then my burrow would lie open, and anybody who liked—please note, however, that quite uncommon abilities would also be required—could make his way in and destroy everything for good.

—Franz Kafka, *The Burrow*

Only the misfortune of exile can provide the in-depth under-standing and the overview into the realities of the world.

—Stefan Zweig

Working in the Covid-19 era has placed many of us in a state of mental exile from the familiar world as we thought we knew it. The social and mental distancing from our usual structures of work and togetherness demanded a quick internal reorganisation, relying heavily on previously internalised object relations and modes of handling overwhelming anxieties. Thus, side by side with the rise in depressive and paranoid-schizoid anxieties and the demonisation of the other, there was also an elusive increase in unconscious archaic anxieties-of-being bearing a concrete, bodily quality. Our sense of existing as well-differentiated, ongoing, coherent, cohesive, and connected entities in time and in a tri-dimensional space has been seriously threatened. To a certain extent, both the symbiotic core of the personality as well as the predisposition to autistic anxieties and defences so poignantly described by Kafka, or as Tustin (1987) called them—"autistic pockets"—have been overstim-ulated. Yet, as Stefan Zweig observed, these turbulent internal realities might provide some further in-depth understanding and mainly com-passion into the realities of such early developmental catastrophes and of the catastrophes of the world in general. I think that the value of psy-choanalysis as one of the last bastions of compassionate passion for the truth cannot be overestimated.

I would like to share some preliminary thoughts regarding three interrelated psychic processes, which I repeatedly encountered in the psychoanalyses of children, adolescents, and young adults during the Covid-19 pandemic. These processes seemed to indicate an intensifica-tion of autistic anxieties and defences not only in those ASD patients who exist in the perpetual traumatisation of their constitution, but also in those who appear to be non-autistic, better organised, and reasonably functioning. There was *an upsurge of osmotic/diffuse anxieties, a breakdown of the psychic bisexual container,* and a *retreat from loneliness to isolation.*

Where does the Covid live?

About a month into the first Covid lockdown in Israel, I was sitting in front of the computer screen for my psychoanalytic session with Ruti, a five-year-old girl. She sat on the other side, at home. Lately we were conducting our five sessions per week remotely in Ruti's room, where she surrounded herself by her toys, crayons, and everything else that reminded her of her beloved, left-behind play box in my consulting room. Ruti, a sensitive, highly intelligent, lively, and very anxious little girl, had been referred for psychoanalysis after the birth of her brother Toby. She became depressed, stopped eating, wet her bed, had temper tantrums, and found it difficult to concentrate and play. Over the last few weeks Ruti started having nightmares. A recurrent one was about getting lost in her own room which suddenly changed and then disappeared. All the walls melted and her parents and brothers turned into water. Ruti would wake up screaming in terror and complain that she's suffocated and drowning. Previously we did a lot of work on her jealousy, envy, and oedipal phantasies directed at her baby brother and parents and the ensuing strong unconscious persecutory guilt. This work proved to be quite helpful. Lately, however, Ruti had become worryingly depressed and withdrawn. She found it hard to participate in her kindergarten's online activities, resumed sucking her thumb, and exhibited severe obsessive-compulsive symptoms.

"Where does the Covid live?" she suddenly asked me. "Do you know?" An answer which was provided by another adult patient that day instantly came to mind: "It's everywhere and nowhere." I was startled by this association, which I kept to myself, and asked Ruti, who seemed very agitated, "Well, what do you think?" "Mummy says it comes from China," said Ruti. "But Dad thinks it comes from bad Orthodox people who don't wash their hands and gather in synagogues and party all day." "And what do you think?" I insisted. Ruti looked at me, approached the screen, and whispered in a conspiratorial manner, "I think it is in the air, the sky, the stars, the water, and the plants, in people, animals, in God, and food. It's even in Toby [her baby brother whose birth a few months ago gave rise to various new anxieties and symptoms]." "How frightening and dangerous!" said I, now making some more sense of my previous sudden association to my adult patient's observation. "It appears to be everywhere and yet, at the same time, nowhere. So how can we protect ourselves? How can we protect Ruti?"

Ruti brightened up and started hopping on one leg across her room, almost falling and bumping into the furniture. "I know!" she cried excitedly. "Let's find a box and prepare a trap for the Covid. We'll give it something nice to eat and then when it's in the box, stuffing its tummy, we'll put the lid back on and throw the box into space!" I agreed that this was a good idea, and Ruti immediately proceeded to examine various containers for the Covid. After much deliberation, she finally settled for a baby crib and proposed to use the doll's house tin potty as the safety lid. "I'll also put a blanket on it, just to make sure," said Ruti, who seemed to be satisfied with this combination of hard and soft covers. "Now we're safe!" she announced proudly.

Ruti's solution of locating the elusive, omnipresent yet invisible Covid in her envied baby brother's crib, proved to be quite fragile, though. It gave rise to new paranoid anxieties and psychotic guilt. Following our session, her mother reported an increase in her obsessive rituals and insomnia. Ruti refused to fall asleep, insisting that she needed to keep an eye on the baby Covid-crib at all times so that it wouldn't escape and kill everyone. When she arrived a week later at my consulting room, following the end of the lockdown, things indeed appeared to be getting worse. Ruti was confused, disoriented, and eventually hid under my couch and sucked her finger violently. She insisted that I put something heavy and soft over her. Her much-loved elderly paternal grandmother, now in a lockdown and belonging to the high-risk group so that Ruti couldn't meet her in person, used to wrap her up in very tight blankets when she was a baby. I became the grandmother and Ruti, in a self-punishing way, became the dangerous Covid baby in the double-covered crib. Ruti often explained to me why she could not meet her granny and get her comforting mantle from her presence: "If I see granny she could die." "But if you don't," I said, "you might feel like you are dying of longing."

I was particularly struck by the way in which Ruti was trying, unsuccessfully, to locate and localise her anxieties which, like the dreaded

Covid, seemed to be everywhere yet nowhere. As was the case in her recurrent nightmare, the walls just seemed to melt down and disappear, leaving Ruti exposed in a saturated, deadly, toxic-waste "space". She felt vulnerable and permeable, without the presence of even a good part-object to protect her. Soft, vulnerable babies seemed to be especially prone to being permeated with the Covid's deadliness. Her localisation process relied consciously on her parents' and her own geographical and social zones and categories (China, Orthodox Jews, synagogues and parties, sky, air, water, plants, etc.) and, unconsciously, on her internal objects and her turbulent relationship with them (her envied baby brother). Her ambivalent feelings towards her brother and the resulting unconscious guilt and attempts at manic obsessive reparation had all been previously interpreted by me. Yet, all these desperate attempts at localising her anxieties (with my former interpretations serving as one such localising agent) seemed to fail as she withdrew into a panic-stricken, silent, and shapeless helplessness. The fact that God itself was similarly afflicted and permeated with the virus echoed the presence of a lethal, archaic, persecutory, and unhelpful superego in Ruti, a pure culture of the death instinct. After several sessions, Ruti took the blanket off the "Covid trap" and made holes in it. I interpreted that action to her as an anguished way of showing me how permeable, perforated, and paralysed she felt. I felt that my own presence turned out to be too much, creating further holes in the fabric of her mind.

Martin Buber said that everyone must come out of his Exile in his own way. However, in Ruti's case, and as I was beginning to realise in other patients' cases, too, this coming out, or coming back, was only a superficial layer over deep, diffuse, non-localised anxieties, a sort of "nowhere-ness" (Durban, 2017b) which emerged and for which the Covid-19 pandemic was just a trigger. The nowhere-man, plagued by osmotic/diffuse anxieties, survives in a perpetual state of Exile. I was also preoccupied by the way my own mind seemed to become osmotic, with contents seeping-in and leaking-out uncontrollably. Thus, unconscious contents from my adult analysand were osmotically pressuring my interaction with Ruti. I became a soft, permeable blanket full of holes. The hard cover, the tin lid, was discarded. As a consequence, Ruti felt disoriented and unbalanced, hopping on one leg and frequently falling and getting injured.

Non-located anxieties and the disintegration
of the psychic bisexual container

"One illness exposes other illnesses," said David, the adult analysand who invaded my session with Ruti, a few months after the outbreak of the Covid-19 pandemic. He went on to explain in his didactic, paranoid, and over-elaborate way, that this holds true not only for bodily illnesses but also for the mental and socio-political ones. When I asked him what he meant by other illnesses, he said that most people experience not-knowing and the accompanying fear and confusion as an illness. "Knowledge is clear, hard. Confusion, dependence, and not knowing are soft, vulnerable, and therefore dangerous. It all has to do with death anxiety, you know," he added.

I felt that he was highlighting something which I encountered daily in my practice during these strange, uncanny times, when the abnormal has become the "new normal", as Irma Brenman Pick commented (2020). The chaotic rhythm of not really knowing much about the virus and its multiple facets, as well as fear, confusion, disappointment, anger, and longing, together with the different anxieties these emotions give rise to, have replaced the background rhythm of relative, albeit precarious, safety. The bodily and the concrete, saturated with anxiety, has overtaken the mind. Autistic-like withdrawal, loneliness, and isolation, accompanied by bizarre, obsessive rituals or a false omniscient position (as in the case of David) have, all of a sudden, become regulation-sanctioned realities for all.

As a child psychoanalyst working with many ASD and psychotic patients, I cannot help but notice how working remotely, online, has turned me, too, at some unconscious level into an ASD analyst: claustrophobic, sense-oriented, and firmly glued to the visual and auditory modes available online. I have been deprived of my crucial analytic tool—that of registering the complex mere presence of the patient and of the freedom not to think (Lazar, 2017), to engage in an undisturbed developmental reverie, when needed. I kept on working, during and after lockdowns, relying heavily on my internal analytic objects and those of my patients. As Howard Levine succinctly (2020) observed, "Working remotely is, well, just that—remote."

While thinking about Ruti and other child patients, I was reminded of an observation Didier Houzel (2019, 2020), following Bion (1962), recently made about the loss, when working remotely, of what he calls "the psychic bisexual container". This primary bisexual container, based on the maternal identifications of both male and female, allows us to move playfully between the "hard" solid boundaries of the setting and the "soft", malleable, and often undefined contents of psychic realities. Ruti's combination of the soft baby blanket and the hard tin safety lid would be one example of this yearning for a protective bisexual container embodying the primary link between penis and breast. Her paternal grandmother would be another such container. In Ruti's case, due to an overwhelming influx of diffuse, non-located anxieties, this containing failed, and the container cracked and split into its non-integrated components. Furthermore, excessive unconscious guilt and envy rendered the recreation of such a container impossible. In other words, osmotic/diffuse anxieties are strongly related to the attack on the bisexual container and vice versa. In addition, the exacerbations of diffuse anxieties and the inability to hold the bisexual container together catapulted Ruti first into a state of paranoid anxieties, then into an excessive use of manic obsessional defences, and finally into isolated nowhere-ness. This state of isolation, or "being lonely without my self", is different from mere psychotic loneliness (being locked in and imprisoned by her internal persecutory objects) or depressive aloneness in the presence of a good internal object (Klein, 1963).

In its benign version, the bisexual container enables a movement between what is knowable, predictable, and clearly defined and the shapelessness of the enigmatic. It combines the prototype of the paternal with the maternal, the penis with the breast. During Covidian times, and as a result of the upsurge of osmotic/diffuse anxieties, this bisexual container has been attacked, resulting first in splitting and then in minute fragmentation. Thus, some of the children in analysis became overly cooperative at first, sticking to the "hard" contours of the paternal analytic container at the expense of all the "soft" maternal bits. It was clear to me at the beginning that my patients and I have all been trying very hard to keep on going in some sort of a manic hyperenlisting, trying to recruit all that has been internalised and established so far in the analysis. At the same time, this hypercathexis of the changed setting quite often became a fertile soil for resistance and remote attacks on the process itself. The determination to maintain a continuity of care at all costs often created a rather superficial interaction and blocked the deeper, more complex connection established previously. This hyperalertness with its recurrent "Covid-19 fatigue", reported by so many patients and analysts, was an outcome of the prevalent bidimensionality of experience and the threatened, diminished internal space allowing for developmental reverie. "His Majesty the Screen" replaced "His Majesty the Baby", becoming for some withdrawn patients a kind of "a third", enabling a safer approach to the object, while for others it facilitated a persecuting psychic retreat (Steiner, 1993) or an invitation for oedipal acting-out with an attack on boundaries. For instance, once we switched to working on Zoom, Ruti immediately took me on a guided tour of her home ending up in her parents' bedroom where she crawled under the blankets with her iPad (me) on her belly. It seemed that her oedipal yearnings intensified once removed from my presence and protected by the screen.

The facilitating protection of the "hard" inanimate screen proved to be beneficial for Rami, an ASD eight-year-old boy. Rami is a severely withdrawn, non-verbal, and non-communicating boy. He experienced his body as dislocated, fragmented, and often shapeless, much like Kafka's short story narrator—an anthropomorphic, ambiguous burrowing animal of which only the paws and the forehead are mentioned in a seemingly disconnected way.

In the previous sessions in my consulting room, he would usually sit and stare vacantly into space, shoving a hard plastic lizard's tail into his mouth, often causing it to bleed. Once we started meeting on Zoom, Rami simply hid from sight. I was faced with a blank screen and flooded by feelings of isolation and helplessness. Rami would occasionally appear and try to shove the computer's camera up his nose and disappear again. I mainly interpreted using single, disconnected words, his feelings of being no one, nowhere, isolated, and trying to cover himself up with the cold, hard, blank screen. I also referred to another wish of his to get something solid inside, so that he felt he existed. But the hard, solid tail only attacked his soft parts and made them bleed and leak out. After a while, Rami made some extraordinary developments online which vanished once we were able to meet again in person. Once we switched to Zoom Rami gradually approached the screen and initiated eye contact. To my surprise he pushed his face onto the screen, as if needing to feel its concrete hardness, and then kissed it. I said he must be feeling safer with me now that he has the cold, hard screen to cover him and protect his mouth and eyes from being taken away from him by me. Rami responded by shoving his fingers aggressively into his mouth. I said he is probably missing the lizard's tail (which formerly stood for a spikey nipple-penis attacking his oral cavity). I took the plastic lizard and brought it nearer to the screen. Rami became very excited and banged on the screen. I said he must want it so much, but the hard screen which protects him is also keeping him away from me and from parts of his body that were left deserted with me. I added that he longs to unite the hard tail with his soft mouth so that he can feel whole and safe. Rami became agitated, screaming, and banging wildly on the screen. I felt a growing panic in me, feeling that this barrier between us was impenetrable. I told Rami that I can teach him a trick that would bring the lizard closer to him. I said, "If you open your eyes and mouth wide, like I do, and you look at the lizard and me for a long, long time, you could swallow us both with your eyes and mouth, and then we will be with you." To my surprise, Rami took up my rather crude suggestion for a phantasised bodily incorporation. He opened wide his eyes and mouth, then shut them tight, and slid his fingers gently into his mouth. He seemed relaxed and calm. After some time, he approached the screen again, this time with a small, soft ball in his hand which he tried to push towards me. I was moved by this initiation of a mutual game and repeated the "lizard swallowing" procedure imitating Rami's previous actions.

When Rami and I resumed our sessions in the consulting room, all these new and important initiatives disappeared. The safe, inanimate space created by working remotely gave way to a flooding of indiscriminate anxieties. Rami would either scream, bump into things, self-stimulate with the help of various hard objects, or retreat into complete withdrawal. I think that Rami's attempts at bringing me into his safe, autistic screen retreat were related to his ability to modulate and regulate the different proportions of "hard" and "soft," "near" and "distant", with the screen serving as a protective "other". Once confronted with the reality and excess of his and my real "otherness", Rami was again overwhelmed by his osmotic/diffuse anxieties and isolated himself. It is interesting to note that over our last year of work Rami was either pressing against things forcibly, as if trying to push himself through them, or splash water all over the room and on us so that everything became slippery, blurred, non-located, and fluid. For many ASD children this is a frequent defensive manoeuvre aimed at annihilating what is perceived as a traumatic premature separateness from the object and maintaining an hallucinated symbiotic union with it. I, however, have come to understand this as a simultaneous enactment of the horrors involved in being subjected to and permeated by diffuse, non-locatable anxieties. Once I started sharing this understanding with Rami, he calmed down and was gradually able to create some well-defined, distinct persecutory and dangerous part-object. Later on, he found and created new, combined objects with which he tried to repair the broken down bisexual container. The lizard's tail was gradually replaced by a clown whose head was made out of hard plastic but whose body was soft and cuddly. Rami tried to squash both parts together into a ball and then spread them apart.

I think Rami's online and offline reactions demonstrate the collapse of the bisexual container, the resulting upsurge of osmotic/diffuse anxieties, and the attempts to defend against them, as well as the role of "the screen" in trying to establish an externalised, superficial, shell-like container. This screen container, in turn, becomes saturated with osmotic/diffuse anxieties leading to further withdrawal and autistic isolation. However, if the screen can become, through the analyst, a humanised, shared object, emotional communication might be re-established, the bisexuality of the container restored, and the diffuse anxieties alleviated and better localised.

This brings me to the question of technique. A main difficulty resides in finding the right "positioning" for the analyst vis-à-vis the osmotic/diffuse anxieties. Thus, the questions of sensitively "*dosing*" the analyst's interpretations and presence, resisting seductions for symbiosis, and detecting ways in which the patient tries to turn the situation around, trying to use the analyst's mind as a site for depositing toxic material without allowing for any differentiation or working-through, are crucial. Many times, empathy, alongside analytic neutrality and a certain wall (or a screen) of impersonal aloofness, helps create a sense of security in the patient. Closeness, or deep transference interpretations, are experienced as a threat. Interpretations might be quickly echoed or co-opted as a certain mantle by the patient, only to hide deep panic and confusion. Alternatively, the patient might try to permeate and confuse the analyst's mind. The need for *"empathetic aloofness"* and careful dosing of the analyst's presence can be seen concretely in the following example taken from a recent session with Rami.

Rami brought an empty bottle to his session, which he shook, banged, and bit. Initially, I mainly interpreted to him his use of this autistic object as aimed at preventing contact between us and blocking out my existence, thus preventing any perception of separateness. It was only later in that session that I realised that he was showing me, in a very concrete way, his perception of himself as being an empty vessel, which might be invaded and filled-up in an osmotic way and without any control. Thus, for instance, he would immerse the bottle in water and scream with terror. I was then able to say, "Poor baby Rami bottle is drowning. There's water everywhere and baby Rami does not know where the water is coming from. Is it going in or out? Up or down? It's all confusing and dangerous. Rami will drown." I then turned off the water, saying, "I know where the water was coming from, so I can save baby Rami." Once I started interpreting this, with my back turned to him, some contact began to be established, followed by his first words, "No, out, Rami gone."

Osmotic/diffuse anxieties and isolation

Herbert Rosenfeld (1987) first used the term "osmotic pressure" to describe a phantasised intrauterine situation where the maternal unmentalized toxic psychic contents (i.e. depression) infiltrate the foetus, breaking its stimulus barrier. Rosenfeld described a relatively clear distinction between inside and outside, dependent on a budding ability to employ the mechanism of splitting and thus achieve some form of categoric functions. My experience with ASD infants and children and with adults suffering from autistic anxieties and defences led me to believe that these osmotic anxieties or "pressure" (which, as Rami demonstrates, is indeed experienced very concretely and bodily as such) often mask a more primitive form of diffuse anxieties that surface in hypersensitive and hyperpermeable (and therefore hypervulnerable) individuals. These anxieties seep in and leak out in a diffuse way into space. Because of their non-localised nature, neither in self nor object, these anxieties are experienced as being simultaneously "everywhere and nowhere". Thus individuals and, in fact, whole environments, might be experienced as infectious, polluted, mad, bizarre, and threatening in a non-specific way. The attempt to localise them somewhere is already an advanced formation of a paranoid-schizoid defensive organisation based on splitting and projective identification, which often fails. Thus, "organismic panic", as Grotstein (1990) described it, is replaced by a precarious, random paranoia.

The individual prone to diffuse/osmotic anxieties unconsciously feels in a very concrete, often bodily danger of dissolving, liquefying, freezing, burning, falling forever, breaking, falling into bits, having no skin or a skin full of holes, becoming bidimensionally flat, and losing orientation. Although such anxieties are common in early developmental disturbances such as ASD and childhood psychosis, they may exist, as in the following case of David, to a certain extent in seemingly much better integrated adult patients (Levine, 2013) who can utilise "hard" pathological organisations.

I chose to refer to these sets of anxieties together since, usually, the osmotic anxieties hide more diffuse anxieties. Thus, what initially presents itself as a more organised form of anxiety, experienced as being infected by invasive, invisible substances located outside, in an object or part-object, soon gives way to a panicky collapse into a diffuse kind of non-located anxiety where danger is experienced everywhere and nowhere. Recently, after failing to localise the virus somewhere, Ruti became confused, disoriented, and violent, screaming that the Covid was "in space". She pushed her fingers into her throat in an attempt to vomit and thus evacuate and place the dangerous Covid "out", then tried to burrow under my couch. When that analytic shelter failed to calm her down, she withdrew from contact and seemed vacant.

The current Covid-19 situation, with the collapse of many external and internal structures and the concomitant self-isolation, has given rise to these osmotic-diffuse anxieties in an alarming way. In Israel, for instance, this also manifested itself in a defensive strengthening of extreme, paranoid "hard" points of political and social views, often resulting in actual violence and accompanied by mindless, paranoid, and obsessive rituals. David, the patient who experienced his anxiety as "everywhere but nowhere" asked me recently, echoing little Ruti's question, "Where exactly is this Corona virus? It seems to be everywhere but yet nowhere. Small wonder all and sundry come up with all sorts of theories and meaningless rituals based on so little fact." He then went on to describe a demonstration he attended in order to attack the anti-government protesters. He described the protesters or "lefties" as dangerous viruses, infecting and infected. In the following session he oscillated between trying to localise his anxieties in various left-wing political elements, resorting to "hard", extreme ideologies accompanied by evident paranoia, and "softer" moments which gave rise to non-communicable anxieties. He described this feeling as "sticky jelly". David added that this sticky-jelly sensation reminded him of a dream he had had a few months previously. In many adult patients who can maintain some measure of integration, the osmotic/diffuse anxieties are often "localised" in their dreams.

I shall refer to that session:

> I am in a spaceship with other astronauts. The spaceship had been invaded by a space plankton which makes you apathetic—you want nothing and do nothing except crave this plankton. It is a deadly addiction. At some point, I don't know why, I venture out into space to try and fix it. I disconnect the air hose. Somehow this seems the way to put things right, drain all the air and thus get rid of the plankton. When I want to re-enter the ship, they do not let me in. They are all infected and mindless.

I ask him what comes to his mind when thinking about this dream.

David: It reminds me of something I saw on the Nature Channel about zombie ants in the Amazon river. There's a mushroom which grows on trees there. It finds its way into the ants' brains—their heads—and they go mad. They climb up these trees, sink their jaws into the bark and explode and thus the mushroom spreads … It also reminds me of my sister's high cholesterol and the danger to her blocked arteries. She doesn't seem to care that she's in danger; it's like the plankton got into her and made her apathetic. We also had some poisonous mushrooms in our garden. My wife said it must be the new Palestinian secret weapon against us. (He laughs.)

I suggested to David that his dream was both an important insight as to his current internal situation as well as a psychic biography. In order not to disappear in his nowhere-ness David created a hard metallic shelter (the spaceship). In the past he had referred to his mother as cold, hard, and indifferent though efficient and protective. This should have given him a home but soon turned into a new danger. The invisible, pervasive, and invasive quality of the plankton stood for the diffuse, non-localised, and lethal quality of his anxieties.

It is important to add, although I did not propose it to David yet, that I thought these anxieties might have also infiltrated into David from his mother who was hospitalised twice due to psychotic breakdowns, once before he was born and again soon after his birth. David's mother often blamed him for her failure to breastfeed him as a baby, claiming that her nipples were "too soft" and his gums "bit into her like a vampire".

I continued, adding that these anxieties had turned him into a zombie ant, addicted in a blocked, self-destructive way to the sedative allure of mindlessness. This resembled his sister's not caring about her blocked arteries. Later in the dream he is faced with an impossible dilemma: allowing the analysis to "fix" him means being expelled from the mindless safety and mafia-like protection of his group. He feels the solution is murder and/or suicide. It is all confused since disconnecting the infected air hose from the "mother" spaceship/me might save him but kill the others. But by killing the others—the analysis included—by depriving it of its "air" (he was often late and silent) or depriving the other astronauts and himself of their own toxic cure, David will be shut out, isolated, and eventually die.

Facing such an impossible dilemma, either murder or suicide, has become a daily occurrence in these Covidian times. Physical proximity, closeness, and intimacy have literally become equated with the danger of killing the other. Distance, withdrawal, and isolation have become a psychic suicidal equivalent. This internal impossible situation is the daily norm for our "nowhere" patients who conjure their own self-generated and self-administered cures. Following an observation made by Irma Brenman Pick (2020), I call this "the impossible dilemma of cure". Steiner (2011) has pointed out the dangers of emerging from pathological organisations, or psychic retreats. In ASD children, for example, as the analysis progresses, losing one concrete cover or mantle without yet having a new, better integrated, bisexual, and adjusted one can pose a real danger of decompensation and confusion and further arouses diffuse anxieties (Durban, 2017a).

Epilogue—a safe place for the Covid

"I found a safe place for the Covid," announced Ruti, securely lodged on her favourite spot—the couch in my consulting room. "That's great," I said. "Would you like to tell me?" "Only if you keep it a secret. The Covid is very naughty and knows exactly what people think." I wait. "Noa's mummy is a nurse and her father is a doctor," Ruti tells me. "They said that the best place for the Covid is in hospital." "Really?" I ask. "How so?" Ruti laughs and rolls over on the couch. "Stupid, don't you know? The Covid is sick! That's why. It was sick and feeling very, very bad and that's why it's been so naughty 'cause of the bad feeling inside. It didn't know it was sick. It thought everyone was sick and tried to be friends with them!" "Ahhh … So," I said, "being friends is the cure?" "No," giggles Ruti. "Being friends didn't help. It needed treatment and a laboratory. A doctor who is clever, big, and strong, and especially a nurse who can sing and play with toys and knows how to give an injection without you even feeling it." "I get it," I say. "So only if there's a strong, clever doctor and a kind nurse working together can we help the poor Covid get better and send it on its way." "Yes!" says Ruti triumphantly. "It can go back to Virussia [Ruti's beloved grandmother is originally from Russia]. It is Virussia, the virus land in the North Pole where they're cold and freezing all year round and that's why they come here. They need some warmth. That's why they like lots and lots of people, because it is nice and cosy and warm." "Right," I agree. "Just like every little boy and girl. They need a daddy and a mummy, some warmth and tenderness, and not being left alone." Ruti seems to be perturbed. "And grandmas and grandpas need that, too," I add. "Yes," says Ruti. "And now enough of talking, let's play."

Ruti provided me with her impressive insight, following our analysis of the different manifestations of her paranoid and osmotic/diffuse anxieties and manic obsessive defences. She intuitively understood that concern and compassion for the vulnerability and loneliness of the deadly virus, under the protection of a safe, creative union between the maternal and the paternal, might be the way to alleviate her anxieties and localise them in a benign way. She was developing a growing willingness to accept the facts of life or as Roth (2020) described it—becoming resigned to reality. This process of de-demonising the demon, often quite impossible when flooded by anxieties, is central to child psycho-analysis. In fact, simple compassion has never been declared as a valid psychoanalytic tool, nor has interpretation as a compassionate act. It is my hope that the Covid challenge and the now widespread experience of the anguish of helplessness and isolation we all occasionally share might change that, even in some small but significant way.

Joshua Durban
September 2020

References

Bion, W. R. (1962). *Learning from Experience*. London: Heinemann.

Brenman Pick, I. (2020). Personal communication.

Durban, J. (2017a). The very same is lost: in pursuit of mental coverage when emerging from autistic states. In: H. B. Levine & D. G. Power (Eds.), *Engaging Primitive Anxieties of the Emerging Self: The Legacy of Frances Tustin* (pp. 129–150). London: Karnac.

Durban, J. (2017b). Home, homelessness and "nowhere-ness" in early infancy. *Journal of Child Psychotherapy, 43*: 175–191.

Grotstein, J. S. (1990). Nothingness, meaninglessness, chaos, and the "black hole" I—the importance of nothingness, meaninglessness, and chaos in psychoanalysis. *Contemporary Psychoanalysis, 26*: 257–290.

Houzel, D. (2019). Splitting of the maternal container, psychic bisexuality and autistic sensation shapes. Paper presented at the IPA international congress, London, July 27.

Houzel, D. (2020). Private communication.

Klein, M. (1963). On the sense of loneliness. In: *Envy and Gratitude and Other Works 1946–1963*. London: Hogarth, 1984.

Lazar, R. (2017). Introduction. In: R. Lazar (Ed.), *Talking about Evil: Psychoanalytic, Social and Cultural Perspectives*. Abingdon, UK: Routledge.

Levine, H. B. (2013). The colourless canvas: representation, therapeutic action, and the creation of mind. In: H. B. Levine, C. S. Reed, & D. Scarfone (Eds.), *Unrepresented States and the Construction of Meaning*. London: Karnac.

Levine, H. B. (2020). Private communication.

Rosenfeld, H. (1987). *Impasse and Interpretation*. London: Routledge.

Roth, M. (2020). Transference in the time of Corona: working through under a shared reality. In: L. Giuseppe (Ed.), *Environment Crisis and Pandemic: A Challenge for Psychoanalysis*. Italy: Frenis Zero Press.

Steiner, J. (1993). *Psychic Retreats*. The New Library of Psychoanalysis. Hove, UK: Brunner-Routledge.

Steiner, J. (2011). *Seeing and Being Seen*. London: Routledge.

Tustin, F. (1987). *Autistic Barriers in Neurotic Patients*. London: Karnac.

Part VI

Conclusion

CHAPTER 15

Covidian life

Howard B. Levine
Cambridge, MA, USA

G iven the enormity of the threat and disruption posed by the Covid pandemic, the abruptness and brutality of the vulnera-bilities, the social disparities, the emotional, cultural, economic, and political upheavals, and the sense of danger, disorder, and disloca-tion that these have produced, it is best to begin by cautioning that it is probably too soon for anything more than provisional first impressions about its impact and opportunities. Time, thought, and more patient consideration will be needed before categorical or definitive conclusions can be reached. What follows are some starting points and hypotheses that we, as citizens and as a profession, might find interesting or use-ful to help begin the much longer period of investigation and dialogue that will be needed to reach significant hypotheses and substantive conclusions.

The undisguised brutality of our time

We are in the midst of a global and national[1] crisis of what may in the end well deserve to be called a *traumatic actual neurosis*. The combination of a new and previously unknown life-threatening pandemic—requiring radical and abrupt changes in our daily lives, overwhelming our poorly prepared public health capacities and medical facilities, coupled with perverse and deficient national leadership, continued disinformation, enforced social isolation, reality-based distrust of each human contact as a potential deadly carrier of disease, the prospect of economic hardship and collapse, and more—has threatened lives, underlined economic inequalities, political avarice, rapacity, and indifference, and exposed the weaknesses and limitations in what we once supposed was a democratic and egalitarian social compact.

The helplessness and anger that have resulted—some justified and some dictated by desperate attempts to hold onto or regain positions of power, discriminatory advantage, and privilege—have produced counter-responses and the reflexive resort to unthought action in our culture, in society, and in ourselves. It is a psychoanalytic axiom that there are two general categories of action and response. If attached to and guided by a considered reality sense, action can be *adaptive*. If we encounter and recognise a problem or obstacle to our comfort and well-being, we may take steps to try to alleviate or remove it. If driven by panic or wishful thinking in the service of denial, action is *evacuative*. The difference between the two may not always be clear, immediately recognisable, or easy to discern, but the consequences are significant.

The Covid pandemic challenges and has exposed our "normal" denial of the fragility of life. For some, including many of the political leaders upon whom we must depend, the initial response to that challenge has been to encourage us to disregard the danger or to seek out fictitious "enemies" to blame for the crisis. For others, it brought an awareness of mortality, a sense of anxiety and fear, accompanied by a depressive realisation of the vulnerability and fleeting quality of life.

---

[1] Inevitably, certain remarks and descriptions in this chapter will be offered from within the American societal and political contexts. I leave it up to readers from other countries to decide their applicability to their own national and local situations.

These have contributed to the increased sense of worry, strain, and fatigue that so many patients and analysts have reported in the initial weeks of the pandemic and have driven many to extreme ideological positions or blind or impulsive action.

In America, for example, we have seen initial rampant denial—Covid is no worse than the flu; these elderly would have died anyway; more people die each year from the flu;[2] xenophobic or partisan political conspiracy theories—claims that Covid was a "Chinese virus", a product of the CIA gone awry, a Democratic party attempt to disrupt Trump's reelection; hopes that inexpensive, readily available remedies like ultraviolet light treatment, quinine, or household bleach (!) would offer sufficient protection. Perhaps most striking of all is the pro-business calculus that talks about the effects on the economy vs. the need to curtail Covid spread, as if "business" and "the economy" were somehow independent of the health and welfare of people, who are the workers, distributors, and consumers of economic activity!

Did we really need to panic-buy toilet paper or greedily empty supermarket shelves of canned goods and pasta in the first weeks of the pandemic? As psychoanalysts, we might wonder about this sudden "me against you" upsurge of competition for seemingly dwindling resources that violates any humanitarian instinct of "How can we be sure that all of us survive, because we are all in this together?" What unconscious "dirt" were we thinking we had to wipe away, cleanse, and protect ourselves from? Racism? Classism? Colonialism? Envy? Greed? What might the phantasies be that are somehow related to the social, economic, and opportunity disparities that have been even more brutally revealed across America in the past months?

In addition to its premonitions of physical illness and death, the pandemic has also summarily revealed the existence of long-standing social, economic, and mental health problems secondary to governmental indifference and an unequal distribution of wealth. Although not the

---

[2] As if the brutality and neglect involved in the failure to provide adequate universal health care and attempts to undo the meagre health insurance plans afforded by Obamacare were an acceptable "status quo" against which the pandemic should be measured! This in a nation that usually leads the world each year in domestic gun possession and gun related fatalities … America first (sic)!

expectable subject of psychoanalytic discourse, these, too, require our profession's recognition, study, understanding, and address. There is a dispiriting shock having to face how superficial the ideals of progressive liberal democracy are in comparison to the racism, classism, xenophobia, hatred, neglect, and greed that lie just beneath the thin social veneer of many Western countries. To echo the words that Freud (1920) used to characterise the devastation wrought by the 1918–20 Spanish flu that followed upon the carnage of the First World War, Covid has laid bare and contributed to "the undisguised brutality of our time" (p. 327).

A greater incidence of mortality and morbidity has fallen upon the shoulders of the working poor and people of colour, exposing the oft denied problems of racism, classism, and callous abuse of others that exist throughout the world. These are the kind of social issues that Freud attempted to address in "Thoughts for the Times of War and Death" (1915b), *Why War?* (1933b), *Civilization and Its Discontents* (1930a), and other writings. Regrettably, we have not as a profession adequately turned the attention of our unique perspective on human emotions and behaviour so as to successfully understand, explain, and address these problems. Perhaps the Covid crisis will force us to refocus our efforts in an attempt to do so.

At the moment I am writing this, these problems are painfully evident in the United States, where the unwarranted murder of George Floyd, Breonna Taylor, and many others[3] by police has caused a tremendous upsurge of protest, exposing the latent brutality, racism, and repressive behaviour of American law enforcement. The Black Lives Matter movement is only the most recent attempt to underline the oft-denied fact, borne out by the history of the American Labor movement, that at moments of great social change, police forces usually act at the behest of the dominant capitalist ruling class.

We can no longer deny the dependence of the wealthy and upper middle classes on the supply chain services provided by the working class and poor and the gross inequities that exist in access to adequate medical and hospital care, education, comfortable living conditions,

---

[3] Sadly, the list seems endless and just to name some of the more current victims, includes Sandra Bland, Philando Castile, Freddie Gray, Laquan McDonald, Tamir Rice, Walter Scott, Alton Sterling, and far too many others.

social mobility, and the distribution of wealth. Nor can we continue to deny the damage done by xenophobia, isolationism, and the paranoid blaming of "others" in the face of an international public health crisis of this magnitude. Hopefully, as we begin to process the impact of the pandemic, we will enlarge our appreciation of the life that we *do* have and recognise that we are all interconnected and interdependent, all in this together, that *all lives matter* no matter what their ethnic or religious background or the colour of their skin, and finally seriously take on the long-overdue attempts to address global warming, climate control, the nuclear arms race, and other existential threats to continued life on earth.

So perhaps the first lesson that we should take from the pandemic is that life is precious because it is precarious. This was the point made by Freud (1916a) in his essay, "On Transience". Even under the best of circumstances, life is a game of chance that we adapt to in various ways, including some degree of normative denial. Bion (1962) talked about "learning from experience", but as a tank commander in the Great War, he knew that one first had to *survive* that experience and that survival was often a matter of chance. When he refused a prestigious medal for heroism in combat, he said that the only difference between the men who received medals and those who were condemned as deserters was the direction that they ran in when they were terrified.

The consulting room

The *frame* (setting) is a metaphor used by Jose Bleger (1967) to describe what he believed is an essential metapsychological component of psychoanalytic treatment. Derived from concrete, factual elements—for example, the role of the analyst, the structure and place of meetings, the starting and ending times of sessions, payment arrangements and fees, schedule, goals, and "rules" of the treatment, etc.—the frame refers to how non-process features of the clinical context and surroundings function silently as containing structures for what otherwise might prove to be potentially disruptive, explosive, even psychotic forces within the individual and the analytic dyad. As I shall attempt to show in a later section, I believe that Bleger's description can also be extended to apply to the everyday social frame within which we conduct and live our ordinary lives. This frame, too, has been severely altered by the threat and safety requirements of the pandemic.[4]

Under "ordinary circumstances"—to the extent to which these might exist in any analysis!—the frame is an invariant, a silent background that "is never noticed until it is missing" (Bleger 1967, p. 512). In the analytic situation, it is the frame that helps demarcate a transitional space within which the most private thoughts, moments, and feelings of the patient's innermost self may emerge and be shared and in which transferences may be lived out, experienced, noticed, and explored.[5] It is also the metaphorical container for "the most primitive part of the personality, it is the fusion ego-body-world, on whose immobility depend the formation, existence and differentiation (of the ego, the object, the body image, the body, the mind, etc.)" (Bleger, 1967, pp. 514–515). When the frame cannot be maintained or adhered to, when it is altered or traumatically breached, then unruly, unexpected consequences may erupt, produced by the unleashed, uncontained forces of the psychotic part of the patient's personality.

Because it works silently as a container for the psychotic parts of the personality, the frame plays an essential role in the *analytic* situation that may reach beyond its psychotherapeutic possibilities and exceeds its superficial, administrative components.[6] The frame provides the backdrop and "screen" against which the "as-if dream processes" of psychic

---

[4] Parsons (1999), discussing Green's work, goes even further, saying: "The structure of the [classical] analytic setting is itself a representation of internal mental structure. It not only gives access to internal structure, it embodies it" (p. 64): "… the lying down, the frequency and the silence [of the analyst] are all examples of how the analytic setting is set up to embody the negation of ordinary reality" (p. 69). And he concludes: "If the analytic setting represents in its external structure the internal activity of negation, and if … negation is essential to the creation of psychic reality, this means that the structure of the analytic situation represents the process by which psychic reality is constituted" (p. 69).

[5] McDougall's (1985) "theatre of the mind" and Green's (1980) "framing structure" are related concepts.

[6] I am assuming here that while psychotherapeutic processes are part of every successful analysis, there are unique and important analytic therapeutic processes that may be harder to reach in less intensive and other, non-psychoanalytic psychotherapeutic modalities. See also Green (2005), who suggests that in psychotherapy, in the absence of the classical analytic setting, the role of the setting must be superseded by the analyst's internal psychoanalytic frame and function.

reality may unfold. Bleger's message for these times—and that is equally applicable to when the pandemic will be brought under control and it is deemed safe to return to our offices—is that changes in the frame and the effects that they produce should not be taken lightly or without careful thought and examination of our accumulating clinical experience.

No doubt influenced by his own difficult childhood and horrendous experiences as a tank commander in the First World War, Bion was wont to say that psychoanalysis, like much of life, required "making the best of a bad situation". The precautions required in the face of the explosive spread of the Covid virus—social distancing and quarantine, restrictions on travel and assembly, the use of masks, etc.—have radically changed the setting of the analytic clinical encounter. As an emergency measure, psychoanalysis and psychotherapy have been forced to leave the office and go online. Telemetric treatment, once the exception, has become the rule.

The challenges this presents contain liabilities as well as opportunities for adaptation, growth, learning, and change. To the surprise of many clinicians who had not had previous experience with telemetric treatments, unexpected continuity and therapeutic possibilities emerged within the varieties of virtual contact offered and/or required within the altered settings. Online seminars and conferences have afforded us new learning and study opportunities. Perhaps the positive lessons learned of what is possible in regard to inter-regional conferences and seminars will help us to redress some of the provincialism and cultural and language silos that have impeded the evolution of a truly international psychoanalytic movement and dialogue. Truly substantive telemetric dialogues in a variety of forms and settings may obviate some of the expense and time constraints that have beset previous psychoanalytic congresses and meetings and prove to be the germ of a future psychoanalysis spawned in the twenty-first century.[7]

---

[7] I say "some" but not all, because I do not believe that online meetings can fully replace the intangible benefits of in-person meetings, where collegial friendships and dialogues can begin and be strengthened, substantive discussions can continue over coffee, drinks, and meals, and the social context and living conditions of other places can be experienced first-hand in an otherwise unmatchable way.

At the personal level, as clinicians, we have been very fortunate, because most of us have been able to continue our work and earn our living by resorting to telemetry and so the latter has been to our advantage. But are there differences between the immediate gains of therapeutic necessity in an emergency situation and the fostering and utilisation of an analytic process in the service of an analytic cure? If so, can we learn to specify under which circumstances and with which patients these differences obtain? And what will we learn about the possibilities and limitations of psychoanalytic training and formation when conducted at a distance?

As with any other crisis situated in "the real", there are immediate measures that must be taken to try to calm and contain ourselves, our families, our patients, and our immediate worlds. Continuing with patients via telemetric modalities has clearly been helpful. Once containment is achieved, each of us may begin to psychically elaborate the meaning of the concrete and brutal "facts" of the pandemic in a deeply personal and subjective way. For each of us, this elaboration may prove adaptive, evacuative, or, more probably, reflect elements of both. I have wondered, though, about a hypomanic quality to some pronouncements that telemetric settings were now "proven" to be functionally equivalent to in-office treatment, that one no longer needed to leave home, pay rent for an office—or change out of one's pajama bottoms!—to conduct business …

Nearly nine months into the Covid crisis, at the beginning of the second surge within the US and faced with the prospect of what could prove to be another year or more of virus dictated precautions, many analytic clinicians are calling telemetry and virtual contact a "new normal". Some analysts talk of going beyond crisis models to never going back to in-person visits or employing "hybrid" models. Based on the clearly salutary *therapeutic* effect of telemetric measures in the initial crisis, they espouse virtual treatment as "proven to be equivalent" and a solution to the realities of the many other demands—work, traffic, children's activities—of modern life. These are claims that may in fact be borne out by experience, but they are in need of careful study and yet to be determined.

The reality of the spread of the virus and the virulence of its destructiveness have shattered the illusory protective shield with which we lived our pre-pandemic lives. Psychic space, in our patients and ourselves, has become compressed and flooded with worries and fears, accompanied and unrelieved by continual, obsessive searching for news and information and often an irritable reaching after false solutions. In the face of this flooding, an analyst's first task may be to try to help restore a space for clear thinking in our patients and in ourselves. This is a point that Captain Bion would probably have agreed with. Before a commander (or analyst) can successfully lead his troops into battle, he may first have to help them settle down and begin to think clearly.

Helping an overwhelmed patient to calm down and begin to think—and to free associate—is not inconsistent with doing analysis. Rather, it is a prerequisite. *There needs to be flexibility in the application of a broad analytic technique that respects the need to respond to the patient at the moment-to-moment level of the patient's capacities and existential needs.* Once this psychic space reappears, we can begin to see the ways in which each individual's psyche, assuming that they have the capacity to do so, begins to create and assign meaning and nuance to the more general—and generic—threat of the pandemic in line with each individual's personal conflicts and idiom. The appearance of this space may well serve a kind of diagnostic function, indicating that the potentially traumatic "forest fire" of the pandemic is coming under some control and being integrated alongside one's more usual set of conflicts and concerns.

In writing about the treatment of patients who are at the limits of analysability, I made the point that the *analytic process often begins and must be sustained for long periods of time inside the mind of the analyst* (Levine, 2010). This is true no matter whether the analysis is conducted in the office or via telemetry. It may only be as an analytic function becomes internalised by the patient that what we think of as the analytic process can be recognised in the discourse that emerges between the pair. Most analysts have learned that some useful therapeutic work can continue by computer modalities or by phone. Whether the depth and extent of this work will prove equivalent to in-person analysis, are suitable for training purposes and for which analyst–patient pairs remains to be determined. My assumption, pending proof or disproof by subsequent experience, is that the analytic effectiveness that is available through the change in setting in this crisis situation will be correlated in part to the degree to which an analytic function exists or can develop in either patient or analyst.

One patient in quarantine who suffered from the tragic, premature death of her spouse and was in analysis in part to deal with the consequences of an arrested grief reaction, looked out of the window of her once bustling, now deserted city and remarked: "It looks like a graveyard." Another patient, whose father lived in constant danger of being arrested remarked that social isolation was "like prison". These unconsciously chosen metaphors were "signals from the field" (Ferro, 2002) that indicated how each patient was beginning to contain and metabolise the impact of the threat and the isolation in their own particular way. They were creating and attributing personal and subjective meaning to the cruel and impersonal chaos of the pandemic; beginning to unconsciously assign symbolic value *après coup* to events associated with the actual trauma of the pandemic, weaving what were now becoming symbolic, signifying events into the associative fabric of their lives.

Trauma and the social surround

The two previous examples refer to patients who had each, prior to the pandemic, had a considerable amount of in-person analysis and had internalised capacities for free association and self-observation that supported some degree of autonomous internalised analytic functioning. Not all patients have this capacity or have been able to elaborate elements of the Covid crisis in this way.

For many, the first weeks and months of the pandemic produced what I would call a *traumatic actual neurosis* marked by anxiety, strain, and fatigue, followed by hypochondriasis, sleep and eating disturbances, and minor somatic distress. Actual neurotic symptoms initially have no symbolic meaning. Although Freud restricted the use of the term, actual, to disorders of a sexual origin—dammed up libido, excess masturbation—there is good reason to extend it to non-sexual events that assault and shatter our psychic regulatory capacities—what Freud (1920g) called the ego's protective shield. The changes in setting required by the pandemic have drawn our attention to the level and degree of each of our patients' capacities to work analytically and offer us an opportunity to more closely study the means by which self-reflective and elaborative capacities are developed within the analytic situation.

Trauma in psychoanalysis is always an economic matter: a question of the balance or imbalance between the offending stimulus and the mind's capacity to contain, metabolise, and detoxify its impact and consequences.[8] And containment, as we have seen with Bleger (1967), will depend in part on the effectiveness of the containing function of the setting, both analytic and sociocultural.

In the case of the pandemic, the stimulus has been an invisible, life–altering, and life-threatening pathogen about which little is known and for which neither adequate treatment nor immunisation is yet available. The lack of clear knowledge of what we are up against or how to deal with it magnifies the terror and strain that all of us have been feeling and has stimulated the resort to panic buying and other wishful, magical "solutions". In the light of this uncertainty, the denial, posturing, and anti-science rhetoric of governmental leaders has only added to the confusion and made things worse. Who and what do we believe? Who do we trust?

The lack of knowledge and the lack of leadership along with the silent, undetectable spread of the virus have made it almost impossible to locate the Covid menace "somewhere". We cannot easily attenuate its threat by having a "there" and "not there". We can barely demarcate a safe zone in which we can truly relax our guard. The closest that we can come to successfully doing so is near-total isolation and sequestration at home. This strategy may offer some sense of comfort and control, but at a terrible cost. The fact that Covid can be spread from person to person has created a fertile ground for suspicion, avoidance, and paranoia. Social isolation for some has become a solitary existence. For others, it is a version of Sartre's (1955) *No Exit*. Still others feel it as the low-grade imposition of an experiment in sensory deprivation.

Its wearying impact alerts us to the fact that we have been living almost without noticing it in the broader structural setting of our social milieu. It reminds us of just how much psychic and emotional support we ordinarily obtain from ordinary social contacts and exchanges and their regular, expectable, unremarkable occurrences: the small talk we

---

[8] See Levine (forthcoming).

make with the clerk in the dry cleaning store; the greetings and brief comments on the weather every afternoon with the man who sells the homeless newspaper outside my office building; the puns and movie tips I exchange with my trainer as we work out together.

All of these contacts and more are an important part of the ordinary fabric of our lives, hardly noticed in the passing, until they are interdicted by orders to quarantine or shelter in place. Their sudden removal from our lives reminds us of the extent to which

> ... each institution is a portion of the individual's personality; and it is of such importance that identity is always, wholly or partially, institutional, in the sense that at least part of the identity always shapes itself by belonging to a group, institution, ideology, party, etc. (Bleger, 1967, p. 512)

I have previously suggested (Levine, 1990) that in normal development, the young child acquires an internalised sense of unconscious invulnerability based on actual parental protection and provision of love, food, clothing, and shelter. Good enough parenting fuels the internal development of an unconscious, omnipotent protective internal object that fosters unconscious (omnipotent) expectations of security.[9] Later versions of this expectation are seen in the "invulnerability" of adolescence; the assumption that "it won't/can't happen to me" in young adulthood; the idea that death is something that only happens to one's parents' or grandparents' generations; and the general denial of death as part of life that we see in many seemingly secure adults, until they experience the loss of one or both parents or someone else who is significant and close. Even then, although the inevitability of death may be recognised intellectually, it may not be until much later, if at all, that it will escape the category of being "unthinkable" and become, to whatever limited extent is possible, a reality to be reckoned with.[10]

When Freud introduced the couch, it was already a familiar staple in the consulting rooms of many Viennese physicians. Once established in the rest of the world as a psychoanalytic norm, it began to accrue a

---

[9] See also Sandler's (1960) background of safety.
[10] See De Masi (2004).

set of meanings and a mystique, along with other aspects of the office setting of analysis, and became part of the *social ritual* of psychoanalysis. Has this "normalisation" obscured the fact that it is only *for those patients who can tolerate its use*, that it allows for the development of a more inward concentration, a greater freedom of association? It can liberate some patients from the narrowing of focus inevitably produced by attention to the analyst's expression and face. For other patients, the loss of visual contact on the couch can precipitate an excessive, traumatic anxiety or withdrawal that interferes with the treatment process and may not be "analysable" as a defence (i.e. removable), but needs to be recognised as an underlying condition and vulnerability that must be respected, met on its own terms, and overcome in an often prolonged face-to-face treatment.

As the setting has changed, some patients have required specific options such as Zoom or FaceTime as opposed to the telephone in order to see our faces. To whom have we offered them? It has been interesting to hear that some analysts instruct their patients to lie down during tele-sessions and set up their computers to offer the analyst a couch-like view of the patient. I suppose there are many reasons for doing so, but I wonder if this gesture is necessary and helpful—especially when it is used at the analyst's request—or does the suggestion contain an attempt to hang onto the ritualised past and deny the enormity of the crisis and change?

The change in setting has revealed how much we tend to depend upon ritual in general to structure and perhaps stabilise ourselves and our lives. One patient, whose problems involved very early infantile maternal misattunement that left him struggling with powerful, unconscious forces aimed at merging with and being absorbed by his object, described feeling dislocated by the loss of the time and space between the end of the analytic session and his work life, which he experienced when he began having his sessions by Zoom from home. He described an invasive quality to the feeling of the period immediately after the end of the session that had previously been diluted and kept from awareness by the commute back to his office.

Another patient, who suffered from similar problems, but who protected himself from his intense merger longings by having a much stronger and more rigid schizoid retreat, had, for a long time, been in a rather dull and repetitive position in his in-person analysis on the couch.

The increased distance afforded by phone sessions initially seemed to depressurise something. His chronic lateness to sessions disappeared, his attention turned increasingly inward and to more personal emotional matters, away from his struggles with productivity at the office or how his wife and children were doing. The treatment unexpectedly began to deepen. Within a few weeks it reached the heart of some very threatening and disturbing feelings and his discourse became quite anxiety ridden, then tentative, halting, intellectualised, and flat. This sequence, from engagement to anxiety to renewed withdrawal gave both analyst and patient a clearer perspective from which to see the depth of the patient's phobic avoidance of potentially destabilising material.

As analysts, we now all have observations, experiences, and stories like these to share and reflect upon together. What our final conclusions will be about therapeutic effectiveness, the development of analytic competence, and the role of telemetric methods in training, supervision, and continued education remain to be seen. As noted above, it is too soon to separate out and understand the impact of the change in analytic setting and differentiate it from the other impacts—social isolation, economic crises, etc.—of the pandemic threat. But the exigencies of the pandemic have given us a most unwelcomed and unexpected opportunity to rethink some very basic fundamental assumptions as we continue to move our profession forward into the twenty-first century.

Howard Levine
November 2020

References

Bion, W. R. (1962). *Learning From Experience*. London: Heinemann.

Bleger, J. (1967). Psycho-analysis of the psycho-analytic frame. *International Journal of Psychoanalysis*, 48: 511–519.

De Masi, F. (2004). *Making Death Thinkable*. New York: Free Association.

Ferro, A. (2002). *In the Analyst's Consulting Room*. Hove, UK: Brunner-Routledge.

Freud, S. (1915b). Thoughts for the times on war and death. *S. E.*, *14*: 173–300. London: Hogarth.

Freud, S. (1916a). On transience. *S. E.*, *14*: 303–307. London: Hogarth.

Freud, S. (1920). Letter from Sigmund Freud to Oskar Pfister, January 27. In: E. L. Freud (Ed.) *Letters of Sigmund Freud 1873–1939* (p. 327). New York: Dover Publications, 1992.

Freud, S. (1920g). *Beyond the Pleasure Principle. S. E., 18*: 1–64. London: Hogarth.

Freud, S. (1930a). *Civilization and Its Discontents. S. E., 21*: 57–146. London: Hogarth.

Freud, S. (1933b). *Why War? S. E., 22*: 197–218. London: Hogarth.

Green, A. (1980). The dead mother. In: Green, A. (1997), *On Private Madness* (pp. 142–173). London: Karnac.

Green, A. (2005). *Key Ideas for a Contemporary Psychoanalysis*. New York: Routledge.

Levine, H. B. (Ed.) (1990). *Adult Analysis and Childhood Sexual Abuse*. Hillsdale, NJ: Analytic Press.

Levine, H. B. (2010). Creating analysts, creating analytic patients. *International Journal of Psychoanalysis, 91*: 1385–1404.

Levine, H. B. (forthcoming). *Affect, Representation and Language: Between the Silence and the Cry*. Abingdon, UK: Routledge.

McDougall, J. (1985). *Theatres of the Mind*. New York: Basic Books.

Parsons, M. (1999). Psychic reality, negation and the analytic setting. In: G. Kohon (Ed.), *The Dead Mother* (pp. 59–75). London: Routledge.

Sandler, J. (1960). The background of safety. *International Journal of Psychoanalysis, 41*: 352–356.

Sartre, J.-P. (1955). *No Exit and Three Other Plays*. New York: Vintage, 1989.

Index